"Memory is one of the rare privileges of age. With compassion, wise humour, and a poet's eye for the telling detail, George Szanto has given us a sort of Pilgrim's Progress from one man's intimate story to a dazzling meditation on history and nature."
—Alberto Manguel

"A moving and very thoughtful memoir of George Szanto's lifelong dance between literature and adventure, wanderlust and home."
—Ronald Wright, author of *A Short History of Progress*

"Watching his bogland on Gabriola Island as its life revolves around the circuit of seasons has put George Szanto at the perfect vantage point for reflection and storytelling. He delivers both in generous spades of visualization, language, and drama, whether in recalling fishing trips or eye surgery, dreaming the ideal house or bringing a loved parent back to life through reminiscence, watching in gaped-mouth wonder at the antics of birds or digging deep into family photographs. 'The sections of a house,' he writes, 'should recognize and live with each other, bringing a sense of harmony to those inside.' Just so do the sections of *Bog Tender* bring a reader to a sense of recognition of the harmony of one writer's life of relationships."
—Myrna Kostash, author of *Prodigal Daughter: A Journey to Byzantium*

"Part memoir, part travelogue, part meditation on the natural life of the author's beloved bog, *Bog Tender* is a passionately thoughtful book. Szanto writes with wonderful lucidity, never leaving the reader, always circling back to the essence of things. Frog lust and stink cabbage."
—Susan Crean, author of the award-wining (Hubert Evans, 2001) *The Laughing One: A Journey to Emily Carr*

GEORGE SZANTO

BOG TENDER

Coming Home to Nature and Memory

BRINDLE
& GLASS

Brindle & Glass Publishing Ltd.
brindleandglass.com

LIBRARY AND ARCHIVES CANADA CATALOGUING IN PUBLICATION
Szanto, George, 1940–
Bog tender : coming home to nature and memory / George Szanto.

Also issued in electronic format.
ISBN 978-1-927366-08-0

1. Szanto, George, 1940–. 2. Szanto, George, 1940– —Homes and haunts.
3. Authors, Canadian (English)—20th century—Biography. I. Title.

PS8557.U5375Z53 2013   C813'.54   C2012-906801-2

Editor: Rhonda Bailey
Proofreader: Heather Sangster, Strong Finish
Design: Pete Kohut
Cover images: Cattail: Eli Asenova, istockphoto.com
Dragonfly: kokoroyuki, istockphoto.com
Author photo: Bob Meyer

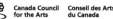

Brindle & Glass is pleased to acknowledge the financial support for its publishing
program from the Government of Canada through the Canada Book Fund, Canada
Council for the Arts, and the Province of British Columbia through the British
Columbia Arts Council and the Book Publishing Tax Credit.

The interior pages of this book have been printed on 30% post-consumer
recycled paper, processed chlorine free, and printed with vegetable-based inks.

1 2 3 4 5 17 16 15 14 13

PRINTED IN CANADA

For Elisabeth and David

Hope and the future for me are not in lawns and cultivated fields, not in towns and cities, but in the impervious and quaking swamps. When, formerly, I have analysed my partiality for some farm which I had contemplated purchasing, I have frequently found that I was attracted solely by a few square rods of impermeable and unfathomable bog—a natural sink in one corner of it. That was the jewel which dazzled me. I derive more of my subsistence from the swamps which surround my native town than from the cultivated gardens in the village.

Henry David Thoreau,
Walden, 1854

The past, recalled, is a flowing cornucopia of visions, sounds, aromas, emotions, gaieties, terrors, faces and places.

We do not remember chronologically, but in disordered flashes. We are not, after all, programmed memory machines. People are less efficient and orderly—but consider the compensations: freedom to associate; to roam and rummage in the attic of our yesterdays; to let one thing lead to another.

The ability to relive those parts of life that have been significant is a gift equal to life itself.

Garson Kanin, *Tracy and Hepburn:
An Intimate Memoir*, 1971

The cottage that we built early on, my writing studio, doubles a few brief times a year as an overnight space for guests. although it covers only 699 square feet, it has two floors. Each floor's space is increased by a balcony that runs along the front, the side facing the bog. From the second floor I can see the length and breadth of the bog, a wetland dominated by spirea, locally called hardhack. The plant is, indeed, hard to hack. Since retiring I have been able to do what I've wanted to do since I was twelve, write fiction full-time. In the summer I work upstairs, in the bedroom. My large writing table and the futon bed are the room's predominant occupants, joined by a filing cabinet and two bookshelves, home to ongoingly used reference works. Lots of light comes in from March to November, through large windows on four sides and skylights in the ceiling. Fresh air as well—with the windows open, cross-breezes enter from any direction. In one corner, a small bathroom.

In the winter I write downstairs, a combination kitchen-dining-living room, a twenty- by twelve-foot open space. A bathroom with a tub is down here as well. Most important, here, too, is the wood stove. Baseboard heating keeps the cottage at eight degrees Celsius overnight; the stove brings it up to twenty in half an hour.

The huge front windows, like the deck outside, allow me to stare with pleasure out to the bog. It's in constant motion, activity large and small, in and around it: deer, birds, red squirrels, snakes, frogs and tadpoles, snails, insects, the occasional mink and river otter. At times when I find myself stuck for the next thought or piece of dialogue or image, my eyes are teased by the nuances of the bog and I find or discover how to invent what I'm searching for.

Rarely do people come down the driveway toward the bog. An occasional lost driver winds down, thinking we are someone else. Some days I'll see a female deer and a couple of her young trot down toward the water; after fawning season, mainly single animals appear. Friends arrive in the evening, but by then I'm no longer at the cottage and don't see their vehicles. Mostly at the cottage there is peace, intruded upon by no others. Only birds and my computer's lightly tapped keys make sound.

From bog watching came this non-fiction project, these pages you are now starting to read. The writing has taken a year and runs parallel to the novel I'm working on. Sometimes the two projects intersect; the one helps clarify some aspect of the other. I have used my bog writing to discover what I am doing here, how I got here. As I've followed the changes in insect, animal, and botanic life, each season has awakened, month by month, long-slumbering memories. Some parts of what I've learned have come to light in the novel, others here, in this exploration of the world of the bog and the world of dormant memories I carry with me, like we all do.

It has been a heady year.

SEPTEMBER

Why begin in September? My life till I retired was structured by the school year, shaped by intellectual work from fall till spring. Also, September was the month that gave us Elisabeth, the start of my happy career as a father. September seems a natural beginning for a new project.

I.

Yesterday afternoon as I walked back from the cottage I saw that the dragonflies are back. They've been gone for the last three weeks. Some lazed in the warm, hard-packed sand of the road crossing the bog, others flitted ten or twelve yards over my head, their huge eyes searching for and finding flying insects. Not mosquitoes. Even at the wettest times there are few mosquitoes here by the bog. In spring, when mosquito larvae would hatch in the warming water, the bog is filled with frogs, whose preferred delicacy is, precisely, mosquitoes in their larval stage. Yesterday the dragonflies were enjoying an unusual September hatch of some other insect, a high-flying species.

I walk this road, our packed-dirt driveway, most days around ten-thirty in the morning. From the house, the road crosses the bog, passes my studio, and ends at the macadam of Chernoff Drive. If I don't stop somewhere along the two hundred yards to the studio, I can get there in about four minutes. My daily commute.

The transition between house and work, however, usually lasts longer. I take breaks along the way, to examine and reflect on overnight shifts. Most often these are tiny, a couple of little pink flowers I'd not noticed before, deer hoofprints in the middle of the road where the dirt is looser, the narrow grove of little alder trees just a few months old, a new brown rut in the hard-packed dirt. At times my breaks are longer, as when the Pacific crabapple buds have overnight sprung to life in a veil of tiny white blossoms, or in winter, when the two inches of rain over the previous two days have raised the bog level to within a half-inch of the road's edge and the potholes have dropped below the waterline, or a heavy winter storm here at the highest point on the island has downloaded twelve inches of wet snow, flattened every hardhack bush, and left us snowbound, unable to drive out, forcing cross-country skis or high gumboots on us if we are to cross the bog.

Yesterday it was the dragonflies, two and a half inches long with a wingspan of three, their bodies a deep, iridescent blue. Dozens of them. Whether their appetite was aroused thanks to some invisible sign that a flurry of savoury insects has just hatched or they've somehow been directed here by a scout of their own, I have no idea. That they have arrived is enough. They're here for one purpose only: for me to admire. Admiring life along the drive is part of my bog tending, a kind of mulling.

The bog is on an island, Gabriola, off the east coast of Vancouver Island. Kit and I have lived here more than ten years. Prior to that we'd enjoyed three years coming to Gabriola for several months, winter and spring. To get to the island from the mainland we take the car ferry from Vancouver to Nanaimo, on Vancouver Island, then another ferry from Nanaimo to Gabriola. I like to think of these transitions as moving from a larger geography to an increasingly smaller one: if we've been away on a long trip we can fly into Vancouver International from anywhere in the world, pick up our car, head down to the big ferry at the terminal in Tsawwassen, a vessel capable of carrying more than a thousand vehicles, two hours later disembark on

Vancouver Island, the Big Island, drive up to the small city of Nanaimo, onto our little ferry the *Quinsam*, with a seventy-car capacity, after a twenty-minute crossing drive off onto petite Gabriola (about the size and shape of Manhattan Island, but with a population of four thousand), head along South Road, leaving behind an equal number of cars that have chosen North Road, our fellow ferry-crossers dropping away a few at a time, then we, too, quit that main artery and head up the hill along a less-travelled road, finally onto Chernoff, a short, wooded street, then turn onto our driveway, down the slope, past the cottage, across the bog, and up an incline to the house. From the great world out there to our refuge here. And, on the other side of the house, far below, False Narrows, the shining Pylades Channel, and beyond it Trincomali Channel, branches of Georgia Strait, home to three dozen dark-wooded islands, the closest being Mudge, Link, DeCourcey, Ruxton, and Thetis. A grand vista.

High up, with a bog. The bog lies between two ridges; there's no runoff, though it seeps from east to west. The bog is perhaps a half-mile long, extending through three properties, and a hundred yards across at its widest. Our property is a long, narrow lot. The bog cuts it in two, extending through three properties. Ours is in the middle; before the bog road, no one walked from one side to the other on our land.

Our coming to own the property is a story in itself. In 1990 I published *The Underside of Stones*, the first novel in my Conquests of Mexico trilogy, and was promoting it across the country. One of the venues where I'd been invited to read was a place I'd never seen, Gabriola Island, in British Columbia. My host was a friend from many years back when I first joined the Writers' Union of Canada, Sandy Frances Duncan. I did my promotional reading. The following morning, a gloriously warm day in mid-February, Sandy and I sat on her deck sipping coffee, listening to birds chirping away, me staring at crocuses, snowdrops, and daffodil shafts all calling out to me, Spring is here! Believe it!

"Mid-February," I said to Sandy.

"Yep," she agreed.

That evening I called Kit at home in Montreal and told her about the wondrous morning. "You wouldn't believe how gorgeous and warm it was here today."

Her excitement was less acute than mine. "You forget," she said, her irony heavy. "I lived in Vancouver most of my early life."

"I know, but—"

"And besides, this morning I shovelled fourteen inches of snow off the car."

We were both still in our early fifties. Retirement, though far off, kept creeping closer. But we waited a year and a half before going out to coastal BC—it looked like a good place to retire—on a scouting expedition: where precisely might we want to live one day, what kinds of house could we get for how much. On one issue both Kit and I were resolute. Whatever we did, we would not buy land and build a house. In Montreal we'd bought an old downtown Victorian row house. For many years it had been a rooming house. The whole place had to be gutted, walls knocked out and replaced, all but the shell of it redone. Our relationship with the contractor was, well, complex. So we'd had a rich taste of the building process, and would never go through it again.

In BC we began in Victoria, then planned to head up the east coast of Vancouver Island, check out Nanaimo, cross to Gabriola and spend a couple of days with Sandy, then head farther north along the coast to Comox and on the ferry over to the mainland, down to the Sunshine Coast, down to Vancouver. In Victoria, a young real estate agent acquaintance of friends there took us from Sydney to Brentwood Bay, from downtown out to Sooke. The wife of the couple we were staying with gave us an excellent suggestion, as is clear now but we didn't follow it: buy waterfront. Why? Rarity value. There's little of it left.

In and around Victoria we reconfirmed that the city or the suburbs were not for us. The agent suggested that as we drove north we consider the area around Mill Bay and Duncan, even Chemainus and Ladysmith. We did. They each felt, somehow, not quite for us.

On Gabriola, Sandy had organized a realtor to show us house possibilities. We saw a dozen houses in a range of prices, each less viable for us than the previous. But along the way we were getting a taste of the island, finding it satisfying and lovely.

Our weary agent must have sensed this. He asked if we would consider looking at some acreage.

We said, as one, "No!"

In the evening, talking with Sandy, we thought our response through. What to lose, looking at land. I'd done some demographic research, and it seemed clear that, as baby-boom Canadians from the east, or even from Winnipeg or Calgary, began to retire, there might well be a surge of people slightly younger than us—we pre-date the earliest boomers by half a decade—out to the West Coast. We did want to live here, we had by now decided, and it'd be a good idea to have bought into the market. Whatever we invested in we'd likely be able to sell at a profit and then buy something else later on.

We called the agent. We saw small lots and ten-acre parcels, the lesser ones too close to neighbours, the larger ones too expensive. From a cliff one hundred and twenty feet above the sea, overlooking Georgia Strait, the snow-capped coastal mountains on the mainland and the treetops below us, we glanced down as a couple of eagles floated by. The price? Well beyond our range. Oceanfront land seemed impossible, but to live on an island without seeing the ocean seemed, somehow, a decision we might come to regret. We had lived for the first six years of my full-time teaching life in Del Mar, California, a small beach cottage a forty-eight-second walk from the beach. Bought at a price that seemed a touch out of our range at the time. Sold when we left for near to triple what we'd paid. (Sold again seven years later for about thirty-five times what we'd paid; we've never been good at holding on to investments.) Our time there had given us a strong desire to live close to water.

"How about an ocean-view lot, then?" asked the real estate agent.

We shrugged him a kind of collective Sure, why not.

He took us to half a dozen places. On one short road on the island's highest point was a lot he wanted us to see, around five acres. We walked down a drive through a deep cedar wood, the imposing trees' ancient arms embracing the dirt track and ourselves as in caring protection. We reached the cleared space designated as a possible house site and knew we'd arrived in a peaceful, generous place. We caught a glimpse of the sea over low trees—a superb vista ready to be opened up, as we discovered a few minutes later by breaking through the woods to the empty cottage next door: below us lay an immense spread of ocean punctuated with islands, glowing in the sun. We returned to the lot for sale. Stillness, the air soft and hushed. The notion "magical" is not part of my active vocabulary, but in this instance to have called that space magical wouldn't have been inappropriate. Resinous breezes stirred limbs and treetops. The filtered summer sun felt warm, clean. Birdsong, and the wind. To get the view, our agent told us, we'd have to fell some of the trees down the slope. A grand spot. But no! We were not going to build a house. We were not mad. We would find an existing house somewhere.

We walked back without speaking, and at the car agreed the place did seem wonderful. And yet, and yet.

The agent said, "It's been for sale for fourteen months. They'd probably accept a reasonable offer."

I wondered what was wrong with it. "Would it in fact keep us in the market?"

"Always hard to tell," said the agent, "but I think—yes, it would. Of course," he added, "to make the most of the land you'd want to build."

No. And to create the view, we'd have to cut down some of the very trees that gave the site its immense sense of peace.

The next morning, as we drove farther up the coast, I realized why I didn't want to live on Vancouver Island itself. Earlier, between Victoria and Nanaimo, the hum and thunder of internal combustion engines had been omnipresent. Eastern Vancouver Island is dominated by the coast highway, which runs from Victoria up to the northern tip. We had in fact considered the communities along the highway but discovered that at many points, even three or four miles inland or toward the ocean, we could hear traffic—the echo of truck roar, wailing sirens, a steady flow of cars. On Gabriola we were far enough away. Though sound often carries well across water, the rumble of traffic hadn't reached us there. Inland from the highway lie vast, silent wilderness tracts, but there's little community in those parts. We headed on up to Campbell River, seeing towns along the way that didn't capture our imaginations. We took the ferry to the mainland and headed south to visit a friend on the Sunshine Coast. We'd look for houses there.

The houses of the Sunshine Coast were easily fifty percent more expensive than their equivalents on Vancouver Island and Gabriola. We borrowed the friend's boat and headed out onto the strait, trolling for salmon: an avoidance technique. We talked about the houses we'd seen, the prices. Where in fact did we want to live? Kit said, "Should we reconsider—" just as I said, "Maybe it wouldn't be such a bad idea—" "That piece of

11

land?" "That piece of land." We turned the boat around. Just as an investment, of course, we both agreed. On shore we called Sandy. No, she hadn't washed our sheets yet; yes, we were welcome. We crossed back to Vancouver Island, down to Nanaimo, called our agent. He'd meet us at the property. We ferried over to Gabriola, drove up to the land. His small car awaited us. In front of it, a large sedan. He believed it belonged to another agent, someone he knew who worked out of Nanaimo. We walked along the drive. The tranquil beauty of the place was indisputable. At the house site, three people. The two agents greeted each other. We all agreed it was a pretty piece of property. We walked back toward the road. Kit and I conferred for the best part of five seconds. Yes, we were prepared to make an offer. We took ten percent off the asking price. Our agent phoned it in.

Another offer had been made twenty minutes earlier. First offer in the fourteen months it had been on the market. We had to wait, see if the other offer would be accepted.

Meanwhile, said our agent after glancing through his listings, how about checking out a different piece of property for sale on this same road, the same ridge, a few lots farther along, five acres, described as "an Engineer's Challenge." Just for comparison's sake. Also high up on the island, it was a long, narrow lot, one hundred and fifty feet by nearly a third of a mile, standing beside a one-hundred-and-sixty-acre tract to the west, privately owned forest land. Like the cedar-rich property, this lot was situated between two short roads, the one we had entered from and the one lower down the slope.

The challenge was one of access. We walked onto the land, breaking through the woods. A couple of hundred feet in, fifteen to twenty feet below us, was the nature of the challenge: a wetland crossed the entire property, extending well into the forest land to the west, cutting the property in two. No way to traverse the bog. We drove around to see what it all looked like on its lower side. But the steepness of the slope—about thirty degrees—made building a driveway prohibitive; cutbacks across a ribbon of land barely wider than a suburban lot would obliterate the most desirable aspects of the terrain itself. The house site was inaccessible. A shame.

More than a shame. Exploring Gabriola, we found the island gave us pleasure—its gentle geography, the sandy or sandstone beaches, the climbable hills, the marinas where some day we might tie up a boat, the people we'd met. It had also become clear that Nanaimo was well served, with two major ferry terminals connecting to the mainland and an airport providing regular fifteen-minute flights to Vancouver International. With our kids and our siblings back east, the combination of living pleasantly distant from the many downsides of North American civilization while being able to return there with ease made Gabriola ever more of an intriguing possibility. We returned to Sandy's. In the early evening we learned the other offer on the first property had been accepted.

Back in Montreal we found ourselves, to our surprise, devastated. At not being able to offer a large amount of money to buy a piece of land without so much as a cabin on it.

We decided I'd go back for a few days in the fall; new houses might be on the market, maybe this time . . . In mid-November I rearranged my teaching, took a long weekend, and flew out to the West Coast. I rented a car, ferried over to Gabriola. Met our agent. He showed me waterfront houses, woodsy houses, acreages. By myself I walked the property we missed out on buying, between the grand silent trees. No one had begun building. I returned to the Engineer's Challenge and walked through the woods—the trees there far more scraggly, skinny firs and wobbling arbutus, than on the other lot—on down to the wetland. I sat beside the water, much deeper than

13

back in August. The ruddy, woolly flowers of the hardhack had gone brown, now rich, loose-hanging bundles. From deep in the bog I heard a plunking noise, as if something had jumped in; a satisfying sound. The water wasn't open enough to be a real wetland, and it didn't have the feel of a swamp. Not a marsh, either—marshes make me think of mud. Later other ways of describing it would perhaps come to mind, but at the moment it seemed to be an unadorned bog, simple and gentle.

I stayed for a while beside the bog, listening to a half-dozen variants of birdsong. Watched a pair of pileated woodpeckers, each over a foot and a half tall, peck their way around a dead tree fifteen feet off, their red crests burning in a shaft of sunlight. Listened to, then saw on two separate branches of an arbutus tree, a pair of ravens cooing to each other. Stared at four Douglas firs swaying in the wind, singing to me. Then I heard one of the woodpeckers speaking—kick-kick-kickkickkick; as I turned to them they flew up, the bright black and white undersides of their wings flashing. Every few minutes a red-winged blackbird had appeared. Deep into the fall the air was still soft and smooth. Silently I said to the bog, *Could we live here?* It didn't answer, as if telling me to make up my own mind.

From back on the road I walked down to the neighbouring house. The bog began just to the right of the eastern side of its drive, crossing it minimally. There I met Andy. He said that he had built the house, with the help of a few friends. He took me out to his broad deck along the south side, facing Vancouver Island. Between the big island and Gabriola lay the ocean, a view similar to the one we'd seen in August, now a late autumnal glitter of grey-blue sea sprinkled with those dozens of deep green islands. I could stare at this all day, I thought: morning as the sun rose across the water, midday as storms roared the water white, evening as the colours dimmed. I thanked Andy and returned to the Engineer's Challenge. First I heard birdsong

I couldn't identify, then I sat in silence. It had been a sunny early afternoon when I left Andy's; now suddenly the sky had gone grey above, golden still to the west. I stared at the bog for easily a couple of hours. My mind had wandered through segments of the past, memories, images. I imagined pieces of a possible future here. This could work, I thought. I needed a lot of advice.

We had met a friend of Sandy's, Vic, a smart and highly rational retired engineer. He and his wife, Phyllis, had built their house; everyone seemed to be doing it, I thought. Maybe with an intelligent builder on the job, making a house grow up from the ground wouldn't be so difficult. Vic advised me to speak with Gordie, known locally as the artist with the backhoe. Everyone knew Gordie, everyone had been helped by Gordie's imaginative solutions to ornery problems. I met him, we spoke of the bog cutting the property in two. He knew the spot, McGuffey's Swamp, as a kid he'd hunted up there—hey, they used to grow potatoes up there.

"Can one build a bridge of some sort or a road across the bog?"

"Sure. How you think they build roads up north? It's all swamp up there."

He'd lay a base, branches and stumps with roots from the trees that would have to be cleared for a house site, then fill and cover it with the sand and rock that would come out of the foundation hole. With a little care the road would stay in shape for a hundred years.

Gordie argued a good case. Vic agreed the solution made sense. That evening I called Kit. "I'd like us to make an offer on the other lot on that same road."

"The Engineer's Challenge?"

"A challenge that can be met." I told her about Gordie, and about Vic. She remained dubious, but we agreed to make the offer. A large chunk of money for a piece of property cut by a bog. The offer was accepted. Gordie built the road. The dollar value of the land has multiplied. Its value to our daily lives is beyond estimation.

Our bog is, at first glance, a curiosity. It doesn't appear special. But our bog's ongoing transformations give me a way of dealing with whatever is immediate and unique, with the local as it exists here, now, and nowhere else, filled with its private mysteries. I look into the September bog, under the water—what's down there in all that murkiness? And in my own shadowy storehouse of memories? Living here on the Engineer's Challenge, I've come to sense that my memory, too, is a kind of bog, obscure on the surface, at times clearer when waded into, at times murkier. Living by the bog has given me time to wander about in my past; I report what I discover or recover, I write down snippets of memory. Often I merely mull about what could be down there, back there, in my memory bog. The bog beside the road has its own kinds of secrets, long invisible, unsmellable, unheard, till the season comes for it to release one or another of them—a deer trail here, some lily pads in the newly open water, a thousand frogs mating, ten thousand tiny crabapples heavy on the boughs—whatever is ready to burst forth at its moment in the cycle. Our bog has given me the pattern, seasonal, monthly, an external, imposed structure for this memoir.

2.

September arrives with a double purpose. First, it's annual medical checkup time, followed by the ongoing tests of bodily fluids. Followed by whatever the results advise. Second, there's a little travel; the larger travel happens in October, visits east to our families.

From our first September after coming to live permanently

on Gabriola, medical appointments became etched onto our annual patterns. We'd found a family doctor who, at my first checkup, asked me, How long since your last eye examination? A while. But my eyes were better than ever: I no longer needed glasses for reading, or for working at the computer. Now reading in bed meant I could drop my book and close my eyes with no fear of flicking the glasses to the floor and stepping on them in the morning.

But with any silver lining, look for the cloud. My eye exam confirmed my improved reading vision, and no, no change in distance perception as long as I got increasingly strong lenses. Then the optometrist dilated my eyes and examined the retinas. He made noises, "Hmm . . ." and "uhhmmm . . ." and "hunnnhh."

"What's going on?" I asked.

"Dunno," he said, looked some more, and said, "Never seen anything like it."

"What is it?"

He sat back. "Strange pattern on your retina. Lots of the pigment's there, some isn't."

"What's that mean?"

He shook his head. "Means you'd better see a retina specialist. We'll make you an appointment."

Great, I thought. "You figure it's serious?"

"No idea."

So a couple of weeks later I met with an ophthalmologist in Nanaimo. More dilation, chin on pad, bright light into my left eyeball, full examination of the backs of my eyes. Glance toward your right shoulder, right hip, toes. "Hmm," she said, "yes," and "yes" again.

"What?"

I needed first to look again toward my left hip, shoulder, ear, top of head, right ear. Light deep into the other eye. She pulled back, made notes.

"Can you tell me anything yet?"

"I think, birdshot retinochoroidopathy," she said. "I've seen a few cases like it."

This sounded almost funny. "What's birdshot retin—?"

"A pattern on the retina, as if some of the pigment's been blasted away, like by a shotgun. Like when you walk in the woods and you see a sign that says NO HUNTING, and it's been spattered with birdshot."

"I don't hunt." For the moment it was the best response I could find.

"Nobody's ever told you this before?"

At my previous eye exam everything had been normal. I told her the optometrist hadn't been looking for birdshot, hadn't known what it was.

She said it was a good man who admitted to not knowing what something was if in fact he didn't. The condition could be new, could have been there for a while. "Is it dangerous?"

"Yes. Unless you do something about it."

"What?"

"You better see a retinologist who knows." At the Vancouver Eye Institute, a research centre associated with the University of British Columbia. Two ferries from Gabriola. A drag.

As it turned out, the BC health system allows travel to be compensated if one who lives in a remote area like an island has to head off to a specialist for a consultation—the patient, the car, and, in cases like mine (can't drive with dilated eyes), an escort. A free trip to Vancouver for Kit and me. And quickly organized— five days to get seen. Impressive health system we have here. Or maybe my ophthalmologist figured it for some kind of emergency she hadn't mentioned.

The first retinologist I saw was a man honoured for his ongoing work with eye diseases and part of a team dealing with precisely my syndrome. He had been monitoring birdshot patients for more than a decade and had come across barely two dozen cases in the area. I was a rarity.

He dilated my eyes, he stared in. Yes, birdshot. Outside chance it had something to do with the TB I'd picked up in Mexico fifteen years before and it hadn't been detected till I got back to Montreal.

Another retinologist colleague had to see me too. Or, rather, my retinas. More chin-rest, more probing lights, luckily no more dilation—the previous dab had done me. He stared into my eyes. Yes, birdshot. An intern stared in, then a graduate student. None had seen the syndrome before.

It would have to be monitored for the rest of my life. Birdshot retinochoroidopathy is an autoimmune disease. No one knows where it comes from. I could have had it for years or decades, or it could have come up last year. It is degenerative. Only way to deal with it, daily doses of cyclosporin. Which has its side effects, in this case, hair growth ("Men like that, women don't"), trembling in the hands (not good while fishing), and probable liver and kidney damage. Which of course can be controlled by yet more drugs. Which may have their own side effects. If it remains untreated, that's the end of sunsets.

I tried to track down the syndrome on the Internet. Very little information. It was not seen or at least not described before 1980. Was it a new disease, or just newly discovered? Before 1980 were ophthalmologists blind to it, or not looking for it? No answers. In 2000, only two hundred and fifty or so known cases around the world. It was being researched in Vancouver, at the Massachusetts Eye and Ear Institute, at the Pasteur Institute in Paris. All of these researchers were clear: birdshot gets worse if not cared for, cyclosporin the only treatment. "Zero tolerance" is the phrase used: everyone with birdshot must take it. "I am seeing twenty-two patients with birdshot," my Vancouver retinologist told me. "All are on cyclosporin."

I bought my first batch. Most expensive drug I'd ever taken. I Googled it, read about it. More info about inevitable organ damage, liver and kidney top of the list. I would have to stop drinking—no more wine and vodka. Talk about zero tolerance. Partial control of damage with offsetting drugs. And their side effects. I felt my brain and guts first reel, then rebel. I would not go down this road.

Eugene, a long-time friend from Montreal, now living on Hornby, an island north of Gabriola, had for many years been experimenting with hypnosis techniques to improve healing, specifically for his wife, Jo, a dancer, who, like many of her profession, tended to pulled or sprained muscles or to broken bones. Under hypnosis, Eugene and Jo had discovered, the injured person improved much more quickly, visualizing the wound or muscle and encouraging it to work toward its own healing.

The daughter of other friends, in her late twenties, was diagnosed with non-Hodgkin's lymphoma: projected life expectancy, four to seven years. She studied Qi Gong, a form of traditional Chinese medicine that incorporates exercise and meditation. She practised Qi Gong regularly and she believes this brought the lymphoma into remission. It can always return, she knows, but she has had fifteen good years.

Two alternative ways of gaining control over disease and injury. I thought, If my body has brought this autoimmune birdshot down on my eyes, then I better tell my body, Stop that! With Eugene, I worked up a text that might put my birdshot into remission—in fact, as I wanted to think, into submission. Jo read the text onto a tape, which I could play at my convenience. I put myself on the most strict self-hypnosis schedule possible—once daily, seven days a week, fifty-two weeks a year. I have been keeping to that for more than ten years, maybe once every couple of weeks letting its absolute pattern lapse if I can't get to the tape—or, more recently, to my iPod. My birdshot, my

Nanaimo ophthalmologist tells me, has been steady state since 2000. Until recently I saw my Vancouver retinologist once a year. He, too, declares my birdshot unchanged. "You're still not taking cyclosporin?"

"I did for a week or so, then stopped."

"That's impossible."

He knows I'm doing self-hypnosis, agrees there's value to relaxation (he thinks it's like meditation), but cannot accept that self-hypnosis works.

This September, another eye problem. Over the previous few years I had developed a substantial cataract in my left eye, which blurs and greys my vision, and a lesser one in my right eye. (If both eyes were like the left, I wouldn't let me drive.) At my eye examination the cataract was declared "ripe." As in, I presume, ready to be plucked. This simple procedure is now scheduled for November. It will take only a few minutes. It causes very little eye trauma. But very little trauma is still some trauma. There is an unspoken worry that such trauma could destabilize the birdshot. I try not to think of it.

Our other purpose that first September, after the medical stuff, was a little exploring. So on the first day of autumn Kit and I took a holiday, four days to Vancouver Island's west coast, Tofino and Ucluelet, long, unpeopled beaches, lingering walks through old-growth forests. By way of the Internet we'd found a small cottage on Chesterman Beach in Tofino and used it as our base camp. The west coast, the raincoast, receives about one hundred and fifty inches of rain a year, the wet season beginning in September. So when we arrived to find the beach bathed in sunshine, late afternoon light caressing the wet sand, we knew we'd gotten a bonus. A few of the west coast's sandy beaches lie near to flat, and as the tide withdraws it leaves a sheen of undrained water along its wide departure route. At the moment of our arrival, low tide and late afternoon, the sandy beach, more than a mile wide and a hundred yards out to small breakers, glittered beneath sheaths of a half-dozen different golds. We walked toward the little incoming waves, me shod and Kit barefoot, my feet staying agreeably dry, hers enjoying the pleasure of squishy freedom. Over the next few days we would escape from normalcy, from Gabriola responsibilities, commitments we gladly take on but that have become omnipresent even on a bucolic island.

The beaches and their hinterland south of Tofino, Pacific Rim National Park, make up a temperate rain forest, home to hundreds of acres of old-growth fir, hemlock, and spruce, part of a jungle of vines and mosses, salal, and ferns—bracken, swordfern, lady fern. It's ever damp here, the air filled with light, new perfumes and ancient decay. The park's guardians have built boardwalks through this mild jungle, creating controlled trails through thick forest, others toward and along the sea. One trail takes the walker to the headwaters of a small stream, where in late fall hundreds of salmon come to spawn and die, the tiny fry taking their first nutrients from the decaying bodies of the previous generation. Another trail, now closed but remembered from an earlier visit, tells the story of land reclaiming the sea. We usually think of water and land the other way around, sea eroding the edge of the forest, nibbling away at it. But on a long stretch of shoreline here in the park, logs felled up north had escaped from tug-drawn booms, and powerful winter storms had thrown them against the shore. Over time the spaces between such logs become packed in with seaweed, leaves, sand, the decay of branches, and their own rot, till the space is transformed into a nutrient-rich nurse bed for small forest-edge plants, larger vines and grasses, brush, then small trees, and the once-sandy shoreline becomes a new part of the forest.

The discovery that most impressed me on this visit was the Shorepine Bog Trail, a stretch of relatively open land covered with stunted trees, small grasses, and a great deal of moss. Not a mosquito to be found, but for a different reason than in our bog: the moss here is sphagnum. It spreads across the surface of the entire wetland. It seemed dry enough till I pressed lightly down. My fingers came away wet. Step on it, sink in—and destroy a texture and terrain that nature has taken decades to build up. The boardwalk trails are so carefully planted they seem to float on the surface. When it rains here, the water is sponged in and becomes acidic. No life-respecting mosquito will attempt to breed in this brew.

The first section of the trail passes through what is called the Gigantic Broccoli Forest, so named for its heavily stunted shorepines. Theory has it that the acid in the soil destroys the phosphorous, which is necessary for the tree to develop height. As a result these trees grow wide, branching sideways. Some trees, more than three hundred years old, are only a few yards high. The same tree maturing under more normal circumstances is found throughout the Canadian Rockies, there known as lodgepole pine and rising as high as a hundred feet. Here in this bog the trees do resemble giant broccoli plants.

Unfortunately, but in another way happily, the only day of our trip that wasn't washed in sunshine turned out to be the afternoon we visited the Shorepine Bog. A light mist surrounded us as we started through the broccoli patch, becoming a solid drip. At the half-point—as always, going back no better than pushing on—the rain waterfalled down. But it was the right moment to watch the mosses actively drink down the rainwater. On the mossy surface, no hint of puddling or drainage. We stood in the middle of the rain, watching it keep the bog alive.

Our leaving day dawned grey, but by the time we'd cleaned

up the cottage the sun had returned. So back to the Shorepine Bog. In full sunlight the moss glowed greenish gold. A brochure told us the bog could be as much as four hundred years old at its peaty bottom a couple of yards below the surface. The bog's acidity keeps bacteria from thriving; without them, dead plants can't rot and release nutrients, so the cycle found in the rain forest doesn't exist here. The next generation can't flourish on the bodies of its forebears, as the salmon do. The result, stunted trees and shrubs. And acid-tolerant plants: bog dandelion, a distant relation to those prevalent in lawns and fields; the drying leaves of skunk cabbage, often growing in hollows, far smaller than its cousins in the rain forest; and sedge, a grass that sinks its roots deep into the peat, used by coastal First Nations people to weave elaborate watertight baskets.

We sat in the sunshine. No birds, no insects. Below us, less than six feet down, under the peat moss, lay clay hardpan who knew how thick. Under that, glacial deposit. Only these two layers are similar to our more tender and generous bog.

3.

Another September, another voyage, much longer by far. Another arrival at a new place. We were gone for ten months.

On September 18, 1985, we drove into Tacámbaro, a hill town in the Sierra Madre Mountains of central Mexico. We located the house we'd rented for a year, shopped for basics, and cooked a light supper. We went to bed early, woke before the sun. We washed, we boiled water for coffee—

The world shook. Walls swayed, graceful and mysterious, for more than three minutes. From our rooftop patio we watched women hugging babies, children running in all directions. We had lived through a massive earthquake. In Mexico City the quake had collapsed hundreds of buildings, killing more than ten thousand people.

The clock on Tacámbaro's cathedral dome said 7:19. It would remain 7:19 all year.

The previous December, end of 1984, on a scouting mission, this time looking for the ideal town to spend a low-budget year in the state of Michoacán, Kit, I, and our then seventeen-year-old son, David, had come to Mexico for two weeks. The car rental agency had armed us with a map and directions westward. After losing our way several times we climbed up from the bowl that held the capital city. The non-divided six-lane highway switched left and right a half-dozen hairpin times, us in the inside-most lane. To our far right, buses spewing brown smoke crawled up the incline; between us and the buses, trucks crept upward. Coming toward us, vehicles of all sizes and ages roared downhill; we were white-knuckle driving into a strange land. Slowly the sky grew brighter. Half an hour later we pulled off. Below us lay a grey-brown sea, thousands of cars, trucks, and buses rising from it, no city visible.

As we headed west the air became clearer, the sky a light blue. After Toluca the road diminished, two lanes winding through dry brown countryside. At the occasional stream, women washed clothes, hanging them on scrawny bushes under a high sun. We crossed into the state of Michoacán. Zitácuaro, two hours away, seemed the best town for spending the night. David read the guidebooks. "Hey, there's no mention of hotels in Zitácuaro."

"There have to be hotels," I said.

Second- and third-class buses lined Zitácuaro's main street, their engines blasting versions of purple-brown exhaust. A block off the main road we did find a couple of hotels. I didn't say, You see? because the hotels, even their signs, looked weary. Recorded ranchero guitars shrilled from competing loudspeakers. But we'd come as far as energy allowed, we were in non-gringo Mexico, we needed a room for the night.

We checked out the entryway of the first hotel—wind-blown

trash in the corners, no clerk in sight. In the second, its tiny lobby also short of clean, the clerk took us up two flights, pointed to a bathroom in the hall, faucet dripping, and led us to a room: two beds and a motionless fan. How much? I translated his pesos into six dollars. David checked the sheets. "No way, Da."

We headed for the car. "Just one night," I said. "We'll walk around town. We'll enjoy it."

"I won't."

I explained to Kit: Well within budget, right in the centre, must be lots of good restaurants.

From the back, David expanded: Spiders, dirty sheets, dust and sand everywhere, and the air dated from last week. "Look. Next year when I'm at university and you're here by yourselves you two can play at being hippies. But this is my vacation too."

Kit should see the room—

David glanced up from a guidebook. "There's a hotel three miles away. Rancho San Cayetano. Clean, quiet, simple, the book says. That might mean cheap, Da."

No, I wanted to hear people talking, get the language moving in my brain—

Kit said, thoughtfully, "If we don't like the rancho place, we can always come back."

David quickly agreed. I acquiesced.

We wound down a brown hillside. A small sign read SAN CAYETANO. VACANCY. Leaving the hard grey road behind we drove through a gate and along a tropical tree–lined avenue, blue, yellow, orange blooms in pots, vegetable and flower gardens. Less than a hundred yards in, between two buildings, red, yellow, and pink bougainvillea climbing the adobe walls, we stopped. The birdsong-filled air had turned soft. We walked up a few steps. On our left stretched a long building, attached individual units, a roof overhang, outside each door a couple of cushioned chairs and a little table. I called, "Buenos días!

Hello!" Silence. Small birds flew between trees and trellises, and the air smelled sweet. We stared in admiration.

"Buenas tardes." Behind us stood a short man, a large smile on his gentle oriental face, wearing a short-sleeved blue shirt, chinos, sandals. He continued, in simple Spanish: "And where are you from?"

"Oh," said Kit. "Canada."

"Ah. Vous parlez français?"

"Yes—oui," Kit said, adding, "et anglais."

"From Montreal, then," he went on in English. "And you have come to see the butterflies."

I said, "What butterflies?"

This was our introduction to André Claude, half French, half Vietnamese, a resident of Mexico for more than twenty years. We learned later that he was born in Vietnam, where his father had been a colonel in the French Army. He'd learned his English working in the United States, principally for North American Van Lines. What kind of accommodations did we want? A room with two beds, please. We followed him. Three of the eight units were taken, a film crew come to make a movie about the butterflies.

"I'm sorry, we don't know about the butterflies," Kit said.

His small, quizzical glance seemed to ask, Then why are you here? He explained we were now about forty miles south of the winter nesting place of the entirety of North America's monarch population. The butterflies roosted on the branches of a special evergreen tree found at the top of several mountains more than seven thousand feet high. An estimated twelve million butterflies had arrived this year. "You must go," he said. "It is very beautiful."

We agreed we would. Lucky, arriving here in the right season.

He showed us two rooms, the farthest from the office, each with two double beds. Clean, quiet, and simple had become immaculate, tranquil, exquisite: bedcovers in bright reds, blues, and greens; original lithographs on the walls; tiled floors, loomed rugs. A small balcony overlooked cornfields and, in the distance, an extinct volcano. "It is called San Cayetano," André said.

We chose a room. The cost would be the equivalent of twelve dollars. We were impressed. And he could recommend a very good restaurant in Zitácuaro. We unpacked. David merely grinned, noting we could drive into town for supper.

A knock on the door. André. "I think it would be better," he said, "if your son had his own room. You will all sleep much better."

Kit said, "We're okay really—"

David grinned.

André added, "If it's okay with them."

Yes, it was David's holiday too. He had located Rancho Hotel San Cayetano. Twelve extra bucks was no big deal. David took the room next door.

André invited us for a drink before we headed out for dinner. Over a beer we explained why we'd come to Michoacán, away from other English speakers, wanting to live mainly in Spanish—perhaps near Morelia, a university town, a good library, music, movies. Yes, we'd have a car, we'd be driving down from Montreal. He told us how to locate the butterfly mountains. He explained how to find his good restaurant, and which specialties he personally enjoyed.

In Zitácuaro we ate well, walked the loud, crowded streets, tasted exhaust, and returned to the perfumed silence of San Cayetano. Breakfast the next morning became our Mexican ideal: juice from oranges off the rancho's trees, huevos rancheros with eggs direct from the henhouse and covered with the kitchen's own salsa, fresh-baked tortillas, thick café con leche, rolls just out of the oven, and guava jam made from fruit grown in Rancho San Cayetano's orchard.

We thanked André again. He told us about a restaurant along the road where, after the butterflies, we should take our *comida*. He recommended a hotel in Morelia. "I hope you come back next September. I have made phone calls to let friends know you are looking for a place."

We were overwhelmed. Unparalleled generosity.

"No, it is very simple," he said. "We shall see what they find."

Time to leave. He handed me a bill. The breakfasts were inexpensive. I said, "You've not included David's room."

"But of course not, because I don't charge you."

"But we had two rooms—"

"No, you rented one room. The second would have been empty anyway."

We insisted.

"No," he explained. "With that room occupied I could put a NO in front of VACANCY. So my work for the evening was finished."

"But you weren't full," Kit said.

"But I was. You have two rooms. The film crew has three rooms. One of the rooms is where I live. I always leave one room empty, if a friend needs a place."

David the mathematician said, "But there's still one more room."

"Yes," said André, "that is so. There you are."

We all three shook our heads, visibly or less so. I paid, adding a large tip for the women in the kitchen.

The butterflies were stunning, tens of thousands of monarchs flitting golden in small groves, landing on our shoulders, tickling our ears with the light buzz of beating wings, we and the film crew the only ones about. Millions more were hanging on the trees. The restaurant on the way proved very good. The hotel in Morelia, a two-hundred-and-fifty-year-old hostelry—the interior courtyard heavy with flowering bushes and trees, at the centre a fountain spraying veils of water, the air rich with birdsong—was exquisite. We spent a couple of days searching for real estate agents but failed. Realtors are, it seemed, a gringo institution. But we were having a fine time. And in the fall we'd surely find a place to live.

Back up north, winter blasted us, true to form. We made plans for driving into the unknown. In June a letter from André arrived. It contained a photo of a stone-paved courtyard, bright bougainvillea at the far end, covered porticoes around the sides. He apologized, the only house he could locate. It was eighteenth century, cold and damp, he was unsure about hot water, in a small town two hours from Morelia, far from the university, on a twisting road, surely not what we wanted.

But a picture of a very attractive house. We found Tacámbaro on the map: the end of the road. Which, after a stress-filled few months at the university, sounded pretty damn good. I phoned. "André, we'd like to rent this house."

"Ah," he said, "I thought so. I have begun negotiations for you."

I laughed. "It looks very attractive."

"Yes," he said, "it is. Please phone me in three days."

I should have asked the price—

Three days later, I called. "Were you successful?"

"Congratulations, George, you have rented a palacio." I could hear his grin.

"That's great. But how much is it?"

"Ah. When German television came to Michoacán to film the houses from this period, they selected yours, one of the finest examples."

"But, André, how much—?"

"You know, much less than a small apartment in Houston or Manhattan."

My stomach churned. "André?"

"Yes. Fifty thousand pesos a month."

Instant figuring. Rent, two hundred and twenty-five dollars. Far less than I'd feared. And we hadn't expected eighteenth-century elegance. "We'll take it."

"Good," he said. "I have given the señora the first month's rent. You can pay me back when you arrive."

Stunning. André had met us for one short evening. All signs pointed to a great year.

September came. We drove south. From Houston we called him: "Anything you'd like from this side of the border?"

"No," he said, "but you must know, we have rented an empty house."

"Empty?" My voice squeaked.

"Yes, no furniture, no refrigerator, no stove. But do not worry, I have extra furniture. And a truck. Also a driver."

Kit's reactions and mine were similar: What have we let ourselves in for? and: Hey, it's gonna work out.

On September 17 at Rancho San Cayetano we found André in good cheer, our room ready for us, cut flowers on the table. We talked till dark. The following day, truck ready, the ground strewn with furnishings from the hotel's storerooms, we loaded up: three beds, a couple of couches, tables and chairs, linen, curtains, cutlery. We bought a small stove and mini-fridge. André directed the process, loading pieces in place like a three-dimensional jigsaw puzzle.

I said, "Did you learn to pack like that when you worked for the van line?"

He didn't seem to understand. "I loaded trucks only in Vietnam."

I asked, as lightly as possible, "Oh, for which side?"

"But, the French of course."

"Ah," I said. "Of course."

The next morning we drove off, the truck following. André had called ahead, and six hours later the door of our house stood open: a fine mid-eighteenth-century courtyard swept clean, the walkways under the porticoes tiled red, elegant beams supporting the extended roof, brown wooden pillars holding up the beams. Off the courtyard, nine doors to nine empty rooms. Not a plant to be seen, but these we would bring in.

The truck arrived. And with it, a man walked into the courtyard. We would come to know him well. Unrequested, he helped move us in. He participated in placing one of the couches, down here, so the TV—we didn't have one? "Get a set, help you learn Spanish," is what I think he said—could sit with its back to the light.

He suggested the men with the truck might like a beer. I gave him some money. The movers had lugged in our borrowed stuff. They enjoyed the beer. I paid the trucker the amount André had suggested, added a tip, tipped his assistant as well, and they drove off. Kit made up our bed.

My new Tacámbaro friend hung around. Suggestions for plants, where to place the lounging chairs. I finally realized: a gratuity. I reached a thousand pesos toward him. "Muchas gracias."

He stood still. Well, he was either insulted—friendship is not to be paid for—or deeply appreciative—a thousand pesos would buy his family many pounds of tortillas. My feeble Spanish left me with nothing to say. He stepped close, his face inches from mine. He looked directly into my right eye. His hands held my upper arms, squeezing gently. "We are amigos, no?"

I grinned feebly. "Si—"

"I swept your sidewalk before you arrived, I organized your house, I am your amigo. For an amigo, a thousand pesos?"

Not a single exchange, rather a series of stumblings. On both our parts. "I—I don't know." I was feeling afraid.

His grip tightened. "A thousand pesos. Not much money."

That I understood. "Amigo, for your work, how much is the right money?"

No change in his expression. Then my arms were free. His hands rose to my head. He pressed lightly, three fingers of each hand to my temples. "Jorge, I do not know the answer to your question. Only the gods know." He glanced toward the heavens. "The gods will bring you an answer."

Well, the gods didn't bring me a damn thing. Except—give him another thousand. Which I started to do. But after all my tipping my smallest note was five thousand pesos. Still, anything to be rid of him. "I hope this is good."

"If the gods say this, then it is good." No *gracias* now, that would be inappropriate among equals. "Hasta la vista, Don Jorge." He left.

I told Kit all this. We laughed. All this André had wrought for us. We cooked a light supper, went to bed early, woke—

At 7:19 AM, the world shook.

I used that experience as the scene that begins my first novel about Mexico, *The Underside of Stones*.

I came to love this part of Mexico. Michoacán, with its dry, burnished highlands, was where I'd wanted to retire—being there had preceded the Engineer's Challenge by a few years. After the year Kit and I had spent in Michoacán I'd gone back several times for six weeks, a couple of months, again to write. On these return trips Mexican friends would try to get me to buy property, a house or land, to tie me to the region, and so to them. I saw a number of pleasant places, then fell in love with a newly built colonial adobe they called *la casa de Chip*, Chip being the American who for health reasons couldn't live in Mexico any longer. To get to the house one took a skinny five-hundred-yard drive between two other properties—foreshadowing the narrow drive across our Gabriola bog. The *casa* had three bedrooms, complete with beds, chests, brass, tiles, and artefacts of the region. It was selling with all its furnishings intact and came with seven hectares of land, a stream dammed for first a trout pond, then a carp pond. The peace was grand. And the price?

"Chip will charge you only what it cost him to build it," one friend advised me.

"And how much was that?"

"Fifty thousand US dollars, an incredible bargain,"

I could see that.

"Cheaper than a Mercury Cougar," another noted.

"Why so inexpensive?"

"Ah, because of the long drive. For many country Mexicans a house directly on a major road is a mark of status. Far off the road, no one can tell if a fine house stands back there."

Kit didn't want to retire to Mexico. We both agreed we wouldn't stay in Montreal. Though we much loved the city, summers had become too hot and humid for her, winters too cold and the streets too icy for me. For years we'd been spending as much time as possible in our small country cottage on a lake in the Laurentians, north of Montreal, at first getting away on the weekends and sometimes, when possible, leaving Thursday after work and not coming back to the city until Monday morning. Kit had grown up in Vancouver, I largely in suburban New England. Neither kind of place seemed right for our retirement. We agreed, Mexico was not going to work. When we did reach retirement age, our health demands would increase, and we had seen the insides of Mexican hospitals. Also, our insurance in Canada would be cancelled if we were out of the country for more than six months.

Chip's house slipped away, over time's disappearing horizon. We came to the Engineer's Challenge instead.

Late this afternoon I walked back across the bog to the house. The dragonflies had departed. I was remembering the glimmer of their bright blue wings and wondering if they'd eaten their fill of insects so didn't note another presence until I was within a couple of yards. I caught a blur of brown movement as a head rose to stare at me. Between the carport and the wood-shed stood a fawn, no more than a couple of feet tall, sharply jointed, skinny back legs tense, white spots beginning to fade. He (?) stared at me as I stared at him, surprised, fascinated, each of us unsure what to do next. Most surprisingly he was alone, no mother in evidence. Neither of us moved. Slowly he lowered his head and nibbled at the grass by the side of the shed. Then he checked me out again, and walked a couple of feet to the edge of the drive where there's a bit of a drop-off.

We put branches down there for deer, arbutus leaves being their special treat. For arbutus, deer come from every direction like, one might say, dragonflies to a hatch. I've seen two dozen deer around a fallen tree. In the morning they'll have cleared all the leaves they can reach. I had, a couple of days earlier, tossed an arbutus branch into the drop-off. Now, nearly no leaves. The fawn began to nibble at the leaf stubble, only a few stems left but a small feast for the little guy. The whole time I hadn't moved my feet, only my head turning to follow his movements. Then, in the high salal and ocean spray beyond the drop-off, out of the corner of my eye, I saw a moving shape. The mother. I would leave, let them feed in peace. I moved one foot quietly. The fawn sprang—a cliché of a bound—into the brush and disappeared.

OCTOBER

I.

This morning, the first in October, the leaves of the broadleaf maple look more golden than they did yesterday at the end of September. A few have fallen. The flowers in pots on the cottage deck still need watering. The neighbour's meadow, leading down to the bog, is at its greyest brown, the bog at its driest. Our neighbour Alan, Andy's son, says he's seen the bog level drop ten inches overnight, as if someone had pulled a plug. I've yet to witness this, so it remains a good rural myth.

October is my hardest month, the time in the year my father comes back to me most vividly. It was in October that he died. I don't feel much psychic association with the day of my father's birth, August 6, but the time around his death lives on with me.

The satisfaction, and the sadness, of remembering. Dad lived into his ninety-first year. After the funeral a friend asked my brother what Dad had died of. "Everything," Jeff said. This was correct. When he died, all his systems had given out. He lost most of his sight in his one good eye some years earlier; the nerves of his other eye had been mangled when he was fifty-nine by the pressure against them of a large benign tumour. He'd been going increasingly deaf since his late sixties, his beloved classical music become groans and squeaks. His heart, lungs, and arteries had been so reduced in function he needed ever-increasing oxygen, ever more powerful pacemakers. His urinary system and his intestinal system had failed him a couple of years earlier. His skeleton had shrunk—five-feet-four as an adult, down to barely five feet. He took much of his frustration over his declining abilities out on my brother and his wife. But with me, who only dealt with him for a few days once a month, he remained at his core a lovely man.

In his last years he lived with my brother's family, near Philadelphia. I was in Montreal and tried to visit him for four or five days every three or four weeks; I'd been able to arrange my teaching schedule to make this possible. In September before school started I'd visited Dad, Jeff, and his family, then had gone again in early October over the Canadian Thanksgiving/US Columbus Day weekend. Should I return once more in October? Maybe once a month was enough. But I knew Jeff's difficulty in caring for Dad—lots of day help, but Jeff was responsible at night. Relief of just a few days was valuable. More, Dad clearly had very little time left, which meant I had little time left with him. So I would fly down at the end of the month.

The day before I left I had a call from Jeff. Dad was in the hospital again, and it didn't look good. "Not that it's looked good for months," Jeff added. I arrived and went straight to the hospital. Dad lay on the bed, still and silent, tubes entering and leaving his body. I kissed his forehead and said, "Hi." His skin felt dry and cool. He didn't respond. I sat on the side of the bed and took his hand. Two of his fingers curved around mine. He had always had a hard grip, and now his bony fingers squeezed hard. It was a grasp like a baby's, a four-month-old grabbing a finger and holding tight. Now his grasp took three of my fingers, thumb and pinky excluded, and pressed. I can sense the pressure as I'm writing this, the cool, hard hand amazingly arthritis-free, the hand that taught me to cast a fishing line, his thumb rubbing the skin between my knuckles.

When, three weeks earlier, I'd been with him at Jeff's home he'd sat there in silence, his eyes mostly closed, his breath coming shallow. When he had to get up I grabbed his hands;

he'd lock his elbows tight and I'd pull him up. On his feet he would wobble, find a balance, then take my elbow with one hand, my wrist with the other. He'd advance, each step six to eight inches. We'd walk like this for a few feet and he'd stop, perhaps halfway to his destination—the bathroom, the table. Halfway was half a victory. He'd have to sit again. He'd say, "Just let me catch my breath." Catch was the right notion because his breath eluded him; he would gasp for it until at last there'd be enough so his throat could stop rasping. He'd sit, wait for the breath to come right. He'd take my hand again, my fingers, as if they held the air his body needed.

I half remembered, and wondered at it, that I had once held his hand this way, nearly fifty years before, walking down a path in the garden, stopping as he showed me the marigolds starting to break from bud to flower. I must have held his hand earlier too, two or three fingers anyway, as I was beginning to walk, and he was the support then. This was during the war, in Northern Ireland where I was born, and then in England.

I know he once held my hand, squeezed it tight till I felt the pain, to stop another pain. I was four or five, we'd gone fishing. I was riding on the padded rack at the back of his bike, holding on to the top of his pants. We'd been out in the countryside. I remember walking through ferns under trees toward a brook, an overcast day, the woods dark. I wore short pants, and one part of the forest floor abounded with nettles. Dad helped me avoid them, picking me up if there was no other way. Dad fished and at first caught nothing. He let me hold his line and I caught nothing either. A bit later he caught a couple of trout, then let me take the line—and suddenly I had a fish on. He helped me reel it in. I now think the fish had already been on the line when he handed me the rod, but then it was my first fish. And we'd been out on an expedition together so everything was good. It was dusk when we quit, though not cold. I was tired so he carried me part of the way to our bike. Somewhere back in the city, me holding on to him, I must have relaxed into sleep. My sharp memory is of falling, yet not quite dropping to the ground because my foot had gotten caught in the spokes of the bike's wheel. There was a commotion about us, grey people, me sitting on the curb. I can remember crying. But mostly I remember the pressure of his hand, very tight around my hand, both my hands. The squeeze was so tight it reduced the pain in my foot and ankle. Years later I could imagine him feeling awful at his part in this incident, angry with me for having fallen asleep and getting my foot caught between the spokes, worried I might have broken my foot in a way that could never mend, scared at what my mother would say when he got me home, how it was his fault; but from then I remember only the pressure on my hands, tight, holding me there, with him, to him.

We had been living in England, in Manchester, for a year or so, having come from Londonderry—or Derry, depending on one's politics, then as now. We'd taken the ferry from Belfast to Liverpool, as I learned later, and the crossing was rough. In open waters we were a target for any Nazi air and U-boat raid. I knew about the raids; I'd been hauled from my bed often when the sirens went off. My parents knew far more than raids—they had escaped Hitler's Vienna only five years earlier, a story that has its place later in this memoir. Out in the middle of the Irish Sea the thrust of waves terrified me and I remember calling, "Mummy, your hand!" We were in bunks in a kind of ferry dormitory, my father in an upper berth and my mother across from me below. But it was my father's hand that reached down and found my fingers. When I think back on it, Dad must have been hanging from the bunk to find my hand, his hand grasping mine, from above somewhere. He might have come down and lain beside me because I felt much calmer after that. When I woke we were in England.

As I sat beside him that early October, Dad's breathing was so shallow as to be invisible, and his sleeping face looked like a death mask of itself. His hands lay on his chest, so little flesh on the fingers, skin over bone. On his right hand the index finger twitched, one of the few signs telling me he was still alive. I reached out, stroked that hand. He opened his eyes and grinned. He couldn't see me anymore, and his hearing aids were beside the bed. He said, "Hi, George."

"Good morning," I said.

He tried to push himself up on his elbows. He was too weak, he fell back. "My god," he said.

"Shall I help you up?"

"What a life, Georgie. What a life."

"I know, Dad. It isn't great."

"I'm not myself."

"How about some coffee."

He reached up a hand, and I took it. He said, "I wish I could fall asleep and not wake up."

I could only say, "You will, Dad. But not yet."

"What time is it?"

"Ten-thirty."

"My god. I thought it was twelve."

"No," I said and sat at the edge of the bed. "Ten-thirty."

"Still some time to live," he said.

2.

A dream about Dad, a couple of nights ago. We are in a car, me behind the wheel, in a long rural ferry lineup preparing to cross some stretch of sea water that isn't familiar to me. He decides he wants to get out and heads over to the shop by the side of the road, to go for a pee, buy a sandwich. I wait in the car. I become worried. The lineup starts to board. I get out, wave the cars behind me to drive around. The last of the vehicles

40

and passengers have boarded the ferry. I'm in a panic, have no sense where he's gotten to. I head into the shop. A men's room, a sandwich bar, but Dad isn't there. I describe him, ask if anyone has seen him. A clerk points to the back door. I walk out. Behind the shop is a small body of water, not connected to the sea, a little freshwater bog lying flat. Lily pads grow around the edges. A few yellow lilies reach out of the water on narrow stems. I see a small fish rise, leaving tiny rings in the water. Dad sits on a rock on the bank, staring at the water, watching it. In his hand, motionless, a fishing rod. Dad, studying the water.

I'd never been there with my father. But we had visited many places much like it. There, in the dream, the familiar part was Dad, watching the water.

The dream, I know, is as much about me as about him. When I was very young, still in England so it would have been before spring of 1948, he and I had travelled by train out into the countryside, to fish. I have long forgotten where it was or what we caught, but I still remember vividly the train trip back. We stopped at a small town. Dad said he'd get off for a minute to find us each a sandwich, and that I should wait for him in the compartment. I did as told, three-four-five minutes. What if he didn't get back in time? Suddenly the train did begin to move and he wasn't there. It picked up speed. I was panicked. I stared out the window. I saw him, running hard. But the train pulled ahead—he fell back, he was gone. I jumped into the aisle, I had to tell someone. I remember trying to talk to a woman, not being able make the words come out of my mouth, crying and gesturing. Then suddenly I was picked up and crushed, and I knew it was Dad, speaking softly: "It's okay, it's okay, okay." When I'd stopped crying, was sitting again in my seat, he asked me which of the two sandwiches I wanted. He told me he'd seen the train start to move but hadn't paid yet, then left more money than the price of the sandwiches and was running only so that he, too, would be moving when the train door was parallel to him, and he jumped aboard. All was okay, okay. But to this day I feel a small panic when someone I love isn't there as the ferry is about to leave, the bus about to depart, the gate to the plane about to be locked. This fear of separation has stayed with me for more than sixty years.

Dad watching water. Studying it. That dream brought to the fore the image, one I knew but long hadn't remembered: a picture of a man trying to look into the water, under its surface, to see what kind of life goes on down there. More than just the fishes. The entire underwater system. To an end of catching one of these fish, yes. But the catching is best done when one knows where the drop-offs are, the sunken logs, the weed beds, the stony ledges. When one understands the whole underwater system. When one knows you have to run as fast as a train in order to jump aboard.

Dad taught me to fish properly only after we came to the United States in 1948. Before I got my own rod, he gave me his old one from England, a trout rod. It came in three pieces, each about two and a half feet, each tapered. For me at age eight, a rod more than seven feet in length was way too long. The rod connected with ferules, the bottom of the middle section sliding into the top of the butt piece, the tip sliding into the middle section. Dad wrapped tape around the bottom of the tip, to fatten it, and slid it into the butt piece. The result, a five-foot rod for me. With the little crank reel, I was ready to go.

We had sailed on the *Queen Mary* from Southampton to New York in March, and spent the summer with various members of Mum's family in New York while Dad looked for work through his professional organization, the Knitted Outerwear Association. He was a designer of women's sweaters. In August he found a job that suited him, in Lowell, Massachusetts. We moved into an apartment above a store, Allard's Grocery, on

Chelmsford Road. In September, on the first day of school, I arrived wearing, as I always had in England, short pants. I was laughed at all day. It wasn't until the weekend that my mother bought me my first pair of long pants. And not until we were settled in, a few weeks or so later, did we begin exploring the neighbourhood—that is, the other side of our heavily trafficked road. So it wouldn't have been till October that Dad and I walked a few hundred feet and crossed the road to a large piece of hilly land that might once have been a pasture. I remember I wore my less-good pair of long pants. A dirt road ran along one side of the field. Beyond the little hills, not visible from the road, we found a stream, slow-running, surrounded by high grasses and cattails. We reached an open area, and Dad stopped. He sat on a rock and watched the water. I remained still, feeling something important was happening. At last he nodded. "Let's go and find our fishing rods, then we'll come back."

So, armed with the rods, some hooks, and a tin can holding a dozen or so worms we'd dug up in the small garden behind the store, we returned to the stream. At first we walked a little way up the stream, then back and downstream, Dad ever staring at the water. We came to a wide spot in the stream and studied it. He asked me if I thought there'd be fish here. Eager to start, I said yes. Where in the stream, he wanted to know. I had no idea. I asked him what he thought. He said maybe the edges of the stream were best, there the water moved the slowest and branches came out, giving the fish shade and protection.

He fashioned a float for me out of a short, stiff twig and tied it onto my line, a hook at the end, a worm on the hook. He showed me how to throw the line out—not casting it, my reel was incapable of that refinement, but stripping a few feet of line from the reel, holding the line in my left hand and flicking the float out over the water with my right. It took me a few attempts, but for the first time I was fishing on my own—in

England, Dad had always flicked the line out for me. Now he watched, not yet fishing himself. Despite his clever theory of letting the float bob along the stream's edges, it always ended up in the middle, in the faster-moving water. But I was pleased that I could manage to let the line out. I was fishing by myself. It must have been my fifth or sixth flick that I suddenly saw the little stick-float dive sharply under the water. I called, "Dad! Dad!" and Dad said, "Well, reel him in." But my fingers were having difficulty with the reel handle so I could only back away from the water, dragging the line and float up to the bank, the little fish trying to return to deep water, yank-yank-yanking the line against my pull. My first American fish was a seven-inch bluegill. Its gills truly were blue, a light steel-blue fading to black-green along its lateral scales. Its ventral scales were gold flecked with red, almost to its anal fin. I'd never seen a bluegill before, and neither had Dad. But it was a fish, so it could be eaten. When I close my eyes I can still see it clearly. And I can still sense an itch of the happiness I felt when we got back to the apartment and Dad showed Mum the fish and said, with pride, "He caught it all by himself." We ate it that evening. There couldn't have been more than a bite or two apiece.

In New Hampshire, where I spent my so-called formative teenage years, October was often our best month for fishing— not necessarily the best fishing, but the most serene, as most late-season fishermen and -women had quit by mid-September. So it was a good time of year for Dad and me to be out on the water, our only company each other. On a Sunday afternoon in 1952, we drove out to Manchester's nearest lake, Massabesic, which Dad referred to as our house lake. Boating and fishing were allowed, but no swimming, as the lake was the city's reservoir. Around the lake on the far side, along a winding and narrow road, a slow-moving stream flows into what's called the back lake. Down a bank on the lake side of a bridge was a rowboat hostelry. We always called ahead to reserve a boat—in October hardly necessary, but on arrival we didn't want to first check in with the owner, a chatty character; we were always eager to get out on the water. We piled our gear into one of the half-dozen boats, grabbed a set of oars, rigged up, pushed off, and rowed slowly into the stream. Easy work heading toward the lake, as we let the current take us.

In this section of Massabesic we fished for pickerel (*Esox americanus*, to distinguish them from walleyed pike, *Sander vitreus*, which get called pickerel in Ontario), the smallest member of the pike family. (A bit of further confusion: the walleye isn't a pike at all, but a member of the perch family.) The most successful bait for pickerel fishing is a shiner, a minnow around three inches long. Dad had taught me how to poke a thin hook into a shiner's flesh just under the dorsal fine. Placement of the hook is crucial. It must pass through the flesh above the spine; hitting the spine with the hook point kills the shiner. And it has to be set in the back rather than through the lips because a pickerel will grab a shiner crossways. The bait's length is the easiest target. Other fish will take bait headfirst, but the pickerel prefers to grab the bait, swim some small distance, turn the shiner in its mouth, and swallow it. We each fished with bobbers—no longer little sticks of wood but plastic balls an inch or so in diameter, half red, half white—with three feet of line below to the hook. This way the shiner could swim about in circles, drawing attention by its unusual movement, suggesting it was wounded and so an easy target.

We worked the stream edges, casting gently, rowing only to keep the boat at the centre of the stream. We watched the bobbers float silently on the flat dark water. No action in the first half-hour. Most of our past success came at the stream's end, a large round pond some two hundred feet in diameter. Over decades, possibly centuries, the stream had washed a mass of silt and soil down toward the lake. The silt had piled itself into a dam with an outlet only the width of the water upstream. It was in the pond, punctuated with groves of lily pads and patches of scrub bushes, that the pickerel lay waiting.

Here had been my introduction to bog fishing. In those days I began to call a bog any body of water that was small, shallow, weedy, had uneven shorelines, and abounded with life. For the bog to be perfect the day had to be wind free, the water still, flat, and dark. That October afternoon with my father, temperature in the mid-forties Fahrenheit, the sky clear, the sun low and cold, the pond was a quintessential bog.

Only one flaw. We were not alone. Halfway across, toward the pond's outflow, another rowboat. Two people, sitting quietly, fishing like us with bobbers. A man and woman. They looked very old to me. Now, seeing them still in my mind's eye, I'd guess them to have been in their fifties. About Dad's age then, but in those days I never thought about how old he might be. He was my father, he had no age. Every few minutes we could hear the man or the woman mutter a few words to the other. With the lake so still the sound of their shifts of body or any activity around their bait came to us across the water with harsh clarity.

Dad tossed his bobber over near a clump of lily pads. Pickerel will seek out these protected places because that's where small fish search for safety from kingfishers and other fish-eating birds. Dad's bobber suddenly disappeared, pulled under by the heft of the fish that had taken his shiner. Dad waited, waited, let the pickerel run, then stop. I could picture it turning the shiner in its mouth, getting the hook to a point back in its mouth where the barb could bite in and hold. I, like Dad, knew this was the moment, and he pulled his rod tip back hard to set the hook. The fish was on. Its first tactic was to take to the air. It came up, broke open the flat water, ruddy gills flaring red in the low sun, sides green and yellow. A good fish, sixteen or seventeen inches, I figured. It swam parallel to the boat, some thirty feet away. Dad worked it slowly, keeping it from wrapping the line around lily pad stalks, keeping it high and out of the weeds. I had the net in hand. The fish was tiring, no longer making headway, coming toward the boat now headfirst. At the boat it dove, a sudden yank causing the drag of Dad's reel to squeal. Just for a couple of seconds. Then Dad had the fish again in control. He raised the tip of his rod, the bobber on the line two feet above the surface. I swooped down with the net and swung the fish aboard. A long, narrow, gleaming fish, meant for speeding through water. A keeper.

A few minutes later my bobber went under and I brought in a small one, which got tossed back in with our usual admonition, "Send us your grandfather."

Then the woman on the other boat had a pickerel on. I heard her muttering, "The net, the net—" and the man murmuring, "I know, I know—" He netted it for her. It looked small. They kept it. We fished on for more than an hour. I finally got a keeper, though not as big as Dad's. On the other boat, nothing new. Dad and I glanced at each other, our code that said, We should be getting back. Ten more minutes? Five more casts. Okay.

Moments later we heard a splash and the man was standing in his boat, playing a large fish. A couple of minutes and he had it close. Now he was muttering, "The net, get the net," and she had it in hand. I heard him say, "Okay. Now." She swooped with the net. She must have missed but hit his line. Suddenly his rod was straight and the line slack. "Gone," she said. And then his words rang sharply across the disturbed water: "You goddamn fool!"

We lifted the anchor and rowed upstream to pay and leave the boat behind.

Here on Gabriola there are no fish in the bog. I'd thought of stocking the pond Gordie dug when he'd put in the road across the bog but had no idea how fish would alter the ecology.

Gordie had built the bog road in October when the water stood at its lowest. Sandy took pictures of the progress and sent them to us in Montreal. Over the previous summer we had talked further to Gordie about the road. He would dig a six-foot trench across the bog a few feet at a time, and lay tree roots, trunks, and branches down ahead of him as he went. Every few feet he'd dump a load of stone and gravel on top of the wood. The new piece of road then served as the platform for his excavator, for dumping the next load of roots, trunks, and gravel.

I had told him I'd like it if he could dig a small section of the bog deeper, a stretch nearest to the cottage maybe fifteen feet across and fifty feet long, big enough for ducks to land. I wanted it to have the feel of the pickerel pond on Lake Massabesic, the kind of place where Dad could have sat to study the water. Though he'd died a year before we bought the Engineer's Challenge, the pond was for him. As to putting any fish in, bass or perch were the only fish that might survive and reproduce in this kind of water. Trout need moving water for their eggs to be fertilized. But, it became clear, a bad idea to stock it, as great blue herons and kingfishers would finish off any introduced fish.

Gordie and I had checked out the area beside the crabapple trees, in late summer so dry we could walk on that part of the bog bottom. Halfway along the length of the planned pond we found dried leaves that looked like lily pads. Gordie said he'd make sure their roots survived his excavation.

When we returned in January the pond was in, flat water and a peninsula for the crabapple trees. I'd forgotten about the lily pads. Then, in late March, as I reached the cottage end of the road, out there in the pond, new green shoots. By early June we had lilies, larger than on Massabesic, the leaves larger too, big yellow bull lilies. Satisfying to find them here, natural to the bog, as if waiting for Dad.

3.

The voyages of October lead east. Most of Kit's family live in Toronto and Ottawa, our son, David, in Montreal. Daughter Elisabeth, her husband, Tom, and their son, Jacob, live in Massachusetts, in Cambridge. My brother, Jeff, is outside Philadelphia, but he and Gillian also own a cottage in western Massachusetts, in the Berkshires. They would drive up, and we and our young would join them there for the long weekend, Columbus Day in the United States, Canadian Thanksgiving, the weekend sixteen years earlier when I had made my next-to-last trip to visit Dad. Jeff and Gillian's cottage is on a lake. I looked forward to a little fishing with Hilary, Jeff and Gillian's oldest son. We'd likely fish from our old canoe. It now lives at Jeff's place, freighted there from our cottage in Quebec by Hilary when we moved to Gabriola.

The trip east began well. We'd spent the first night in Vancouver at an airport hotel, our flight being early the next morning. We get a special rate there, being semi-regulars and over fifty-five. As I registered, the young desk clerk noted I was getting the fifty-five-plus rate. He said to me—I swear—"Sir, may I see a picture ID?"

I gave him my driver's licence, he glanced at it, I asked, "What do you need that for?"

He glanced back at me first, then said, "I'm sorry, sir, you just don't look fifty-five." I hadn't been carded in over forty years.

The next day in Montreal, after we'd passed through immigration (no direct flight Vancouver–Boston anymore) we were waiting in the customs area, and another young man asked in that pleasant but wary customsy way, "What is the purpose of your trip?"

"To see my daughter in Cambridge."

"Oh," he said, "is she going to school there?"

I laughed. "No no, she's been out of school a long time, she's been working for years."

He wrinkled his brow. "Uh, how old is she?"

"Forty-four."

He stared at me. "You've got a forty-four-year-old daughter?"

I nodded. Shaking his head, all disbelief, he pointed to a customs line for us to stand in. Two flattering remarks in two days, and I was high on them.

End of the good part. When they opened our luggage they discovered my fishing equipment—the rod that broke into parts, my reel, and lures. No problem with the rod, but the lures—"You can't take those through." No more being addressed as sir.

"Listen, I've taken these through customs a dozen times in the last few years." The hooks were size 8 and 10, the shanks at most three-quarters of an inch long, the barb a third of an inch from the shaft. Hardly weapons of mass destruction.

"No, those can't go through."

What, my favourite bass lures, some of them over fifty years old? I was mighty irritated; I check regularly with Air Canada and again they'd told me there'd be no problem. I tried to think of alternatives—"I'll go back out and find an agent and send my baggage through."

No, not possible, once past immigration you can't go out again.

"Could you mail them to me? I'll give you my name and address and twenty dollars, please send them to me at home."

No, not allowed, once within this inner sanctum anything threatening had to be destroyed.

But some of the lures had belonged to my father! I was panicky now. "Could you put them in lost and found? I'll pick them up on my way back."

"Not permitted."

The only possibility was for an Air Canada agent to come through immigration, pick up my suitcase, and ship it through for me in baggage. They even had direct-line phones for this. I had forty minutes before departure. I called Air Canada. They wouldn't be able to send an agent for at least an hour. I asked to see the custom's supervisor. I said, with decreasing calm, "How do we resolve this?"

A large shrug from him. "There is no way. Nothing we can do."

I was as close to losing it as I've ever been in my life. They were actually going to confiscate my father's lures! It was all I could do not to burst into tears. Or bash someone. And time was passing—now barely fifteen minutes to departure. I thrust the box of lures at them, cursed under my breath, and Kit led me away.

I wasn't sure how I'd deal with this, but even now as I write I'm still furious. When in the quiet of the night I think about those minutes before boarding my blood pressure skyrockets. My face would no longer be mistaken for someone to be carded.

Far worse than losing lures has happened in the world. New York had usually been the October destination for my parents, Jeff, and me to connect with those of my parents' families who remained, those who had made it out of Austria, aunts and uncles and their US–born children. As Dad grew older he remembered mostly those who hadn't made it. On one of my visits to Jeff's place I remember sitting with him, he muttering, "Guter Gott. Oh guter guter Gott." Good god, oh good good god: the tip of his mind's iceberg, the part of the conversation he was having that I could hear. I knew from previous times with him that many of the sub-conversations leading to his plaint were bitter memories. Of his extended family, many years ago. Of his brothers Willy and Herbert, who were killed in Theresienstadt. Of my mother, who had died on Dad seventeen years earlier, changing him forever. He now trying to think with some clarity. Even as his words failed, the memories never left him.

Willy and Herbert Szanto had in fact fled from Vienna ahead of my parents, in early 1938, and settled in Paris. They were working to bring my parents out, as well as my two grandmothers. Then in 1939 Hitler and his henchmen concocted a plan that, purportedly, would get rid of all the Jewish orphans in Austria—if Jewish men who had left the country would return, to take responsibility for the children, then the children and their guardians would be given safe passage out of the country. Willy and Herbert were two of the many who volunteered for this service. Back in Vienna they presented themselves to the Nazi authorities. And were instantly incarcerated. They disappeared, and were never heard from again.

Many years later I was leafing through the *Theresienstadt Todesbuch*, the camp's *Deathbook*, and found their names: Herbert Szanto. Wilhelm Szanto. Among hundreds of thousands of other names. The Nazis were nothing if not thorough. Willy and Herbert died in 1942. Dad spoke of them less and less as he grew older. But they lived on, deep in his memories.

Today a phone call from the eye surgeon, giving me the date for my cataract operation: something to look forward to.

During the months before Dad died, the times I was visiting, I'd sit with him, saying little, keeping him company, telling him what was happening outside his window. Those days were similar to our times on a boat, rods in hand, watching the water, the weeds, the birds, our bobbers. In the silence, I made notes of some of what Dad said, when he actually spoke.

About his home care nurse: "She's stupid and rough. But when she washes me she wakes me up."

One time, after ten or so minutes of silence, he said, "All day I stare into blankness. When you talk to me, it awakens my senses."

"Good," I said.

He added, "A bit."

I was taken by the guilt of remaining silent.

Another time, sitting beside him on his couch, I felt the weight of his hand caressing my nape. He said, "Just a little bit longer."

"What?"

"I'd like to be around."

On my first visit that October, as I sat with him on the deck at the back of Jeff's house, on a warm early autumn afternoon, I watched him stare out into the large backyard, his head turning lightly as if shifting his gaze. I am rarely given to writing poems, but that day I jotted down some lines. I cite them here because it's as good a memory of Dad's last days as I can summon.

OCTOBER LIGHT

Look, Dad. There's so much light now—
a deep rent in the cloud quilt.
It feels all right now.
Cloud sheets tilt by.

Such fine light now. A pure display.
A finch in the feeder cracks a seed,
sun low behind him, his feathers gleam.
A fledgling grosbeak flaps the finch away.

Once Dad's favourite time. Sherry on the deck,
warm in late sun, on his lap a closed book.
New clouds. Double layered. One sweeps, the
    nearer strays.
See, now! The sun again. Look!

Dad has no light now. His eyes recall its traces
on the deck in times before, and in other places.

Halloween marks the end of October, and on the island the
pleasure of Halloween is taken seriously. The roads of the densely
populated subdivisions crawl with kids pretending to be other
forms of life—sometimes of death—parading from door to door
demanding handouts. Here the time for filling the bags with
candy goes from about five-thirty to nearly seven, a few kids
carrying on longer, preferring a larger haul to being present at
the major public event of the evening, fireworks on the beach at
Taylor Bay. The beach is one of the Twin Beaches, a provincial
park set on either side of a narrow neck of land connecting a
rounded peninsula to the main island. If with global warming
the sea level were to rise three feet, the peninsula would turn
into an island.

To get to the fireworks we'd left the house before six—no
trick-or-treaters ever come up to Chernoff Drive, the houses
being so long a distance from the road—noting as we crossed the
bog a mist hovering, appropriately ghostly, above the low water.
We took North Road, through a stretch of it known locally as
the Tunnel, where fir and arbutus grow tall along the sides, their
branches overhead meeting and intertwining. On sunny days
or near to full moon the road is dappled by light and shadow.
This dim evening a different kind of illumination played on the
verges—jack-o'-lanterns. No homes lie along this stretch for
three or four miles, the land being mostly Crown property, but
grinning and leering and scowling orange faces, huge pumpkins
and tiny ones, sit on stumps, on rocks and ledges, lodged on or
suspended from branches, or on the ground in groups of three
or four as in amused or amiable or devious conversation. They
appear as if by magic, but in actuality a number of islanders
carve them, bring them out to the Tunnel, light them, and go

away, leaving dozens of jack-o'-lanterns for the enjoyment of all who drive by. They have a playful reality of their own and set a generous collective mood for the evening.

Usually Halloween is cold. This last night of October was no exception. Luckily we have a good friend who owns a home on Taylor Bay. His living room windows look out over the water and down to the beach. Kit and I, our host Ian, and three others including Sandy, armed with glasses of wine, waited for the fireworks in the fire-warmed room, munching pizza. The show began with high round starbursts, shots of blue and yellow stars, then multicoloured stars, followed by whining rockets leaving a red trail before exploding into hundreds of specks of green and gold, then silver fountains turning into gold stars, spinning wheels in the sky, crackling stars, and rounds of flashing comets.

The first fireworks I saw were in England, in 1946, on Guy Fawkes' Night. Dad had bought two and explained what they were, that when it got dark he'd light them and they'd make a beautiful coloured explosion. But explosions scared me because I remembered all too clearly the real explosions of only a couple of years earlier, also at night, when Mum—never Dad, he was already out there in the night, an air-raid warden leading others down into shelters—would wake me and guide me, sometimes carry me, into the cellar and we would huddle under the stairs, carpeting nailed to the brick foundation walls both to keep the space a bit warmer and to provide a little protection against splintered glass or bricks. The night would fill with the blare of sirens. They'd last for a while, then go silent. We'd listen for the whine of a buzz bomb, always hoping it would continue and pass over us. The whine ending meant its engine had cut out and the bomb was falling. And would explode. Luckily I, under the stairs, never saw any blast from these.

Dad had brought two little rocket fireworks into the house.

No, I needn't be frightened. In fact I should be excited, they were hard to find but he'd managed to get these two so soon after the war. When it became dark I was told to go to my room on the second floor. I stood by the window overlooking the back garden. The rockets stood upright, a stick in the ground supporting them. Dad waved up to me and Mum beside me, she holding my baby brother Jeff. Dad lit a match and brought the flame to the fuse of the first rocket. I saw a burning string. The flame reached the base of the rocket. And went out. Dad waited. Silence and stillness. He reached out for it, which scared me again—would it explode in his hand? I saw him shaking his head. He knelt again, another match, lit the fuse of the second rocket. It caught, he stepped back, the sputtering light reached the rocket, again nothing—then suddenly the rocket took off on a low angle and exploded amid the bare branches of a little tree, showering the air with tiny sparks of yellow light. A small explosion but scary, too reminiscent of the buzz bombs during the war. I wondered what he did, afterwards, with the first rocket, but never asked.

Down at our beach, the last of the fireworks blazed into the sky, quadruple starbursts in red, gold, and green, and suddenly the outside night was again dark. The whole of the show had lasted nearly half an hour. We finished wine and pizza, and all of us went on to the last event of the evening, the Haunted House, the home of a friend transformed for one day of the year. Each year there's a different motif, usually literary. This year the house showcased snippets of *Macbeth*, a production with over two dozen actors. We walked through the space a small group at a time, past the talking trees of Birnam Wood shivering out in Gabriola's own Scotch mist, muttering, "Birnam Wood is on the move, Birnam Wood is on the move . . ." and greeted the witches at their cauldron, "Bubble, bubble, toil and trouble—" There was Will Shakespeare at his desk, murmuring to himself as he jotted words on paper with a quill, then Duncan's bloody corpse as Lady MacBeth's words, "Will these little hands e'er be clean again?" were repeated over and again. And out the other side. Deb and her husband, Jim, spend most of each October preparing the event.

Back along North Road as the jack-o'-lantern spots of friendly light glowed beside the road, once again up our hill, down our drive and across the bog, the thin wet air still glowing an eerie gold in the car's headlights, and we are home.

Home is a strange notion. I have lived in many places. When I taught for a term in Brazil, in Salvador, I had a room in a house, which for two months I called home. And then there was that lovely *casita* in Michoacán. For twenty-five years we were in Montreal, the longest period of time I've lived anywhere; it's a wonderful city, but it never fully felt like home. In southern California we owned the beach cottage, which, had we stayed longer with our growing kids, would have become too small to be our home. In Laramie we rented houses—harbours of warmth against the bitter Wyoming winters, not quite home. As my parents' son in Derry, in England's and New Hampshire's Manchester, I had a room, shared with my brother. In each of these places, these houses, I often realized I didn't feel quite at home. Right now, here beside the bog, I feel closer to where I want to be than any place I have lived. I feel at home.

Dad died at the end of October 1991. In the months before, knowing he was approaching his end, knowing a funeral awaited, I had read through my notebooks where I'd written down some of his phrases from time gone by. I knew that soon I'd have to say something about him before they lowered the coffin into the ground. I'd been looking to see if I could find some phrase he'd said that I could make reference to. When the moment came, I had to talk about his hands.

At our cottage in the Laurentians I would help him into the boat. I'd row to a place where there might be fish. I would cast a line for him, hand him the rod, let his hands feel the vibrations of a fish nibbling.

He gave me the woods, the ponds, the lakes and bogs. Handed them to me, with a fishing rod.

NOVEMBER

I.

This November 1 dawns clean, bright, crisp. The kind of day that defines autumn. The sun is taking its time sending its shafts through the south-facing windows. But when it reaches the outdoor thermometer's level, around ten in the morning, the hand on the apparatus points to twenty degrees Celsius, sixty-eight Fahrenheit. Both of these readings lie. They do imply, though, that the day will warm up. Outside on the deck the air on my skin feels more like eight or nine Celsius.

Back in the kitchen, time to make my lunch sandwich: lots of green (three kinds of lettuce leaves, plus arugula, cilantro—all these still from the garden—and scallions and a sliced jalapeño) on my own whole wheat bread. I've been making bread since coming to Gabriola. I cheat, though; I use a bread machine. One of the finest aspects of living in Montreal had been the array of bakeries available throughout the city. We'd learned enough about Gabriola and commercial Nanaimo to realize that good bread would not be easy to come by. (No longer true—now there is a first-rate bakery on Gabriola, but expensive compared to homemade bread, which, also, we've come to prefer.) So, while we lived in the cottage by the bog as the house was being built, we planned out uses for its many corners and crannies. We decided one counter in the kitchen would be lower than the rest, to make kneading easier—hard on the back and shoulders for relatively short people like Kit and me to press down heavily for fifteen minutes on a counter the normal thirty-six inches high. The builder understood where we wanted the lower counter, as did the cabinetmaker who would install it, and the man who'd lay the countertop tiles knew exactly what needed to be done. We left Gabriola for our last months of teaching in Montreal. We returned on the final day of the year, headed to the cottage to unpack, then to the building site. A framed structure when we'd last been here, it had been turned into a true house, the overall shape and the bits and pieces no longer images out of our and our architect's imagination and from her plans, but a remarkable realization of our projected home.

Except: In the kitchen, in the bread-kneading niche, the counter height was consistent with the other counter heights. A problem. We brought it to the attention of the builder, the cabinetmaker, the tiler. All of them remembered; conceded, were embarrassed; agreed to tear it down, redo it. Kit and I talked this through. The mess that would result. The time that would be lost. Would it always look like a last-minute change of mind? How much did we want to make bread anyway, someone had said the Village Market now had a pretty good new bakery. We'd heard from friends for years about bread-makers but had always kept ourselves superior to such machines. Stuart our builder suggested we give one a try. We bought, we baked; we've not looked back. You get less upper arm exercise with bread-makers, but they do save a lot of time. And there's a small but intense double pleasure in setting the time delay at night, knowing what awaits, then waking in the morning to the scent of freshly baked bread wafting up the stairs. So today, like every writing day, I look forward to my sandwich. It's packed up with a cookie, also homemade. By Kit.

Around ten-thirty I headed across the bog. The bog road functions as a kind of sundial, not for the hours of the day but for the months of the year. The road runs north–south. In

June and July, late morning, the shadow cast by the trees at the south end is so minimal it barely spreads beyond the woods. The tracks of the road, yellow-brown sand divided by a foot of weed, suck in July's warmth. From the house side to cottage side the road is baked solid, suggesting terra cotta strength. This morning's shadow stretches two-thirds of the way across. As I head out of the shade, no wind, mid-autumn, the pristine sunlight feels warm on my back. On the bog, after a clear cold night, no ice yet. It will come.

The cottage itself, this time of year, this time of day, sits in shadow. In the afternoon, as the sun pushes westward, light will pour in through the windows, low and bright. I'll have to draw the blinds so I can work at my computer. But at eleven, as I turn up from the bog around the corner into the shade to the entry door, it's dark enough for my advance to trigger the motion detector light. A friendly greeting.

Ten days into November, heavy winds overnight, and in the morning the crabapples beside the bog road are denuded of leaves, the branches now scraggly and bare. Usually with such winds we lose power, but this time we got lucky, no outages on Chernoff. Parts of Gabriola went dark—Sandy was without electricity for over twelve hours—and many parts of Vancouver Island as well. Yesterday a rock slide across the Island Highway north of Campbell River closed a long stretch of road up there, and power lines down between Campbell River and Courtenay wiped out another forty miles of highway. As it's the only road that connects the towns and cities along the east side of Vancouver Island, most of the northern third of the island is dark.

On the other hand, behind the house on the somewhat protected east side, the Nearly Wild rose is still producing flowers, the miniature rose bush at the top of the garden is sending out little splashes of colour, dozens of bright red buttons, and down below in the garden behind the boules court the blackcurrant is, perversely, in bud. None of them know how cold it's still gonna get. I tell them this, but they don't listen. I checked out as well the bed beside the boules court that fills first with daffodils, then in the early summer with daisies and poppies. In August when the poppies ended I covered it with black tarp to keep down the fall and winter weeds. This morning I lifted the tarp. The daffodils have sent up green shoots. November. Oops.

I am in countdown mode. The cataract procedure is in three days, the necessity of putting drops in my eye has begun, and I can sense the reality of the knife.

I'm not squeamish about such things, Buñuel's *Un Chien Andalou* with its razor blade and eyeball scene notwithstanding. A couple of decades ago, when we were still living in Montreal, we'd gone to our cottage in the Laurentians. I was splitting logs for kindling. A tiny splinter leapt up and lodged itself in my right eye. It didn't hurt, it didn't seem to harm my eye, but it was an irritant and I wanted to rub away the itch—clearly not a good idea, no sense pushing the splinter deeper in. We left for the city immediately, half an hour packing up and heading across the lake to the dock and the car, another hour to the emergency room at the Queen Elizabeth Hospital. A young doctor, likely an intern, saw me immediately. He examined my eye gently. He put a droplet in my eye, which he said would freeze the surface. He got me to lie back-down on a gurney beneath a bright light focused directly on my eye. He told me to relax and stare straight up. I saw his hand coming toward my face, the pincers he held, the fingers of his other hand holding my lids apart, the pincers huge. I felt a touch of pressure and the splinter was out.

"Got it," he said.

"Great," I said.

"You want to see it?"

I did, though I felt I'd been looking at it for the whole trip down from the cottage and would have believed him if he'd now held up a small log. He helped me sit up. The culprit splinter was the width of three hairs and maybe a tenth of an inch long.

I remember he said, "You were very brave."

"What choice did I have."

The cataract operation is, I know, a simple procedure. A quick cut, the old lens is out, an implant set in place, and it's over. Six or seven minutes, I'm told. Many people have it done, and the change afterwards, they say, is immense. Although yesterday someone mentioned I shouldn't expect too great a difference in anything but the elimination of blur—the most dramatic results are found in patients whose cataracts are far more advanced. For months I had weighed the decision to have it done now against waiting; do nothing can also be a piece of valuable advice. Do it earlier rather than waiting was the advice I listened to, that it's a simpler procedure when the lens is still soft. Now I just wish it were done and over.

2.

I have been given my procedural marching orders. Tomorrow at 8:10 AM I am to present myself at the outpatient clinic of the Nanaimo Regional General Hospital. I've met my eye surgeon, Martin Spencer. He has the high respect of my ophthalmologist, of my family doctor, and of a retired ophthalmologist friend turned mystery novelist living here on Gabriola. I have researched Dr. Spencer. He's introduced a couple of innovative techniques to his field and written papers about his work.

I recognize I grasp only in the most rudimentary way what will happen tomorrow. A man I barely know will take a knife and slice out the lens of my right eye, one of two organs that let me see what is out there in the world. I am asked to trust him. I have read his credentials and his papers, and in fact I do trust him. I remember my students read my credentials. I know I helped some of them, possibly many of them. I know I failed some of them. Hmm. My reason says he'll do well by me, but . . .

Cataract Day began early. Up at 5:00, to get to the ferry lineup by 6:30 for the 6:45 to Nanaimo. Fifty minutes or so before departure would have been necessary for the 7:50, but I've been told there's an unwritten agreement that those who regularly take the 6:45 don't compete with each other to make sure they're on. So getting there at 6:40 might be soon enough, I thought. Except our regular ferry, the *Quinsam*, isn't running these days; it's out for repairs. The replacement ferry, the *Bowen Queen*, takes about fifty-five cars to the *Quinsam*'s seventy, a cargo difference that had to be considered. In the end we chose not to take chances, made our decision, and got up the twenty minutes sooner. A light breakfast, on the advice of the outpatient's directions sheet. As we crossed the soggy road, our headlights turned the mist above the water and low-looming hardhack into an opaque soup. By the time we reached Chernoff Drive the mist had turned to heavy rain, huge, splattering, close-together drops, near-tropical. The hard downpour continued along South Road all the way to the ferry. At 6:30 we were seventh in line. Too dark to read. Kit shut her eyes and napped. I didn't want to close my eyes, superstitiously thinking that might be a foolish thing to do. So I stared out, wondering who was in those cars ahead of us: people who travelled this route daily or others like ourselves crossing today for some special occasion? I wasn't prepared to interview fellow passengers.

The *Bowen Queen* approached and docked. It's a much higher ferry than the *Quinsam*, with two passenger decks above the car deck. A couple of years ago when we'd had the same replacement ferry, in the cabin someone a seat away from me noted to his friend that for safety he preferred the *Bowen Queen*: "If it sinks while we're crossing everybody can rush to the top deck and stay dry." I climbed up to the higher deck, both for its men's room and for some light to read by. The cabin was whirling and gurgling with school kids between twelve and fourteen, off on a field trip, their parents and teachers trying for control. I heard a teacher say to a parent, "I can't find six of the kids." I stared at my book, faked reading, listened to kids arguing or just gabbling, in a couple of instances flirting, me enjoying their energy at this hour, not yet 7:00 AM, and glad I had responsibility for none of them.

We drove off and headed straight for the hospital, the outpatient service, arriving forty minutes early. The appointed time, 8:10, came and went. I decided I'd make notes detailing the procedure. Now 8:20 came. And 8:45. If we'd been on the later ferry I could've had an extra hour of sleep.

Into the nurse's office at 8:50. She explained the procedure. She froze my left eye. She told me the surgery had been planned for 10:35 but was pushed up to 10:00 because there'd been a couple of cancellations. I returned to the waiting room. The psychology of surgery—come early, wait, get irked, wait some more, try to find out what's going on, keep waiting. By the time I'd actually be taken in I'd be too bored to worry about it. But first, wait.

Finally into the receiving room. I lay back on a wheeled stretcher, head on a towelled brace, underside of knees supported by a pillow. A nurse placed a blanket over me. Along came the anaesthesiologist, introduced himself, explained he'd first put some more drops in my eye, and then some anaesthetic jelly. This would numb the nerves around the eye so I would feel nothing during the surgery. Seemed fine by me; boredom was working. A couple of minutes later my surgeon arrived.

He asked if I was ready. Bored, I wanted to say, but refrained because I didn't want to admit to losing the psychology battle. I mouthed something profound like, Ready as I'll ever be. I asked Dr. Spencer if he would let me know along the way what stage in the surgery he had reached. He agreed.

He personally wheeled me into the operating room, leaving the stretcher positioned so that my head was directly below an overhead contraption, a large, ultra-bright light. He told me it would, to begin with, be very hard to look at but that after a minute or so the light would seem to dim. If anywhere along the way I felt pain I was to say so, and the anaesthesiologist would administer additional freezing jelly. He tested my eye, the right, first with his gloved index finger, then with a metal probe, and asked if I could feel anything. I couldn't. Next he took an instrument that looked like pincers that might grab a small object like an ice cube, but, he told me, it worked the other way—this was a clamp to keep my eyelids apart. Which is what he immediately used it for. Then he placed what seemed like a thin, green, lightly padded pillow over my head—"To mask your face." At the point directly over my covered right eye I could sense light beyond some plastic. He cut the plastic away, exposing my right eye. Then he turned on the light. Brilliant beyond bright. I saw a dark central spot. Around it danced an aura of shifting, gliding, glowing lilac-purple light, with yellows at its boundaries. Modifying versions of this would continue till he finished.

He told me he was about to begin. (If, reader, you are squeamish about such things, you might want to continue a couple of paragraphs down.) He said I'd likely feel a bit of wet dripping by the side of my head because as he worked he would be flushing both my outer eye and the hollow he was creating. Okay, he made his first incision into the lens. "The outer part of the lens is hard," he told me. "Taking it out is the longest part of the procedure." He remained silent for a couple of minutes. I felt no pain, only a little ongoing pressure. I mentioned this. "That's normal," he said. "I have to press hard to get through the outer lens." A few seconds later he explained that the outer lens had gone, and he was now working on the much softer inner lens. I heard him say, "There. It's out. Here comes the implant."

It suddenly occurred to me that I had no idea what the implant was made of. I asked him.

I was certain he said, "Cellophane." Another few seconds and he said, "Okay, you're done." The overhead light went off.

I said, "What do you do with my old clouded lens? Can I see it?"

He removed my green cotton mask. "It's pretty much flushed away in the rinse water." I wanted to know what it looked like. "Sort of like thin milk as I take it out," he said, "and when it mixes with the rinse it looks like dirty dishwater." Dishwater.

He set some gauze over my eye, placed a clear plastic patch over the gauze, and taped it in place. I had to leave the patch on till he saw me later in the afternoon. He and a nurse helped me from the stretcher to a wheelchair, and the nurse rolled me out. Kit arrived with my coat, she and the nurse helped me stand, and we walked out. From lying down on the stretcher to departure had taken seventeen minutes.

I felt a little shaky but had no trouble walking. By the time we reached the car I felt steady, except I had no peripheral vision. It was 10:30 and we couldn't see him again until 2:45. What to do? What we do every time in Nanaimo, we ran errands. I needed to replace my watch battery. Kit had to pick up a plaque for the Gabriola Museum to which she gave a lot of volunteer time. We'd earlier decided to treat ourselves to a gourmet lunch at the best place around, the Wesley Street Café. It was early, but we were both hungry and decided to go just at noon—after all, we'd not eaten since that light breakfast.

But on Monday, it seemed, the restaurant was closed all day. Thwarted, we went instead to a nearby healthy food (rather than health food) restaurant and feasted on comfort food.

The first follow-up, at 2:45, took four minutes. Dr. Spencer took off the gauze, looked at my eye, found all was well, added more drops to dilate it further. I had a final question: I hadn't felt or seen any stitching, so what holds the new lens in place? The iris, he said. It's pushed apart during the procedure, and when the lens is implanted the iris closes in around the new lens and keeps it there. Brilliant.

Later, back at home, I reread the material I'd been given regarding my procedure. Having it over and done, its various parts took on more resonance. The itch I feel in the eye is normal. So would be a momentary residual blur. Also, I realized I'd misheard Dr. Spencer. The implanted lens is not made of cellophane but of silicone.

I slept with the plastic eye patch on. It will be there over-night for a week to keep me from accidentally rubbing my eyes. In the morning I took it off. No more itch in the eye, and in the still grey daylight I could see clearly a much greater distance than before. Strange, though, that electric lights give off bright beams in all directions, as if they were stars with shafts. Quite beautiful. This will go away in a few days, I'd been told.

Norm in the village fitted the right side of my specs with clear glass. It will take a few days, possibly a week or two, for me to blend the images seen by each eye, but I seem well on the mend. It'll take at least a month to determine any possible shift in the birdshot.

Two days after the surgery and the new lens is well in place. My concern now is that there be no macular edema in the eye—either eye, since the trauma would have challenged the birdshot in both.

This morning the bog road is white with hoarfrost. The day is cloudless and the air brilliantly clear, as after a heavy rain, but the white is dew that has frozen. At the house there's been no frost, neither on the south-facing side looking down the strait nor on the north front. Trees had kept the thin precipitation from settling, and likely their warmth helped as well. But on the road, frost. And I see it clearly.

Often after a winter rainfall, puddles will form on the bog road. At night the puddles freeze over. But the road has good drainage so puddles don't last long as the water seeps down to bog level. In the morning as I walk across, the tops of the ex-puddles have a sheet of clear ice over them, the space beneath hollow and dry. The thin layer is shot through with freeze lines set at sharp angles to each other, forming eclectic geometric patterns. It always seems a destructive shame to drive the car along the road, crushing the delicate designs.

3.

The property here, as I have said, is long and narrow. As such it cuts through three separate micro-ecosystems. Between Chernoff and the cottage the land is dry with almost no top-soil over a sandstone ridge. The firs growing here are thin and scrawny, called pecker-poles in this part of the world. When we first lived on the island, a slash had been cut into the ridge behind the cottage to bring a water line down from the well. Kit and I tried to fill in the bare space by transplanting salal and Oregon grape there, as well as small alder, cedar, and fir. Without constant summer watering, the transplanted trees died. Before we fenced the area in, the cedars and alders didn't have a chance to die—the deer chomped up the little seedlings with delighted gusto.

Not until the drive reaches the cottage beside the bog do either fir or arbutus have any substance. This part of the land, stretching from the cottage to the ridge in front of the house, is damp, partly because of the bog itself, partly because the soil about it is thicker. Heavy salal grows well here. The canopy is too thick to allow any other undergrowth, though on the south side for a short stretch after leaving the bog, electric-green moss carpets the terrain. At the far end of this second system the other ridge rises lightly, as if floating. At its top the sandstone sits on the surface, an unrelenting dry stretch similar to that behind the cottage.

The third little ecosystem begins below the house and carries on down the slope to the road below. The upper part of this area we cleared when the house was being built, down to a fence we ran to discourage the deer. Here are the flower and vegetable gardens, the fruit trees—plum, apple, pear—and the blackcurrant bushes. Before we moved in, many a fir and arbutus had covered what would become the building site. There'd been some good trees back this way. A local man with a portable mill turned some of the logs into lumber for us. Part of the decorative wood built into the house came from the land, a couple of cedar eight-by-eights and some fine fir twelve-by-sixes.

With the trees gone the land was so bare we tried to seed it with clover, which, we were told, is the fastest-growing ground cover. A few months later it had taken over, with even greater vehemence than predicted. Before we moved in, we'd vowed not to put in a lawn that had to be mowed. But like alder seizing control, the clover flourished until, a couple of years later, wild grasses finally choked the clover out; the grass now has to be cut half a dozen times a year, mostly in the spring and summer. This fall, an especially wet season, we had thick green grass growing till the end of November.

Back here as well we allowed a few alder saplings to grow, starting in 2000 when they planted themselves. We took most of them out in 2006. Some had reached a height of thirty-five feet, their trunks over five inches in diameter, the second growth ring on one of them an inch and a quarter wide. Below the fence this generous climate continues, some of the fir there one hundred and twenty feet tall. The land had last been logged in the 1940s.

My eyes aren't focusing properly. I see clearly out through my new cellophane/silicone lens, and as adequately as before with the other eye, which has been developing, more slowly, its own cataract. But the two points of focus will not meet. I look out and instead of the image in my glance converging, providing depth perception, all ahead looks flat. It's not as if I were seeing the scene twice, it isn't a double image, more as if I were walleyed. I'm still being told this will right itself as my brain learns how to handle the new lens. My brother, Jeff, called last night to ask how the procedure had gone. I told him about this non-convergence phenomenon, which reduced him to laughter. He said, "I wouldn't have believed anybody would go so far as surgery to get the Jean-Paul Sartre look."

I'm trying to concentrate on these pages, but there's a major distraction. Outside the large windows a plump-breasted robin is pacing the deck railing, literally from end to end, all twenty-two feet of it. He's strutting now, a bob-strut, and his head is turned slightly toward the window, as if he's watching me type. He's been at this parade for easily ten minutes, on the railing much of the time, though twice he's flown down to the bog. Now he's bouncing up to the flower pots outside the window, springing from one to the other, always looking into the window. I suspect he's seeing his reflection as another male robin, and sooner or later he'll be locked in battle for his territory with this newfound opponent. Now he's fluffing up his orange breast as if breathing in deeply. And strutting some more. Now he's back on the deck—and attacking the window! Again! He starts at the bottom and flies upward close to the glass, pecking at it as he rises, half a dozen hard tapping pecks on the ascent. Back to the railing, and more swagger. And again to the bottom of the window.

He's now attacked the front window five times.

And now he's gone, flown over the bog.

When we first came to live on Gabriola, each ferry trip was a bit of magic. We'd stand up front and stare out. To the northeast rise the Coast Mountains, at appropriate times of the year capped with snow, a regal horizon line from Vancouver to beyond Texada Island. To the south and southeast lie Nanaimo Harbour and the city itself. Above it hovers steadfast Mount Benson, and beyond it lies the island's wild interior. In the water, curious harbour seals would poke their heads up to watch the ferry pass. In the air we'd see gulls gliding lazily and cormorants whizzing by, and the occasional dominating eagle. At times the water lay flat and fine. At others strong wind would send whitecaps slapping at the ferry or breaking over the front, sometimes splashing passengers. And all the while we and our car were, miraculously, floating on top of the water.

The twenty-minute crossing is a connection between the largest part of our lives, that spent on our island, and the small part that, from time to time and thanks to the ferry, we gain access to. Others sat in their cars and read, or slept, or talked. No one seemed aware, or if aware to care much, that we were in the middle of a remarkable trip. We felt, in our enjoyment of the sights and sounds of the trip, mightily superior.

Then came winter, driving rain, cold days. It felt good to have a warm car to sit in and read. With spring we'd get out again and stare at the sea, and the horizon. And maybe head back to the car for the pleasure of a little more reading. But after the first couple of years we too began to read or nap our way across. One had to insist on getting out and again gaze at the horizon and the water. For us they'd become daily, normal. If we have visitors with us on the ferry we get out and stare again at Vancouver Island or the mainland, now through their eyes, and the land again looks stern, the mountains massive, the ocean scarily deep.

A few days after my surgery we were returning from an afternoon of errands in Nanaimo. Our car, boarded among the first, sat parked at the front. The ferry approached the dock on the Gabriola side. The doors to the lateral cabins opened, people streamed out and made their way forward. They were, I suddenly realized, participating in a kind of choreographed spectacle, each person with his or her set role in the overall production. A rope barrier hung with removable orange plastic netting holds the passengers back from the off-ramp. They wait, the boat clangs against the side barriers and slides into place. A sense of impatient dance seems to build, the passengers partnering the ferry workers. One crew member steps over the rope to tie the ship fast to the dock, a second crosses the breadth of the deck. He slides the orange netting into a bunch at the far end, then comes back, unhooks the rope and holds it, expectant. With the ship secure, the man carries the rope across, looping it as he goes. Only then do the passengers stream off, each still a member of the disembarkment ritual.

I'd witnessed the whole of the pattern any number of times but never before seen its shape. That afternoon it stood out starkly, maybe the clearer for me because of my new lens.

The pattern is present, too, in the ferry loading. It begins before we leave home. For the 7:50 AM ferry, we'd best plan to be there by 7:15. Except in the summer, when, with the increased traffic, 7:00 AM is necessary. For the 12:15, getting into the lineup at 12:05 is likely okay. Except, repeating, in the summer it's hard to judge. In order not to wait too long, we try to time our arrival to reach a lineup when it's about half full. After seventy car-lengths, a sign: ONE FERRY WAIT FOR CARS BEYOND THIS POINT. Usually there's a bit of leeway, the sign assuming virtually no space between cars, and an additional six or eight can be packed on. It's all part of the dance. And, in a morally absolute manner, one has to get into the line at the end; cutting in front of someone who has left a twenty-foot gap and has been patiently waiting goes beyond misdemeanour, it's a gesture calling for island ostracism, not part of any dance. At a certain moment the cars in front begin to move. Time to turn the key in the ignition—not good form to have left the motor running—and drive down the slope, across the ramp, and onto the deck. There a deckhand signals firmly which of the five rows he wants our car in. I will creep along behind the car ahead, till another deckhand gestures, Just a little more, just a little more, till suddenly, like an orchestra conductor, he'll make that sharp Cut! gesture and I stop, leaving six inches between cars. It's my presence in the ritual. Till that afternoon I'd engaged in all these little moves and gestures without realizing they obeyed a set of rules.

The ritual takes place, unaltered, sixteen times a day on the Gabriola end, sixteen times in Nanaimo.

No, my sight hasn't been perfected, and not only because of the left-eye cataract. My right eye sees the sunny daylight world with crystalline purity, a sharpness of image and intensity of colour that is keenly satisfying. But on grey days or at the end of the afternoon the clarity fades—and at night the sense of depth is thoroughly gone. So I don't drive after dark. My left sees through a blur that I'd believed to be only minimal when it was my good eye—my better eye. And the images still don't meet; the focal lengths remain different enough for me still to have little depth perception. As to the effect of the trauma from the surgery, I know nothing, and won't until late December. Eye drops four times a day, says Spencer. I looked up the drugs online: ofloxacin, an anti-gonorrhea drug— hmmm—but, checking further, also of value against bacterial infections of the eye; ketorolac, to suppress the itch in my eye—true enough, sometimes my eyeball seems strewn with sand; and prednisolone, a corticosteroid, to inhibit inflammatory edema. No, they don't seem to have side effects. In a month my surgeon and my ophthalmologist will check out my eye. In two or three months the other eye will undergo surgery as well.

The robin is back. Once more on the railing, the ongoing swagger. Now he's attacking the large side window, directly from the railing—he flies at it straight on, gives one sharp, loud peck at the image in the window, swerves, and is back on the railing. It's all intriguing, distracting me from work—though right now watching him *is* my work. He's an embattled robin, he will overcome the intruder on his territory, he knows that for a fact. The intruder may be hiding behind glass, but this robin will overcome.

Five days later, the last of November, and he hasn't returned.

DECEMBER

1.

Today, the normal slowness of December. Grey days and early evenings. Large flakes of snow, melting on the wet grey ground, melting in the bog's grey water. The least of life by the bog road, possibly some slow-moving protozoa drifting in the water, not visible, at least not to me. The hardhack has gone brown-grey and looks tired after a productive summer and fall.

At the cottage the deck is wet, which also means slippery. We'll blast it with a power-washer, but not till spring, so it can dry properly demoulded. When it's clean, the deck glows, nearly golden. Now it's a dim brown. Two white plastic chairs that weren't brought in over the last few winters have turned a green-ish yellow: they have to go. Last year we cemented in two tracks running up the drive on the slope from the bog. After a snow-storm we can clear the tracks to improve tire traction. Today the tracks stand bare and grey, as if daring snowflakes to land.

Overnight the weather had been predicted to turn to heavy rain, the product of two systems meeting—our own frozen moisture arriving from the northwest and the so-called Pineapple Express, with its mass of warm rain rushing up from Hawaii. But the Express must have made a slow trip of it and we had heavy snow all day Sunday. Snowbound, we spent the rest of the afternoon and evening reading in front of the fire.

Just before dark we did a bit of winter gardening, in the form of protection. Near the front entryway grows a large rho-dodendron, a mid-spring bloomer sporting heavy red flowers.

But the poor fellow is old, and he'd been brought over to the house from the cottage after five happy years growing there. He doesn't seem to enjoy the soil he's rooted in these days, though we've fed him all the vitamins and fertilizers he's supposed to need. His branches have become brittle, and when the heavy wet snow lies on the broad leaves we have to help him along to keep them from breaking off. So we see it as an ancillary bog-tending duty to go out during snowstorms to brush the snow from the rhododendron leaves. It's a not unpleasant job, about ten minutes in the air, which despite—or because of—the snow tastes clean, if a little damp. Then back to the house, and the fire, and my book.

But the images from outside stayed with me. The flowering plum, bare of its dark-reddish leaves, coated with the wet snow, a suit of white armour on scraggly arms. The summer's grapevines supported by an arbour above the seven-yard-long skylight over the kitchen, the vines, and a few remaining leaves catching the snow, making pristine whirls and motionless eddies. The sheet of white beyond the bare gravel of the carport already betraying a depth of twelve-plus inches. The bare bit of deck under the eaves where Kit has put out small bowls, the residual bird feeders of winter and, as I looked, a satisfying place for two towhees—except suddenly each decided the other towhee was one towhee too many, each snapping at the other, each scaring the other away. The bamboo also by the front door was bent in perfect arches, the bottom ends rooted in the ground, the tips in the snow. On the deck off our bedroom the potted plants, one thick with long trails of nasturtium, until a couple of days earlier the flowers a bright yellow around orange pistils, now lay white-blanketed. I picked four, the last available this year, for our salad. Though their scent remained, they'd gone limp. The skylight above our bed, six hours ago an opaque white, now less than half of it snowed under, the snow melting from the heat of the house. Downstairs, too, the tattoo has begun, melt-drops on the kitchen skylight. And my mitts, drooped over the back of a stool, drying in front of the wood stove.

Another good supper, the TV news, and to bed.

It's Monday morning as I'm writing this. Overnight a heavy wind blasted through. Kit, going to check the car still at the top of the drive, found a large fir down just before the carport. Its roots were on the neighbouring property. It wasn't our tree, only our problem. Luckily this proved to be the sole tree that had come down. Less happily, it'd take the chainsaw to clear our drive.

Last year about this time was worse, I remembered, so I dug out some notes I'd made back then. In early December we had a beastly pre-winter, more snow than this year, twenty-two inches fell in one night on the bog road; half an inch had been predicted. After the snow came the winds, similar to this year in that several storms had met—three in five days, wind velocity from eighty to one hundred and thirty kilometres per hour. The electricity was out most of the time, bringing on the song and dance that goes: repaired, we have power, and it's gone; repaired, power, gone. The Pineapple Express then also, warm winds cooling as they came north, all the time increasing in ferocity.

From the third storm last year we had the additional pleasure of, on the slope below the house, a huge tree down across our phone, cable, and electric lines, the wires a mess of tangled spaghetti. Since much of Vancouver Island was dark, with large population pockets powerless—some of one hundred people, some of eighteen thousand—our tree, one hundred and ten feet of it, trunk eighteen inches in diameter, was low priority. (At the storm's height—or depth—half a million people were without power on Vancouver Island and the Lower Mainland.) We had no power for seventy-six hours. When the repaircrew finally arrived it was an early evening. I saw them down on the slope, with flashlights, and let them go about their work. But nothing happened, the house electricity-free all night. The next morning I saw them again, and this time waded down through the snow. I said hello, then asked, "You the guys who were here yesterday evening?"

"Yep," one of them answered, "but we didn't see any lights at your place. We figured nobody was home so it could wait."

We'd had candles burning. I never did get the sense he was putting me on.

Inside the house the large fireplace and two wood stoves kept us warm. Unfortunately, after the first day of the first storm, the generator stopped working, so we had no lamps except candles and the clip-on lights, fine for reading page by page. Didn't matter, I don't read more than one page at a time. We boiled water and fried eggs on the wood-stove top, baked potatoes in the fire, ate regularly by candlelight, and even broiled a steak directly inside the fireplace. This was necessary because, without electricity, the freezer began to defrost. To make sure the steaks, the rack of lamb, and the chicken legs didn't go bad, we had to eat them all.

Tuesday, and all the present snow is gone, the bog road awash with water, the bog's own water itself risen to within a couple of inches of road level. The telephone and Internet are still out. The hardhack has re-arighted itself, standing tall and ruddy in the high, cold bog.

It took till Wednesday afternoon for the phone technician to arrive. I was working at the cottage. I stepped outside and explained he'd have to access the line from the road below because the lines ran up from there. The cottage has its own set of lines, I told him, and here I hadn't lost the phone. He remembered our house—he was the one who had patched our phone line the year before after the big tree below the house came down. At that time he'd cut so many branches from the tree in order to free the line that he went a step further and bucked up half the trunk for us. Now he drove on to the house to turn his truck. A few minutes later he passed the cottage again. An hour or so after that I headed over to the house. The tree along our driveway had been worked on, the heavy upper obstructing branches and the top half of the trunk sawed away. We again had auto access to the carport. Kit and I agreed—what a wonderful phone technician.

Ten minutes later he arrived and told us to try the phone. It worked. He'd discovered the problem quickly—not at all a line down because of snow or wind, but the connection at the transformer at the bottom of the hill had corroded. The storm wasn't responsible. We thanked him, and added our appreciation for getting the tree off our drive. But no, he'd had nothing to do with it. When he'd driven by, a couple of young guys were sawing away—with a handsaw—through a section of ten-inch trunk. A mystery, but one soon solved. We called our neighbours Alan and Sharon, who explained it had been Alan's son who'd cut up the tree.

We spent last night sleeping above the clouds. The tops of Mudge, DeCourcey, Link, previously islands in the sea, had become islands poking up through thick grey fog.

Fog happens often enough on Gabriola in December, January, February. Till recently we didn't fly from Nanaimo in the winter as the airport had no radar for planes to land by—landings were visual. Mostly the airport connected Vancouver Island to the rest of the world without difficulty, but this time of year the endeavour became chancy. Connecting to a flight out from Vancouver, winter trips began with the ferry. But radar was introduced last year.

Freak fogs happen even in the summer. A few years ago, in August, our daughter, Elisabeth, with husband Tom and son Jake, had spent a week on Gabriola, each day more show-offy sunny than the day before. The blue-skies morning of their departure arrived, we took the ferry to Nanaimo and headed south the ten miles to the airport, where a fog bank had floated in off the strait. We unloaded their bags. The day had gone grey and chilly. Likely no problem, we were told. We waited. The incoming plane didn't arrive. We heard a plane overhead. Nothing landed. Tom went on a scouting expedition. He came back to report overhearing a ground crewman telling a ticket taker: "They've passed over three times and just can't see the field."

The plane flew down to Victoria, its passengers still on board, the Nanaimo passengers still on the ground. For Jake, Elisabeth, and Tom, waiting for the fog to lift and taking the next flight wasn't on, they'd get to Vancouver too late for the Boston flight. They rebooked—back to the ferry, the island, the house—and repeated the attempt the next day. A glorious day, not a cloud or a pinch of fog, a day like August is supposed to bring. They got home twenty-four hours late.

Time to organize a February trip, to Hawaii. We wanted a place with privacy, like a small house. The Internet is a remarkable tool. With the tap of keys on the computer, I was in the gardens of a dozen possible houses; more taps and I passed through bedrooms, bathrooms, lanais, and saw dazzling views from living room windows. A place on the side of a mountain with panoramas of the jungle, the ocean below? A place closer to a town, a short drive back after supper at a restaurant? A place directly on the ocean, the black sand beach just off the deck? Since we'd be travelling with friends and halving the costs, all these places were affordable.

Kit and I, in Montreal, rarely took warm winter holidays. These were for the effete. We'd drive up to our little country place in the dead of January and ski across the frozen, windswept lake carrying thirty-pound backpacks. No road to the cottage, so in the summer we ferried ourselves and our provisions over by boat; in winter, with little insulation and no running water, the cottage on arrival was usually below freezing. But a fire quickly warmed the place up. We hacked a hole in the ice for water. I brought up chips of ice for my Scotch. This was normal, this was winter.

It was also why we'd decided not to retire in the east. On Gabriola today the snow is gone, the sky is blue, it's ten Celsius here, and the flowers bloom. Across, on the big island, Mount Benson is heavily powdered with snow, the branches of all the trees gleaming so white in the sunlight it's as if they'd been sprinkled with a billion tons of icing sugar. It would be a blinding tramp through those woods this afternoon, a different kind of beauty. But, having done the eastern equivalent, we have the freedom of not doing snow now. We are exempt.

But we want a little more of what is good. We live privileged lives, we who have retired after thirty-five or forty years working at professions that in the main we enjoyed, we who have pensions that afford us our houses and studios with fine views of ocean or bog, or both. We who can live each day without the responsibilities of jobs, who take on projects and commitments as part of our service to the larger community, we who find ourselves with choices: which of any number of fine Hawaiian houses should we opt for on our ten-day holiday?

In fact we have the greater choice: go to Hawaii or not go to Hawaii. Or anywhere else. To stay here and for a few days do nothing, nothing, nothing at all to improve the world. A few days ago, at dinner with friends, we found ourselves talking about this, the privilege of living on Gabriola. We are lucky, we were agreeing, to have the company of intelligent people in a fire-warmed living room over a home-cooked gourmet dinner and fine wine as the storm outside howls demonically. Such thoughts come about in almost any company; smart and talented people live on this island. I've met many with postgraduate degrees, I've met intellectuals and artists with no advanced training. Self-reflective people all with the broad experiences of elsewhere who arrive on the island for its beauty, finding the satisfactory company of equals. People of many parts: the chimney sweep sings in the *Messiah*, the priest is a financial wizard, the physician sculpts exquisite furniture, the architect plays the drums, the boilermaker wins poetry competitions. We also have the privilege of staying home, enjoying the fire, friends, books. We are at ease.

At the library I tried to take out a copy of Michener's *Hawaii*. Unavailable in the system; it would have to be brought over on interlibrary loan. How fleeting is fame, even Michener's.

Then we hunkered down for the holiday season.

2.

The end of a year demands not so much a set of resolves for its successor but a reconsideration of the time spent since that year came into being. This, I realized as I walked along the bog road to the cottage, comes to me as a Jewish notion. The Jewish year ends the evening before Rosh Hashanah, usually in late September or early October—it's a lunar time-set. The devout spend the first two high holy days of the New Year in the synagogue. Then for the eight days till Yom Kippur it's time for self-examination: what one has promised to do and not done, what were the failures, what the achievements of the year, what the misdeeds to be corrected. God is asked for forgiveness, and prayed to with requests for oneself and one's family to be given life for another year. All this can happen without a god, but for those who think in god-terms it likely works too. Whichever way, the point is for a while to look back thoughtfully, analytically.

I've been relying on the metaphor of bog tending, of bog tender. Today the metaphor takes on new life. Today a thin crust of ice covers the whole of the bog. It flattens the bog. My glance can't penetrate to the water below—and on a day like this I believe Dad's glance could not have either. I can only remember what is or might be down under the ice. I like to think the bog is making demands of me, making this memory tending, bog tending, more difficult by itself icing over. It's a kind of challenge: thinking backwards made hard. Shiny too, as the sun reflects off the surface. The glimmer distorts and makes me think into recent history with a necessarily more penetrating stare. Break through the ice. It's hard. The ice is thick today, fighting back. I keep hoping to see more . . .

Later, crossing the bog, reaching the house, my glance fell on something more mundane: the woodshed. We filled it full this past year. Memories of bits of this days-long event flooded back, just breaking through my mind's ice. The trees had fallen first in the wind storm, later under the weight of the snow. We'd bucked them up, moveable lengths, got them off the road, left them in deep drifts. In early spring we hired a young man to buck them into log lengths, load them into the truck, and drive them down to beside the woodshed. In the late spring we split them and loaded them in till the five bins bulged with logs, each holding from one and a half to three cords. More logs still unsplit stood in an eight-foot-wide, five-foot-high, four-log-deep serried battalion at the edge of the parking area. These would begin to meet their day when the first bin was empty. Enough logs to keep us warm for four years. Now, staring at the full bins, I remember my sense at the time: some count their wealth in land, some in stocks and bonds, others in real estate. We count ours in firewood. Some of it we give away to friends who also need it.

My best present of the season arrived a few days before Christmas, a session with my ophthalmologist. She checked my eye—actually both my eyes—and was pleased with my new eyesight. She said she could see no edema, but to make sure a technician took me to a lab where a machine attached to a computer tested my eyes. This is a remarkable piece of equipment. It takes photographs of the retina and choroid and blows them up massively. After the test I asked what they showed. No edema, the technician told me. I asked if I could glance at the photos. Sure. I looked at the computer screen. "See? All fine." I saw many small dots, the top row purple, the middle green, the bottom red. "Like a layer cake," she said. "All smooth."

"And what would it look like if there'd been edema?" I asked.

She showed me some photographs on the wall. "First one's normal, just like yours." Then three other photos. In the first someone had hacked a chunk out of the cake. The second showed bulges climbing from the cake and crags in some of the bulges. The third was undermined by frothy shapes, round and elongated bubbles, without colour. "You've got none of that."

"Thank you," I said.

So my cataract procedure did not produce edema, and my birdshot remains unchanged. I was way more than a little relieved. I'm still not seeing perfectly, each eye still retains its different focal length, and there's not much sense getting new glasses until my second cataract is done, sometime early in the new year. Looking forward.

3.

Hanukkah–Christmas–New Year's is coming. We prefer not to travel over this period. But five years ago we did, going east. First a few days with grandson Jake and his parents near Boston, then a couple of days with brother Jeff and his family at their cottage in the Berkshires. And then, the big event, to son David's wedding to his partner, Steve, in Portland, Maine, on December 30. We all liked Steve a lot. The wedding would be a three-day process. First, on the twenty-eighth, a dinner held by Steve's mother, Barbara. The cast of characters: Barbara; her gentleman friend, an intelligent, charming conservative who listens and argues well; Barbara's sister from Las Vegas and her fiancé, the latter a librarian in Vegas and a Sierra Club aficionado ("Las Vegas is the greatest place in the world to be outdoors . . ."); also Steve's two sisters and a brother, each with attachments; David and Steve; and Kit and me. Good will abounded, not least because David had charmed the entire group.

The next day David and Steve held an all-day open house, greeting friends from around the corner and across the continent. And the day after, the ceremony took place with joy, pleasure, and the necessary confusion. Kit's sisters and associated family set up the space, an arts-and-community centre, and organized food and decorations, making possible a series of transformations: first, hide the food, then have it appear after the ceremony, then have the space reconverted into a floor for dancing. David and Steve had written the ceremony themselves. Our daughter, Elisabeth, was the major domo/ stage manager for the day. I overheard her speaking with the woman who'd be presiding over the ceremony:

Presider: "You know, I discussed some possibilities with David and Steve, but they wrote the ceremony entirely themselves."

Elisabeth: "I'm sure they did. They're a couple of control freaks."

The ceremony began with a video, made by David and Steve and starring themselves, projected on the wall. Eight scenes, depicting events in their lives in the months before the wedding, from deciding to get married, the invitations, through questions about gay weddings, to the vows, and the presents. Each was a parody of each of their stances on these issues.

A scene entitled, Which one is the wife?

David speaks to the camera: "Of course Steve is the wife.

I make nearly three times as much as he does. Without my organizing the life of this couple, we'd be nowhere."

Steve speaks to the camera: "Of course David is the wife. He's the cook, he's the one who knows how to shop for bargains and for treats. No question, he's the wife."

Cut to: Early morning. Steve in a dressing gown drags himself into the kitchen, takes a box of cereal, pours some into a bowl. Half of it dribbles onto the table. He pours the milk, a third into the bowl, a third on the table, a third on the floor. He gets a spoon and walks off the screen.

David enters. He sees the mess, finds a rag, wipes the table, the floor, and stares into the camera: "The question isn't, Who's the wife? but, Who's the parent?"

Seven more others like this, friends and family convulsed in laughter, becoming a community of the moment for each other, as well as for David and Steve. As, I think, planned.

Then the ceremony, simple, talking of commitment both immediate and symbolic, around the rings they exchanged. And exchanged, too, the vows each had written. Neither had heard the other's till the ceremony itself. Result, tears from each of them, as well as from many in the group. I said a couple of blessings over the wine, my obvious role, and they were pronounced: Married.

During the ceremony it snowed heavy and wet, fourteen inches by early morning. But all roads had been cleared by noon—they're good at that in the east—and we got back to Boston easily, to bed at nine on New Year's Eve, up at four-thirty for an early morning flight to Vancouver, Nanaimo, and the ferry home. We arrived back mid-afternoon. In the evening we went to a New Year's Day dinner party with the energy of the young.

The past, alive in my memory bog.

JANUARY

I.

On this first day of the New Year at high noon as I head to the cottage the sun is so low it warms the bog road for only a few feet, at its south end by the cottage. There's thin bright sunlight on this small section of the road, and where the light stops the packed dirt lies covered with a veneer of white, iced where tires have rolled over snow.

I come back mid-afternoon; it's getting dark in the fir-cedar wood, but light enough to see, a few feet in front of me, a golden-crowned kinglet, three and a half inches long. No fear of my presence as it hopped up the road, pecking at stones and leaves, devouring seeds or bugs invisible to my eyes. It's a pretty little bird, dainty, olive green on its back, narrow yellow stripes on its brown wings, and as the name suggests, a bright yellow-gold crest maybe three-quarters of an inch long on the top of her head. A female—no tinge of red in the gold of this one's crown. She could be wintering around here, or even farther north—her cousins have been found as far north as southern Alaska. She has two broods annually, from seven to ten eggs each. She feeds her young only the first day, then gets on with the business of producing a second brood. So the father becomes responsible for nurturing the young, and the mother as well, he bringing back to the nest enough food for most of the hatchlings to survive.

This is the time of year when the bog and the land around it are at their tenderest, their most precarious. Before the road froze it had been soggy with standing water. The sieving process that gives the road its strength is also the phenomenon that threatens to undermine it. The bog's water level is still only a few inches below the surface of the road, and the sand has a disturbing tendency to turn to mud. Tires traversing the bog groove ruts into the mucky dirt. One drives slowly, one walks delicately.

But where the road and the bog meet, new life is beginning. The sword ferns are newly unfurled. Sword fern is an attractive plant, its leaf stems up to three feet in length, with dozens of mini-swords three to four inches long extending from the rib of the stem. When they're used as decorative plants in gardens, the old grey-brown fronds must be cut off in the early spring, as soon as the new croziers—the early shoots, beginning life furry brown—appear, before they turn, as already now, bright green. In the woods they trim themselves.

In an earlier late January, while still living at the cottage, we'd partially tamed a pair of mallards. Each morning, coffee mug in hand, it was our practice to go for what we called an estate walk, to see what on the property had changed overnight—a practice carried over from years past at our cabin north of Montreal. Here we'd noticed the mallards swimming on the pond. At first they'd fly off when we passed, squawking in proprietorial irritation. After a while they merely skedaddled away, swimming deeper down the bog to where the hardhack began. Getting used to us? As it turned out, they were guarding their nest.

We'd been feeding birds on a platform on the cottage deck. At times the towhees and golden-crowned sparrows and chickadees would get so vigorous in their food-grab they'd set dozens of sunflower seeds and corn kernels flying onto the bog road below. One day we saw the two mallards come waddling up the road from the pond. How did they know there'd be feed on higher ground? Quickly they located it and gobbled away, scooping up the seeds, vacuuming them in. Later we took a small bowl of seed and dumped it by the pond's edge. The following morning the seeds were gone. We left more, watching for the mallards. Nothing that day, but on the next, out they came. Another bowl of seed and quietly we approached them as they ate. They saw us, took one last beak-full, and clambered back into the water. We watched them swim off. They stopped at the middle of the pond, now floating casually. We made a show of dropping seed at the water's edge and walked away. We didn't see them take the seed, but later the new pile too had disappeared. Over the next days we dropped more seed along the road, bringing little heaps of it closer to the house. It all got eaten. Only one time did we see them actually eating. But now when we passed the pond they didn't rush into the hardhack. We'd drop seed, they'd watch. One day they actually swam toward us, albeit tentatively. For several days we didn't see them.

Then they were back, followed by half a dozen little golden-brown fuzzy feathery blobs, swimming along beside and behind them. When they noticed us they panicked, a wild fluttering of wings as if to drive the ducklings faster, and were gone into the overgrown bog. We dropped more seed and left. They never returned to the bank, as if all that flirtation with humans had been a late-adolescent fling, and now with a family to care for they took no more such chances.

Since 1987, starting in January, usually till early August, my time has been devoted primarily to writing fiction. January 1986 was also for writing, but not in the same separated-out way. That was the year we spent in Mexico, and my writing time had begun already in mid-September 1985. We were in Tacámbaro, Michoacán, I having given up twelve months' pay to be away from McGill. I had been the director of the Communications Program for a couple of years; three of my colleagues had collaborated, perhaps not intentionally, though I was never sure, to drive me so near to madness I knew I needed to get away. I approached the dean of the Faculty of Arts, one of the very few deans in my twenty-five years at McGill it was possible to speak to directly—no layers of politics intervening—and told him I needed to resign as director, merely teach for a year, then take a year off. As I had no upcoming sabbatical, nor any outside means of support, I would teach the following year at half-pay, and go away the year after that, again at half-pay. He understood my situation and made a counter-offer: I should take myself off the next year at half-pay when I desperately needed to be gone, then come back and teach a full year at half-pay. An immensely humane man, and I immediately accepted his offer.

We spent the Mexico year living well on Canadian dollars and Mexican inflation; the fifty thousand pesos we were paying in rent, when we arrived worth two hundred and twenty-five Canadian dollars, dropped to about half its value after we'd been there for five months—our rent had descended to one hundred and twenty dollars monthly. And, given the Canadian and Quebec tax structure, we discovered that half my previous gross pay ended up being, after taxes, about two-thirds of my new take-home pay. We returned to Montreal and for that year I taught full-time on half-pay. We discovered that by cutting back here, there, and somewhere else we could survive, and more. I went back to my dean and explained I wanted to go on half-time altogether. Luckily a precedent for this existed, as several of my distinguished colleagues taught part-time at McGill and part-time at institutions elsewhere. The category was called Full Time, Reduced Load. With of course the reduced salary implicit. I applied for that status, received it, and remained on reduced load till I retired. Which left those years, beginning in January, for writing fiction.

The opening page of my website (www.georgeszanto.com) cites a couple of my basic beliefs about writing:

You only start to learn to write after you've thrown away your first million words.

And, from Samuel Beckett, "To find a form to accommodate the mess, that is the job of the artist now."

I've believed both these notions for a long time. I was likely still in my twenties when I reached the million-word milepost, and while I tossed out most of those words, a few I did not. They hang around somewhere in my files, and once in a while I come across them. I could, possibly I should, at such moments of rediscovery get rid of them. But I haven't. Why not? Possibly to remind myself that I should. That one should.

I began writing when I was about twelve. My first short piece was a detective story. I remember very little about it, except that the murdered man was named Tom Jackman. Because I didn't want it to seem derivative of anything I'd read, I made up Tom's last name. I showed it to my sixth-grade teacher. She had me read it to the class. It was a bit of a sensation—none of her students had ever written a story before. It might have been the adulation I received then that prodded me to keep going with this story-writing business. I could invent all kinds of people, and places, and incidents, create them right out of my head.

Maybe six months later I read a newspaper account about a banker who was receiving a prize for his good works. The banker's name was Jackman. I remember I felt chagrin, a kind of slap to my hubris. But it was a valuable lesson: there is very little one can write that's original. Years later an artist friend, when I referred to a piece of her sculpture as original, said to me, "Originality is a function of the obscurity of your sources." Which is a kind of paraphrase of Pete Seeger's notion, Civilization is built on plagiarism. And along the way, one can have a mighty fine time playing with the possibilities of combining in a somewhat different form some juicy words and situations.

For a long time I've been profoundly taken by the power of verisimilitude, the notion that one can write something that has all the appearance of truth, legitimacy, authenticity, and yet has been fabricated by the author using a quill or typewriter or word-processing program. When the first volume of my Mexico trilogy, *The Underside of Stones*, was published, it received, I was happy to see, a good number of well-thought-out reviews, most praising the book. *Stones* is the story of a Montrealer in his fifties whose wife has just died after a long illness. He takes himself to Mexico for a year, to Michoacán in the Sierra Madre, to escape and grieve. At the end of the book he is ready to return home, his life made whole again. One reviewer wrote, after some laudatory phrases, that he also wished to send his condolences to Mr. Szanto on the death of his wife. Both Kit and I enjoyed the review thoroughly—for this reviewer, *Stones* had achieved a high order of verisimilitude.

I find all parts of writing a pleasure, from mulling over a certain as yet shapeless moment or sense of things, to making notes about the flash of an idea or a fragment of a scene, to piecing together instants and notions that seem to contain their own internal glue, to stopping to consider the aptness of a word—spending time with dictionaries or my thesaurus, lolling over it because I have the privilege of time to do so—to finishing a draft, to rewriting and re-rewriting, many instances of rewriting, polishing, polishing ever more smoothly. And giving it to a reader, then receiving a critique on a section of it that pleased him or her. Or, often better, a part that as far as the reader is concerned doesn't fit; Hosannas that someone found it before it was etched into the stone of print. Best of course when the critique shows me an aspect of the story I hadn't noticed: unplanned, it has entered the story and improved the whole.

Probably it's the rewriting I enjoy the most. Compared with staring at the first blank page, rewriting is bliss. With only some notes and a set of potentials before me, I always feel: Yes, I did finish that other novel, that last one, but wasn't that a freak, an accident? Can I really shape another? But when I have the first draft in front of me I know the project will meet its conclusion. What follows may be three or four times the work of getting the draft on paper, but the project's completion has become inevitable; getting to it is just a matter of time. It's as if, were I a sculptor, I had dragged the stone into the studio and seen in it the shape of the final product. As Michelangelo is purported to have said, "The statue was already there, I merely had to cut away the extra stone." When the first draft is done, I believe I can see where I've overwritten. And, with the advantage of print over stone, I can see what is underwritten as well and so add the words that will put flesh on the shape—to mix two half-metaphors terribly.

I write much of the time. Certainly when I'm at my computer or sitting with editing pencil in hand and manuscript on the writing table, but at other times as well. When I was writing the trilogy I spent considerable time in Mexico, first with Kit, later mostly alone. When by myself I'd be up by seven, at my desk by eight-thirty. But my brain had been writing since four or five—some difficult scene or unbreachable mess from the previous afternoon, an impenetrable problem, resolved without resort to adverbs once dreamwork helped me to stop forcing my way through.

Often I'd forget to break for lunch, and in half a dozen instances I kept writing till I looked up and it was already dark. One time Marta, the *criada* for the house I was living in, came to the door, as she did three times a week. I was deep in my story. She knocked hard. I was so inside the scene I had no sense she was there. She pounded hard, harder. From somewhere in the distance I heard a strange banging, pulled myself away from the computer, and went to the door. I stared at her, recognizing her not at all. She was an intruder into the reality I had until that moment been part of. She was the fiction; only my story was real.

Kit is fond of an anecdote about James Thurber, as told by his wife. The Thurbers were, among eight or ten others, guests at a dinner party. The hostess looked at Thurber, his head to one side, speaking to no one, eyes half closed; she asked his wife, "Is James all right?" "Oh yes, he's fine," said Mrs. Thurber. "He's just writing." I'm not sure I reach such heights of concentration when in the company of others . . .

Back in 1998, we left Toronto the day after Boxing Day for our drive across the continent, to begin my writing time, to continue preparing ourselves for living full-time on Gabriola. We arrived on January 6 and were delighted to be back. The cottage was intact, much as we'd left it. Flashlight in hand we explored what little we could see outside and discovered the new pond Gordie had dug in our absence. Out in front of the deck, under the overgrown crabapple tree, the pond now deepened the bog there from its previous two or so feet in winter to about ten, he told us later. Some thirty feet in length, about ten wide, with a small peninsula built in, jutting out from the bog road. Hard to detail more in the dark.

In the morning, several potential disasters and a real one. I took from my case, which I had carried with me wherever we went, never to be left in the car at night, the envelope that held the first things we'd need on arrival—the house key, the post office box key, the credit union cheque book, the key to the crawl space. Except this last wasn't there. In the crawl space under the house we'd stored nearly everything of importance that we'd left behind; this morning, desperately needed, the coffee grinder. We'd brought our favourite coffee beans from Montreal but had no way to grind them till we found the machine. Until we had coffee, no going on the estate walk, no discovering the assured large changes on the land since August. Unscrew the lock? No, the hinges were inside, covered by the door itself. Tear the whole thing out? We were ready to. But we'd stored the crowbar in the crawl space too. Nothing for it but to unpack each box, each daily-use suitcase, the backpack. Finally the big suitcase, so bulky we'd never gotten to it along the way. And, under books and papers and clothing, we found the crawl space key. Loose. I can't imagine what I'd been thinking—likely nothing—when I'd dropped it there, unconnected to other keys. The grinder, the coffee machine, the well-travelled beans met and produced a powerful and needed elixir.

Steaming mugs grasped tightly, we walked the land. The bog was bright with the sound of blackbirds, though none were visible. The pond, which last night had held a mysterious, magical gloom, this morning looked like a scar, black humus piled along one side, bare bare bare. This will grow over, we convinced ourselves. For the moment, though, it was not a thing of beauty.

But the sun was shining—first time in three weeks, Alan next door told us later. We ambled across the bog up the rise, to the house site. Nothing built there yet. We had decided on the site five months earlier, before leaving for the east. Now, two weeks after winter solstice, we wondered if we'd placed the house in space that might be very dark in winter. No. Light flooded through the trees even in early January. And with the leaves fallen from the deciduous trees, we discovered we'd created a broad new view down to and across the water, and to dozens of islands. High in a tall fir two ravens croaked at each other, romance brewing.

The road over the bog, despite the rain, was strong and solid. As Gordie said it would be. On the way back we could hear Alan in his workshop and stopped by to say hello. He, too, had had a pond put in—since Gordie was on the site anyway—in his segment of the bog. Sharon's kayak sat at the far end, ready for a hundred-foot voyage, their pond being somewhat longer than ours. "Yes," said Alan, "Gordie nearly lost it when he dug your pond. He had his backhoe out there, on logs on top of the mud he'd dug out from below. Pulling out muck, dropping it on the side, building up the bank. Then his hoe caught on something under the water. Well, he tugged away at it. Hard to know if you're picking up two tons of mud or whatever. But when he knew he was stuck down there he pulled, set the weight of the hoe against the logs it was resting on. And they began to crack. And the hoe began to slide, down into the water—it was like whatever was down there was pulling at the hoe. It was scary." Alan grinned. "I couldn't look. Nothing I could do to help him if he went in all the way." It took an excavator to pull his backhoe out.

Later Gordie would tell us it must have been an old tree trunk, buried maybe five hundred years ago, maybe more, intact. Like the trunks and roots buried under our road, holding it up. "Must weigh maybe ten tons," Gordie figured. "Lots of stuff buried in that swamp."

The unpacking continued. As we'd been driving out of Toronto, I had discovered I didn't have my blue wool mitts, knitted by a friend. Though thinning in the palms, they were handy for holding the steering wheel in the early morning when the thing was a circle of icy plastic. Gone.

In the southwest I didn't need but also couldn't find my warm white scarf, and it didn't show up in the unpacking. Also gone, my blue cardigan, my daily schlepp sweater, as great a psychological comfort as for keeping chill at bay.

And, in the afternoon, a greater cause for panic. Before leaving Montreal, in mid-December, Kit and I had organized our available receipts for 1998, that preliminary work for the income tax people. We didn't want to carry all those scraps of paper out to Gabriola, so I'd made lists of our expenses. Now, here on the island, the lists weren't in their file. Two options: fly back to Montreal and look for them, wherever they might be in some box deep in storage; or, being there and not finding the lists, do the work all over again from the little scraps of paper. Okay, we argued, we didn't have to fly back right away. The material wasn't needed till March, and our January–February by the bog would be broken anyway by a trip east. Elisabeth and Tom were about to give us a grandchild. We'd fly to Boston for the baby's birth. I could search for the lists then. Some relief, much irritation.

More unpacking. Piles of other files: house plans, notes for the Canada Council jury I'd be on in February, banking materials, insurance. The pencil-edited manuscript for the novel I was working on. My floppy disks. All in place. Except, where they should have been in with the manuscript, my extensive notes for further changes were absent. I felt sweat on my scalp. I sat, calm, calm, and thought. They had to be there. Just more misfiled material. Likely I'd put them in an incorrect file. I went through each file page by page. And found—the tax lists! A careful check, and all was there. Good, I thought. Surely the novel material is here too. Somewhere. Except, an hour later, it wasn't. Nothing. All the overview material, all the through-lines, all the polishing inserts: all absent. And no further idea where to look. The notes were the one item that couldn't be replaced, years of thinking, of ideas. The manuscript could be reprinted, even recorrected. The notes were unique.

In itchy frustration I paced the property. The trouble with nature, she wouldn't get in my mood. Especially here along the side of the bog, she was so damn optimistic—January 7, and shoots of new green had spread along the bank, the willow was bright red in the low sun, even the little transplanted firs up on the hill had brand new light-lime extensions.

Okay, nothing is unique, even notes could be recreated. Maybe, like Thomas Carlyle's original manuscript of *History of the French Revolution,* deemed old scribbling by John Stuart Mill's housekeeper so she threw it in the fire, they could be improved in the next version.

The following morning we saw movement down by the pond, to the right of the crabapple. Binoculars at the ready. Two, then four, then five large water birds. Big ducks of some sort. We've not seen their like here before. Two were black above the beak, in fact with a mostly black head except for a white triangle starting from behind the eye to the nape, and white stripes on the breast. Three had darker heads, dull brown, but each featured a ruddy tuft at the top of the head. These latter looked familiar. Find our Peterson *Field Guide to Western Birds.* The ducks continued to display themselves, scudding across the water just behind the lower branches of the crabapple, onto the muddy bank, again into the water, again out. The black and white head was the give-away: hooded mergansers. The white and blacks are males, the brown-tufted ones females. Of course. We'd seen such females in our Laurentian lake. Peterson writes, "Note the loose tawny crest of the female." Likely a family from last year. The fog and drizzle had returned, so we put on raincoats and walked outside quietly. Motion on the water stopped. They stared our way. We stopped, stared back at them. And slowly the two in the water paddled out of our sightline; the three on land meandered into the pond and float-drifted away as well.

Major activity for any day of return: laundry. We took it all down to the marina to use the little laundromat's washer and dryer. At the bottom of one of the bags, my blue sweater. Put there to carry it from some motel room out to the car? And forgotten. It, too, got a wash. A small celebration.

2.

The last few days have been deep blue, just under freezing at night. The bog is iced over. The hardhack stands tall, bright red-brown in the sun, but where sunlight hasn't yet reached it, it's a field of brilliant white. Hoarfrost covers every stalk and branch. Even out of direct sun the white glistens. The line between red-brown and white is sharp. The hardhack has no say which it will be, sunlight making all the decisions here. I stood and watched for possibly five minutes, and saw the line move. More correctly, as the sun moved the frost melted, very quickly, on the stalks of hardhack. And once the branches were touched by the sunlight, no going back. At least not till the middle of the night if the temperature dropped and the air again released its humidity—the damp for the frost doesn't come from the bog, as the ice is nearly half an inch thick. The air temperature at night has dropped to minus two. The ice remains.

And the red-winged blackbirds have returned. Somewhere down the hardhack stalks and above the frozen water, they're nesting. Crazy birds. Kit says she's heard them in the dozens, but I haven't yet seen them. Nor do I in the few minutes I watch, neither see nor hear them. I'll listen again going back to the house. Maybe when the air's warmer they'll make their appearance.

Here on the island we get our revenge on mid-winter by eating. Last night we had a birthday party for Sandy at our house, a potluck. This was Sandy's third party in four days, with much overlap of company. But more was being celebrated than Sandy's passage of one more year: some good friends had survived the year.

A couple of months ago a close friend had an abdominal aortic aneurism (AAA). He had read about such things in an article in his monthly wellness letter. The article noted that if one had smoked more than a couple of dozen cigarettes in one's life, one could be a candidate for an AAA. He asked his doctor to do a scan on him. The scan showed an AAA. Yes, he could get an operation in several months. Early the next morning he felt terrible pain in his gut. He reported to his doctor, the ambulance arrived and drove him across to the Nanaimo Regional General Hospital where a helicopter stood waiting— why the helicopter couldn't have picked him up on Gabriola no one seems to know—and whisked him down to Victoria. The aneurism burst as they were opening him up. For a while it was fifty-fifty life or death, but he made it through. Yesterday evening was his first dinner party.

Some years ago another good friend had his hip replaced. Over a period of time the joint deteriorated. An ever-active man, he at first hobbled, then could move only with great difficulty. About this time last year, as he was preparing himself to have the hip done again, he had a heart attack. The operation was put off for six months, to let his heart heal so he could take the trauma of a new replacement. He waited, he was operated on, he had another small heart attack during the operation. For the last months he has been recuperating. Yesterday evening was his first dinner party. He walked without help from our parking space up on the ridge down to the house. The AAA man and the hip man, neighbours, walk together every day from their houses to the mailboxes a few hundred yards away.

For the past few years another close friend has fought thymus cancer. The thymus is a small organ near the heart, important in childhood and adolescent growth for developing the body's immune responses. After it has served its purpose, normally the thymus withers away. For her it didn't, and some years ago it became cancerous. Its proximity to the heart rendered it inoperable. She's had her bouts with chemo and radiation, which have shrunk the cancer, but it won't go away. After the chemo she changed her diet and for the past three years she's been doing hypnosis with a variant of my birdshot tape, rewritten specifically for her. She has remained steady-state and looks very well. She, too, was present at the party yesterday.

The AAA man's wife was diagnosed with breast cancer a dozen years ago, no recurrence. Sandy, who has had a small heart problem, is again healthy. My first cataract is gone, no edema, and my birdshot too remains steady-state. We celebrated last night. My toast was: To aortas, to hips, to thymuses, to hearts, to breasts, to birdshot—may we never hear from them again.

FEBRUARY

1.

It's cold and wet. Some nights the bog road's puddles freeze over, some days they melt into mud. Driving across the road, we make inch-deep tire ruts. They hold water. At night they freeze. All will be smooth come May, but for the moment it's better to sit by the fire and read. Or go away. So this will be a short chapter, not much about the bog or about other Februarys, because our friends Ian and Marilyn and Kit and I are leaving for Hawaii on the third.

Today, February 1, a Friday, around four I drove over the muddy road down to the village, parked the truck, did my errands, returned to the truck, turned the key in the ignition—silence. No response from the battery, not even a dreary groan. I called Kit to come with the jumper cables. I lifted the hood and braced it in place, stared at the engine, at the battery—new last year—looking for what I don't know. A minute later a man I'd never met walked past. "Engine trouble?"

"Battery, I think."

"I got some cables," he said without asking if I needed a boost and headed to his car.

Ten seconds later another unknown man stopped and said, "Want a boost?" I explained I was already getting one. He watched as the first man brought his cables and hooked them on. I turned the ignition. Instant start. I thanked both of them, and I left the engine running till Kit came. Together we drove to the garage where we have our vehicles serviced. I automatically turned off the engine—and felt like a fool. I tried to start it again. As dead as before. The owner, Tim, a talented mechanic who's helped us out many times, was gone for the day—for, in fact, the weekend—and his wife, Joyce, was in the midst of closing down. We explained about the truck. "Hey, no big deal, leave it, Tim'll get to it on Monday." We explained further, we'd be heading off on Sunday for our holiday. "No problem. If I get the time I'll drive it up to your place. If not we'll park it here till you get back."

One of the pleasures of living in a small island community.

The day before we left, as I walked back along the bog road from the cottage, the air was filled with the song, so-called, of the red-winged blackbirds, liquidly lovely for the first four notes, ending in a screech: da-da-dee-da-chree! da-da-dee-da-chree! I still hadn't seen any; unusual, as they were noisily present, probably celebrating the births of their broods. Had the day, soggy and grey, in sharp contrast to the expected clear blue skies and soft warm air waiting for us in Hawaii, been keeping the blackbirds low in their nests?

The first February of our full-time residence on the island, over a period of three or four days, we saw some remarkable bird activity. We took, before breakfast, one of our estate walks: get outside, breathe some fresh air, see what had shifted. Even the occasional minor seasonal disasters—pea shoots being nibbled by slugs, blight on the apple trees, birds digging up newly planted seeds—prove intriguing, especially when, having discovered the problem early enough, I can solve it. So, coffee mug in Kit's hand, tea now for me, binoculars hanging around my neck, we were heading to the bottom of the garden when four large birds came circling the house. One seemed to be prey, the others hunters. The first settled onto a branch of the arbutus tree that hung half over the house. With its totally white head, clearly an adult bald eagle. The other three at first buzzed it, challenging. Then two sat in nearby trees, the third on the same branch as the first, maybe ten feet from him. Through the binocs we could see these, too, were eagles, but without the white head, so juveniles or adolescents; it takes four to five years for the adult head to go white. Slowly we walked closer. The three were giving white-head a hard squawking time, and white-head was emitting small, melodious whistling sounds. They kept up this patter for maybe five minutes, till the first and then the second of the separated pair took off, as if they were now bored by it all. Then white-head flew away, out in the direction of the bog. Finally the last one flapped into the air, but not to follow. Instead he rose high in the sky, swooped around the side of the house, and settled on a branch at the bottom of the garden, about where we'd been when we first saw them. No further drama, so we left.

Then, in the afternoon, they were back, all four. Now they took to flying in circles above the garden. Landing on branches. More circles. "Must be something dead or dying," I said to Kit—and then remembered: the evening before I had buried the head, spine, and skin of a salmon I'd baked for a dinner party the previous day. "My buried fish carcass," I said.

"Buried, but not deep enough," said Kit.

The next day, about sunset, a perfect blue and gold sky, Kit and I were walking from the cottage to the house when a swarm, literally, of male red-winged blackbirds took off out of the hard-hack at the centre of the bog—my first sighting. They rose high, a single unit of maybe a hundred, a hundred and twenty birds. The swarm swooped and rose, dove and turned back up, some-times in a tightly packed group, sometimes lengthening, twice breaking into two parts, separating to maybe a mile apart, then surging back together again, meeting on the fly. This went on for at least ten minutes, as if they were a single organism, changing shape while rushing its way through the sky, all of it over the bog and Dave's fields next door, choreography of the most complex sort, each component of the organism synchronized with the others. Finally they swooped out behind some trees and disappeared. We waited. They didn't come back. It grew dark, and we gave up. As if they had left the stage for intermission. No idea what they were all about, but it was spellbinding. And the next day there was a symphony of blackbirds again in the bog, singing and screeching away.

I located an article in *American Scientist* (vol. 99, pp. 10–14) that examined this phenomenon. Over the years a number of theories have emerged. Nineteenth-century thinking suggested the presence in each flock of a leader who made the decision and the other birds followed. But on examination that proved improbable: how would such a leader of a hundred birds communicate instant flight or a shift in direction? Early in the twentieth century a new theory held that some sort of collective thinking made the birds fly in unison, some sort of telepathy binding them together. No way of proving this either. Since the 1980s it is thought that each bird acts as its closest neighbours act, paying no attention to the overall flock, but responding with immediacy to the birds around it, as they respond to the birds next to them, and so on. Except, as I've seen, for one or two who rebel and veer off, taking others with them. All intriguing.

Also that morning, standing on the deck, we could see, down below over the channel between Gabriola and Mudge, hundreds of gulls, various kinds, flying in tightly packed groups. They had to be at least four hundred feet above the water because we could see them from the house, near to level with us. We'd never noticed this phenomenon before either. It, too, went on for five minutes or so. We didn't go down to the water to see what was happening, but later learned that an immense school of herring had been swimming through the channel, chased by dozens of sea lions killing and swallowing herring fast as they could, with the gulls gobbling up corpses of collaterally damaged fish, a stolen feast.

Back from Hawaii, back to the bog. A fine warm holiday. Jacob's birthday happened while we were in Hawaii, Jacob Michael Szanto Canel, the Michael after my father, Jake's great-grandfather. We called to wish him a happy day. When he was born, he changed something in the world. Like so many times before, a new human being had come into existence, one who had simply not been there before. What he'd do, what he'd be, lay in the realm of the unestablished, the potential. Would this be the small person I'd be able to take fishing? He was unquestionably here. Furthermore, he had changed me, moving me a step higher in the generational chain. He changed his parents the most. They had married some years before, but with Jake's appearance they became a family. Some changes in the human lifeline can be reversed— moving out of the parental house, buying one's own home, moving in with a partner, marrying, or even becoming addicted to drugs. These can be cancelled: move back home, get a divorce, go into rehab. But some changes can't be undone. Having a baby transforms one's life forever. Once there's a new life, one is always a parent, whatever ultimately happens to the child.

Until that moment, change is often a process of distancing. As I grew from childhood through adolescence and became an adult, my parents and brother became, if not of decreased importance, at least more removed. Leaving my parents' home for college was the beginning of my independence—coming "home" for a weekend or for the summer told me that this house was becoming less and less my home. After my BA a year in Europe with Kit was the beginning of full independence. Till the baby arrived.

Having a baby creates a new generation—as much the child's itself as the parents'. The mother becomes a different kind of daughter—her mothering an activity that takes up an immense part of the day, far more time than being a daughter. Mothering, for most mothers, changes a woman forever. The infant is totally dependent on her care, the bond between mother and child, often father and child as well, so intense it can flood the hearts of new parents with its magnitude of emotion. And in some ways the new mother becomes more of a daughter, recognizing the similarities between herself and her own mother, her child and her. Just as the father finds a new relation with his parents.

I say the father, but I am generalizing from myself. Prior to Elisabeth's birth, Kit and I felt self-contained. We needed only one another, our parents people we loved but people we largely lived without. But when Elisabeth arrived in the world we suddenly felt more connected not merely to our parents and siblings but to a larger community as well. After her birth I had become a different kind of son, discovering that my own father had once experienced this closeness with his son, with me, was in fact still feeling it. All this had been invisible to me for years. Grandparenting is an echo of these relationships, watching Elisabeth—and her husband, Tom—now deeply involved with her son, their son, recognizing her love for Jake as a version of our own longstanding love for her, just as for her brother.

Tom and Elisabeth had taken a long while to decide to have a child. Years ago they'd called to tell us their household was about to increase. We were very pleased. "When?"

"Oh, in a few days."

"What?!"

"Yes, we're getting a cat."

They had for a long time been in, as they put it, ideational mode, trying to envision themselves as parents. One day ideation was transformed to conception, to pregnancy, and then Jake arrived.

They would raise him to be a gentle kid, with feminist and socialist principles at the fore. Except Jake, it turned out, was in love with things mechanical and big, like heavy construction machinery. When he was nearly five he and his father were riding on a bus together—not rush hour, the bus mostly empty. Suddenly Jake turned to Tom. "I don't like men," he said.

If it had been me, I'd have asked why he didn't like men, but Tom, working positively, said, "Oh? And what do you like?"

"I like women," Jake said, hesitated a moment, then added, "and cars."

From the seat behind them Tom heard a female voice say, "Starting him early, aren't you?"

2.

Another moment to be noted during our stay in Hawaii: the thirty-third anniversary of my mother's death. I have been wanting to give her as much space and honour as I gave to Dad. But I'm afraid I have less to say about her, and my notes about her rarely take the shape of stories. My memories of her are more generalized—in this circumstance such and such *would* happen, if I said this, or she *would* respond in a certain way. My thinking has been that I remembered less because she'd died sixteen years before Dad, in 1975, when I was thirty-five. I mentioned this to Kit. She tried to draw stories out of me, specific moments from my childhood to match the fishing stories with Dad. But I could find very few about Mum. I felt somehow foolish, certainly inadequate, even disloyal to her. We talked, Kit and I, about the situations I'd be in with Mum: for example, how, when I returned from school in the afternoon, she and I would talk about the events of my day, school conversations, my classes, homework. But from the hundreds, thousands, of hours spent in these kinds of chats, very little stands out. Not like fishing with Dad. Maybe, Kit suggested, I had much less time with Dad, so when in fact we had the chance to be together it was a special and therefore memorable moment, whereas the time I had with my mother was normal, taken for granted, no precision lodged in my memory. I prefer Kit's explanation to my weakly blaming loss of memory on the many years that have gone by.

In many ways Mum was an impressive woman. In her late forties and early fifties she took her BA degree in General Studies at a small Catholic college, Notre Dame, in Manchester. This she followed with getting an MA in German Literature at the University of New Hampshire when she was fifty-six. She'd been urged to do so by the nuns at Notre Dame, who had hired her to teach German at the college starting the fall after she received her undergraduate degree. She got along with them brilliantly, ever full of stories about her colleagues, Sister This and Sister Someone Else. Several times I heard her giggling with one or another of them.

Dad finally retired at sixty-eight, hoping Mum, too, would quit her job so they could travel more together. They did take several long trips, but never in the winter because of Mum's teaching responsibilities. She had not worked since leaving Vienna. Now she had a professional position, some standing in the community, and so enjoyed her job, the work, and the comradeship with other teachers, she wasn't prepared to give it up.

My best remembered adult times with her come from the five years between her first cancer operation early in 1970 and the second, which was closely followed by her death at sixty-seven. Prior to the second she was brimful of energy and hope; she had taught for a couple of years after the first bout, then finally resigned her job to spend time with Dad. After the second operation she abandoned hope—or maybe hope abandoned her. My strongest memories of her, however, belong to the last few months. In the most tangible sense that time I had with her was special, what with ever fewer days remaining as the future and the death it contained roared toward her. It was then that we sat for hours, she sometimes in her armchair, sometimes around the kitchen table, later as she lay in bed, that we tried to build a family tree with both her and Dad's precursors and contemporaries, and she would delve into her own memory to find grandparents and great-grandparents, second cousins, those living and those who died. Dad's sister Louise, who died in her twenties in 1928 of strep throat, a disease that could have been cured twenty-five years later with a little antibiotic; Dad's grandfather Manno Schwartz who moved from Vienna to Budapest, became a successful wine merchant, married Rosa, and magyarized the family name, changing it to Szanto around 1870. He called his son Ferencz. Ferencz comes most clearly out of the past because, aside from the stories Mum got from her mother-in-law, we also have a photograph of him standing on the steps of his large wine shop in Budapest wearing a three-piece suit and a bow tie, his name emblazoned above the door. Beside him, one step down, is a woman wearing an elegant dress, we presume his wife, because on a step yet lower down stands a girl about eight years old—no idea of who she might have been—and another woman, dress more dowdy, head covered with a shawl, holding a boy baby. If this baby is indeed Ferencz's son, that would make him my father, who was the eldest. On the sidewalk below these five people are kids, both girls and boys, sneaking into the photo. Dad's family moved back to Vienna when he was a year old, in 1902. Their name remained Hungarian. Ferencz became Franz.

Mum's greatest love, my most important present to her, was

Elisabeth. Mum hadn't been pleased to learn that Kit and I had married, Kit not being Jewish, and even less happy that we had gotten pregnant—I still had to go to graduate school, how would that be possible with a baby in the house? and so on. Kit and I did just fine, and Mum was completely taken by our little girl. Mum called her the golden child, an apt description of the angelic blond baby we'd produced. Over the years they became and remained as close as a grandmother and granddaughter could be. And they were both always right about what was wrong with me. I became their beloved joke, sandwiched between an older and a younger generation. Kit, Elisabeth, and I spent a year in Provence when Elisabeth was between two and three, and my heinous crime that year was to have taken my daughter away from her grandmother—reminiscent of my mother's comment when, in my last year as an undergraduate, I was awarded a Fulbright Scholarship to study in Germany. I'd be away for a year, and in that country whose people had wreaked such havoc on her family. She was pleased for me, proud I'd won the scholarship, but . . . She said, "One of my eyes is laughing, the other is crying." Sad for her that my parents wouldn't see me for a year, but not as bad as taking the golden child to Provence for the year.

Cancer struck her first late in 1969. An operation and radiation followed. She seemed free of it for nearly five years—the famous five clean years, a strong indication that it wouldn't recur. But it did, a few months before the five years were up. We were in Manchester for the summer of 1974. It was mostly then that she and I began making up the family tree. This, too, was the summer after our first year of Kit teaching at the University of Wyoming, the summer before my taking on the job of starting a Comparative Literature Department at McGill University. Kit and the kids—Elisabeth then eleven, David seven—would stay on in Laramie for 1974–75, and I would try to discern whether or not Comp Lit at McGill was viable. I commuted a lot that year between Montreal and Laramie, three weeks a month at the university, one week in Laramie. On Montreal weekends I would drive five hours down to be with my parents in Manchester. Over the year-end holidays Kit and the kids came east.

We went to Toronto first to be with Kit's family for Christmas, planning to spend time with my parents a few days later. On Christmas Day the call came, that Mum was in a coma. I took the train to Montreal, where my brother picked me up. Jeff had been in Ottawa. When we arrived in Manchester, Mum was still unconscious. Kit flew down to Boston, where I picked her up. She was with me in the hospital a couple of days later when Mum rallied. Her first words to Kit when she walked into the room: "There's some leftover apple sauce in the fridge wrapped in plastic, second shelf from the bottom, at the back. It should be eaten."

David and Elisabeth, then aged nine and thirteen, flew to Boston unaccompanied, having been put on the plane by Kit's sister Joan. Because of the high volume of holiday traffic they needed to fly via New York, there changing planes. The day before David had made a rich chocolate fudge with Joan. At the last minute he had insisted on taking some with him in a plastic bag, which he stuck in his pants pocket. At the airport he was holding the baggy of fudge, now squished and melted. A customs official held it up, stared at it, and said, "And what is *this*?" It could have been many things. After a full explanation the official let him take it on the plane. They had been told to wait in their seats when the plane landed, and a flight attendant would lead them to their connecting flight. They waited, each engrossed in a book, till finally David stood up, looked about, and said to Elisabeth, "Is there a reason why we're the only ones on the plane now?" E. quickly alerted an attendant. Who panicked: the kids were going to miss their connecting flight! Elisabeth remembers being zoomed from the international to the domestic airport on a speeding golf cart, getting to the plane for Boston with minutes to spare.

Mum seemed stronger by the time the Laramie contingent returned to Wyoming and I to Montreal. I spent every weekend of January with her and Dad. End of January, beginning of February I did my week's Wyoming commute. In Laramie I got a call from Dad, that Mum was again in a coma. We all flew east, and she died a couple of days later.

I loved her immensely. But when I was younger, maybe ten, I felt strongly divided in how I viewed her. I remember the four of us in the car, Jeff and me in the back, Mum up front beside Dad. She hummed the tune of a popular song of the time, the verses wordless, but at the end of each verse sang the refrain aloud, "Ain't We Got Fun," with equal stress on every syllable. Her accent embarrassed me, Viennese overlaid with British English, as did, at other moments, her syntax. People, I had been told, considered her accent charming. Charming for me meant some warm and attractive quality arising from someone's distant privacy. I couldn't understand why anyone should consider my mother's accent, so foreign, charming.

My father drove. The two of them, in front, talked. I, sharing the back seat with my brother, tried not to listen to them—it was hard enough retaining control over my half of the back, making sure Jeff didn't invade. I had to be ready at every moment.

She lapsed into silence. Then, a few minutes later, the hum. And at the end of the verse she turned around and sang-spoke the four words. The slang "Ain't" in her accent made me want to hide, my shame controllable only because no outsider had heard. I'd never been bothered by Dad's stronger accent. Mum's did, maybe because she was showing off her colloquial

American, and basking in the pleasure of her life, of being alive, of having escaped Vienna.

She would then have been about the age Elisabeth is now. Dad was driving us back from a lake where we'd been for a long weekend. Only two years in the United States, already they owned a car, could afford to rent a cabin for a weekend, a place for us to swim, to play in the fresh air. Yes, fun. No question. But her insistence, her sung accented insistence of fun, spoiled any sense of pleasure.

But there were pleasures. For them, and for me too. As when they built our house, with money borrowed for the mortgage and for the down payment. My mother laughed—they'd make the last payments the year my father retired. Debt and possession, simultaneous New World realities. Because they now owned a piece of New Hampshire, a quarter-acre of the New World, the first time they'd owned the place they lived in. Their home went up slowly; from poured cement to roofing shingles, it was their property. We've got it all now, my mother said. She stood on the new macadam curbing, and her glance ran from the trees saved after clearing the lot down to the garden she'd soon plant, daffodils and tulips for next spring, forget-me-nots, roses. Her look stopped at the still-unpainted house itself. Her brown eyes, always her gentlest feature, filled with a haze of tears. We've got it all, she said.

Relatives, those whose names weren't inscribed in the *Theresienstadt Todesbuch*, came up from New York and admired the ways of life in suburban New England. I left home, then my brother too. We began families. Little distant units.

When the cancer first hit Mum, she was sixty-two. "We'll fight it," my father said. "We'll kill the beast." He gave up his job to be with her. But he retired too late, too little time left to them for long pleasures together, free from the stresses of work, of illness. I believe he was as horrifically stricken as she was by the monster; he in the heart. It was from her eyes the life seeped first. Sad doe eyes, my father called them.

She died less than a week before her sixty-seventh birthday. At least, said one of my uncles, the social security will cover most of the expenses. He meant Medicare.

She saw only the first house Kit and I bought, our little beach cottage in Del Mar, California. She never saw either of the houses in Montreal, the first a semi-detached old place with a little garden, the second a row house, a greystone. She would have enjoyed both. But, in the first Montreal house, on a late spring afternoon as I was pulling out brown tulip leaves, I heard, clear, clearer than I'd hear myself if I spoke aloud now, her voice calling from the porch, *We're ready*. I looked up. For a tiny moment I saw her there on the back porch; her eyes, really.

So. It seems I've found more memories of my mother than I thought I had in me. Up from depths of the memory bog.

In the mail when we returned from Hawaii, a note from the eye surgeon's secretary. I have an appointment for the removal of the cataract in my left eye for the middle of March. Worth looking forward to.

We spent the second evening after our return not reorganizing our lives—not answering emails or washing our clothes—but having that winter experience we appreciate most about being home: sitting by the fire and reading.

I enjoy the fireplace. I am fascinated by fire. I enjoy moving the coals around to give the burning logs the advantage of more oxygen, then feeding the fire with new logs, staring at the flames, watching the patterns they make. I enjoy the warmth the fire puts out. I would find it hard to live in the country without a fireplace. We even put a fireplace into the living room of the house in downtown Montreal when we revamped it. My parents had a fireplace in the living room of the home they built in New Hampshire. They rarely used it. Three attractive white-birch logs lay on a raised hearth. Over the years they remained decorative and had to be dusted. The two or three times Dad actually made a fire he removed the birch logs, replacing them with less attractive wood. And by the next morning he would have swept out and washed the fireplace, the birch logs back in place.

Still, the living room of my parents' house was unusual compared with that of other houses built in the 1950s in that it did have a fireplace. In most new houses of that era in the United States the living room space previously reserved for the fireplace had been given over to the television set, the space the eye focused on when one entered the room. (My parents had relegated our TV to the den.) In pre-1950s houses, the new television set was often placed in front of the fireplace. Which made a kind of sense, in that both the TV and the fire serve, on one level at least, a similar kind of function, answering to similar kinds of eye demands, the need for movement and change. The flickering flame fascinates, the flickering TV entertains.

We built our Gabriola home with no space in the living room for a television set, a small pleasure in rejecting fifties values. The TV would live in the little spare room next to Kit's study. But we did make allowance for a cable outlet in the living room—hidden away, however, behind a small cabinet. This has allowed us the chance to unhook the TV from its usual site and wheel it into the living room/dining room. Just occasionally, of course. And not in front of the fireplace.

A couple of mornings after getting back, as I walked along the bog road, I heard a double splash. I looked, saw nothing moving, no duck swimming away, none flying either. And the splash was far too heavy for a frog. So it had to be something swimming under water. A couple of years ago I'd seen an otter dive into a hole under the road, quickly out of sight. The hole has remained open, but I've never seen the animal again. Though its path was traceable—from the pond by the road at the cottage end there'd been a clear trail of an animal coming out of the water and dragging its low belly through the grass, crushing it, leading to the opening under the road. And twice in the winter I saw a path through the snow.

Then today, a couple of minutes after the splash, in the middle of the road by the dug pond, a hole going straight down—four inches in diameter and, when I probed it with a stick, about fifteen inches deep before it turned toward the bog. This could be a problem if the animal is undermining the road. We need to fill in the hole with stones, drop sand down through to plug it up. Hope the invisible part doesn't mess up the road between the hole and the bog.

I called Kit at the house and told her to stop at the cottage en route to the village—something she should see. An hour later she got out of the car, opened the door, and said, "I get why you wanted me to stop. I'd never have seen it."

She must have driven right over the hole in the road. I asked her what she meant.

She pointed beside the car, below the bank from the hill at the side. "There."

I came out of the cottage. At her feet, dull brown like the dead grass and the stony bank itself, lay a small dead deer on its side, a young female, visible eye glazed, head thrown far back as if it had broken its neck. We called the RCMP; they'll remove a deer from the road when it's hit by a car. No, unfortunately, this deer was on private property, it had to be disposed of by the landowner. How? Oh, just haul it off somewhere and throw it in the woods, that's what we do. Thanks. Then Kit called GROWLS—Gabriola Rescue of Wildlife Society. No, they just handled live animals; we were on our own. Likely, the GROWLS woman said, the deer had had a hard winter, that sometimes happens. Not enough nourishment, so it had grown weak or diseased. Such a deer would move in close to a house or any place that gave off a little warmth, lie down, and go to sleep.

What to do? Just as the police suggested, toss it into the woods, let nature reclaim its own. Wear gloves, the woman said. Disposable ones, preferably. Most deer don't carry disease, but some just might. So we did precisely that—thin new plastic gardening gloves under old dishwashing gloves. Each of us grabbed two hooves. A small deer. It weighed maybe forty pounds. We dragged it to the other side of the bog road and flung it into the ravine. It was a curious sensation, throwing a recently living animal to a place where it could decompose. Poor little thing, I thought. Part of the processes of nature, but still sad for all that. Kit filled in the hole in the road—it took three wheelbarrows of sand and rock. Busy creature, the otter.

The day after we returned we had headed out to the garage to pick up our truck—Joyce hadn't found time to bring it to the house. But there it stood, had for two weeks, safe and repaired—bad connections at the battery cables, cheap to replace. Problem solved.

MARCH

I.

On the first day of March, as I walk across the bog, the songs of a hundred or more red-winged blackbirds so overlap it's impossible to hear a single discrete da-da-dee-da-chree! All has been reduced, or more correctly heightened, to a blend of constant sound. And loud. The surface of the bog has dropped to three or four inches below the road level, which brings the little cottage-side peninsula into the pond up out of the water. And the birds still haven't made themselves visible in any significant number; I've seen only a couple of males and a single female since we've come home from Hawaii.

The blackbirds had gone silent when I headed back to the house in the late afternoon. But, for the first time this year, I heard the *ribbit* of frogs, sometimes written as *krek-ek*. For now just one or two; but they, too, are back in the water. They are green or brown, about two inches long, have long, slim legs and, on their toes, rounded pads that help them grasp and even climb up along bark. They return to the water to breed. I have recently learned, from Robin Wall Kimmerer's *Gathering Moss: A Natural and Cultural History of Mosses*, that they spend the largest part of the year on land, often high in trees—hence their label, Pacific tree frog, also known as the Pacific chorus frog; their scientific name is *Pseudacris regilla*.

And their choral chanting has begun. It's the great competition for a mate, the meaning of the song. They'll get louder over the month, maybe as loud as the first time I heard them.

In March 1993 I'd come west to assess the progress in the building of the guest cottage. The cottage, my studio, doubles a few brief times a year as an overnight space for guests. Sandy had taken pictures, sending them to us in Montreal, but I wanted to be there personally, to check on the process for myself. She and a friend, Patsy, had been to the site several times, including once in an early evening, and now they insisted on bringing me along after dark, without explaining why. We drove up Chernoff and down to the cottage. As soon as Sandy turned the engine off, the air was saturated with frog song. We got out and stood, and listened. I said something like, Amazing, but no one heard the word, drowned out by the *ribbit* of thousands of frogs, each searching for a partner. We stood without speaking for five minutes. The din grew louder. I felt a strange sensation take me: Yes, these were mating songs, but somehow I felt the frogs were also calling out to me, squeaking, Welcome home, welcome home! Then Sandy clapped her hands hard and instantly the frogs went silent. We waited a couple of minutes. One frog, perhaps the neediest, began its *krek*-song. A moment later, another. Over half a minute new frogs joined in, an ongoing accretion of sound as in a Beethoven symphony, when increasingly new instruments take up the refrain. I felt as if I were being led through a double ritual, allowed on the one hand to overhear frog lust, on the other to hear them call out a welcoming note to me. It's all a grand mating ritual, laid out before me.

Now in the water all is serious business. The males have arrived first, *ribbit*ing in unison to create the wall of sound that attracts females. They mate, and the females drop their sacs of eggs on new or decaying bog plants under the still, cold water. The eggs will hatch in a couple of weeks, producing tadpoles, which after two months become frogs and leave the water until the next breeding season.

I'd been a participant in another ritual in an earlier March as I flew from Montreal to Brazil to participate in the evaluation of the Communications Program at the University of São Paulo. The map in the airline magazine showed North and South America on one page. The straight line of the equator sliced through the centre, below Bõa Vista, above Manaus. It would be my first crossing to the southern hemisphere.

My images of passing over the line came from long ago, from stories of people who made the trip by boat. There'd be a ceremony at poolside complete with deckhands dressed as water sprites, half a dozen mermaids, a couple of trumpeters, a drummer, cymbals. The sprites and mermaids splash through a choreographed routine. Suddenly, a drum roll, and King Neptune appears. The chief sprite announces, "Those who've never crossed the equator, step forward! Pay homage to the great King of the Seas!" A clash of cymbals and the dripping wraiths incant some salty mumbo-jumbo. The initiates, dressed in what they're wearing, are led to the pool's edge and unceremoniously thrown into the water.

We, however, were flying thirty-seven thousand feet above the Caribbean, a little high for a casual shove. I turned to my neighbour. I'd talked to him earlier, somewhere above Savannah. He was Brazilian, consigned to Wisconsin for six weeks to set in operation an apparatus for manufacturing wood veneer, a mammoth machine built near São Paulo. He's been around the world, Russia, Quebec, wherever trees grow in abundance, installing his company's products. Had he ever undergone an equator crossing ceremony on an airplane? No, and he'd flown both ways many times. I told him about my imagined ceremony. "It'd be nice if, the moment we cross, they at least mention it."

"Why not ask the stewardess?"

I caught her as she passed, a pleasant young woman named Savia. In mixed Spanish and English we overcame my lack of

Portuguese. I told her the outline of my idea, joked about not wanting to get dunked in the sea below, but wondered if the captain ever announced the moment the plane crossed the equator.

"I've not heard of such a thing, no."

"Do you think he might, if I requested?"

She considered this. "I'll ask."

My neighbour, as Savia walked up the aisle, chuckled.

I read for a while. Savia came back, mouth set ironic, eyes guarded. The captain was not agreeable. She'd had a small argument with him. Not a sympathetic man, she let on. "But a fine pilot," she added quickly. "He told me, it's clear, we'll cross over about 2:55 AM, long after the film is finished. The passengers will be asleep. An announcement would wake them."

"Not even a whisper over the public address system?"

She shook her head. I tried to figure imaginative ways he could make note of the crossing—have the plane dip half a mile in the air, tell us all to put our seatbelts on—Savia scowled. "I mean," I said, "we won't be going uphill anymore. After the equator we head down."

She laughed a little. Well, she might mention it again. She didn't mind pushing, this particular captain was—she used the English word—"a grouch."

I ate a good meal. My neighbour talked about mahogany veneers. And about flying from Moscow to Capetown, another segment of the equator, no ritual there either.

Savia, when she poured us coffee, admitted she'd failed again. I thanked her and gave up, watched the movie, fell asleep. A sky-high sleep rumpled by glimpses of water-cloud valleys with nothing underneath. Then my inner clock brushed aside my dream-pictures. I forced my eyelids open.

Savia stood next to me. In her hand, a small white paper cup. She smiled. "It's 2:55. We're crossing the equator—" She glanced at her watch. "Now." She raised the cup over my head and turned it upside down. Drops of water dribbled over my hair and down my cheek.

She grinned. "To you, from King Neptune."

At the bog, a repeat of the sighting—or rather the hearing—of the animal I am now convinced is a river otter. I managed an instant of a glimpse, something of such shape and size, as it splashed into the water. I can think of nothing else it might be. Not sure how to get to see it. Spend more time sitting by the bog, I guess. Fine by me.

Also along the bog road, the volunteer willows have begun to sprout. I'd paid them little attention till this year, since last year when they came into leaf they were barely four feet tall. I hadn't noticed how much they must have grown over last summer—one is easily a dozen feet high. Tall but scrawny. And a different kind of willow; some of the buds are only that, but one has genuine pussy willows, white-grey and soft. March, when full spring arrives.

I went this morning to check on the deer carcass and scared away a couple of ravens, one of which flew off with a hunk of rotting meat in its beak. I'd seen ravens down at the bottom of the slope where we'd heaved the deer, and once a bald eagle, carrion carnivores all. Now, as I looked at what was left of the animal, it became obvious how busy the birds had been. The head was still there, minus the eyes and nose, and the skinny shin bones and hooves remained as well. The tail too. The flank and back were gone, eaten away down to ribs and the vertebrae of a spine covered with some hair and dried blood. All the innards were missing. A clear feast, eaten so quickly the animal hadn't had time to bloat. And never did it start to stink, at least not that I could smell. Certainly now no unpleasant, or even pleasant, odour rose from it. And very few insects. I hope the insects arrive, and more birds, and more wind and rain, to clean off the skull. I'd like it for the cottage.

Just a few days now till my second cataract surgery. My right eye is fine, though still itching more than I think it should; over-the-counter drops help. Now comes the left eye. Recalling my doubts and worries before the first procedure, I'm impressed how relaxed I am this time. Tomorrow I start the prescription drugs, two different drops, four times a day each. Not a problem. Except they have become the crux of a different matter. I don't get to put the two drops in back-to-back. I have to wait at least one minute between drops. One minute is a curious period of time. It's barely long enough to read another page, wash a few dishes, pass on a piece of trivial information. But now that minute gets wasted. At my age I find myself resenting the enforced waste of such a minute. I can waste hours, evenings, the occasional whole day with ease. Somehow this kind of waste disappears from my consciousness. But the minute lost, so finite, so precisely measurable, is a period of time taken from me. The same is true for the hour or the day. Once past they, too, are gone, but with that long a period I don't sense that a finite chunk of my living time has gone by, a chunk I'm not going to get back.

A writer friend now visiting the island, Heather, published a book last year, *No Time*, in which she argued that we are all so busy in our daily work and commitments we have no time to live. We furthermore have no time to realize the implications of not having time. We become disconnected from community, even family. For me, on the other hand, time is one of my privileges, a privilege not available to most people. I in fact do have time. I can sit at my desk, writing my stories, writing about my bog in all its ramifications. I have time to look for and test out the precision of what I'm writing. I have time to leaf through my *Roget's*, judge words in the context of each other, play with words, testing and tasting several to determine if this one or that better describes or explains what I'm trying to say. I have time to check several dictionaries to find a word's genealogy, trying to give a sentence its proper historical tone. And I have the time to enjoy that process too. (In this way I learned, some weeks ago, that the word *prostitute* literally means someone who stands in for another person, from the Latin *prostitutus*, the past participle of *prostituere*, from *pro*, meaning for, and *statuere*, meaning to cause to stand. Kinda neat. Something I should have thought of long ago but in fact needed time to discover.)

I can spend hours simply staring at the bog. It's a pleasure, not a waste of time. But I resent the minute that will be taken from me, four times a day for nearly eight weeks, as I wait between putting these drops in my eyes. Two hundred and twenty-four minutes, about three and three-quarter hours over the two months, a recognizable, spanned, assessable loss. Yes, I'm a mite obsessive. But . . .

These days a new phenomenon has put Gabriola on the map: feet. Right feet. Last summer a right foot was found, the foot alone, encased in a running shoe, along the shore of one of the northern Gulf Islands. A few days later another right foot turned up, also in a runner, discovered on a beach here on Gabriola by a nine-year-old girl. When we returned from Hawaii, one of the first items we heard on the news was that a right foot had been found along the shoreline. At first we wondered why this foot business was, months later, still in the news, then learned that a third foot was the object of concern, this one off Valdez Island, north of here. Why running shoes? An expert in such things has suggested that running shoes tend to float, being manufactured of buoyant material. Since they float upside down, the bones of the foot would be protected from birds. Days later we received emails from separate friends, in Anchorage, in New York, and in Memphis: What's all this about Gabriola feet? It turned out that the March 4 *New York Times* had run a story, "In an Answerless Canadian Inquiry, 3 Bodyless Feet," with Gabriola as the site of the inquiry. One island resident opined that "the left feet are probably encased in concrete at the bottom of the strait." So we've all been coming up with hypotheses: That it might be a cult with a gimpy-footed leader who needs to have all his followers hobbled, so removes their right feet. That it might be an advert for a running shoe company: Our shoes will keep your feet afloat! That it might be a gang of left-wing bears who love human meat but feel disdain for the lower right. And so on. Which makes Gabriola known around the world as the foot island. The senior reporter for one of the island newspapers received a phone call from the BBC in London asking him to comment on the three right feet.

Where do the feet come from? No one knows. The RCMP are investigating. Yes, people do disappear at sea, fishermen and kayakers, and float planes have crashed without bodies being recovered. And Nanaimo has been known for its regular summer invasion by Hells Angels, their convocation taking place at Angel Acres, a farm the bikers own outside of town; what they get into there is anyone's guess. And so on.

The level of the bog water has dropped another inch. The hardhack remains grey and stooped. No frogs today, or black-birds—just a lot of silence. The wind blasts across hard. It's strongest when it comes out of the northwest, usually a clearing wind. Not today; this is a southeasterly, bringing damper weather, rain, and fog. But on the bog's peninsula the big yellow irises, though a month from blooming, have sent up strong green shafts, and the smaller blues, both Siberian, are already pushing up delicate little stems. The promises of March.

2.

In an earlier March we first met Judith, she who became the architect of our house. Years back I'd drawn up an outline of our cottage floor plan. Our much-appreciated builder, Stuart, had made working plans from this and the cottage was constructed just as we'd imagined it. But since that time Stuart no longer drew up his own plans. We'd need an architect. We had talked, before Judith, with another architect on the island. There, too, I'd drawn up a basic design for the house we thought we'd like to have, and we'd gone to see her. We were taken to her studio. She sat us down at a table, Kit and I on one side, she and her partner on the other. For a few minutes we made small talk. Then I mentioned I had a design for what we were thinking about. But the architect wouldn't look at it. Instead, she lectured us for forty-five minutes on the house we would get from her, the house that was right for us. She told us her fee would be a percentage of the final cost of the house: ten percent if it came in under two hundred thousand, graduatedly less if over. She had a contract ready. We said we'd have to think about it. We left without her having seen my sketches or even asking what we wanted from our new home.

A few days later Judith arrived at our cottage, somewhat out of breath because her husband had their car and she'd bicycled over, about six miles. We introduced ourselves, chatted briefly about life on the island. We had a table with three chairs. She sat on one side, we on the other. She pulled out pens and a pad of graph paper. She nodded once sharply and said, "Well, I'm listening." As we'd had driven away from the first architect's home, both of us had said simultaneously, "She was completely uninterested in hearing us out!" But Judith did listen, hard. And she had a real sense of our piece of land. Later we discovered Judith's houses were all different, except each was identifiable as one of Judith's houses in terms of aesthetic unity and in

128

its rapport with the property it stood on. Her first words won us over, and for the next three hours we became increasingly certain we'd love working with her. She heard what we said, and heard our unspoken hopes as well.

That afternoon we got to know and began to understand each other. She made many notes on her graph pad. She told us she couldn't design a house for someone she didn't know. She studied my sketches carefully. She agreed this would make a solid house. It was to be two storeys because, as with the cottage, we wanted height in order to gaze down the length of the strait. From the cottage balcony one can see across the breadth and width of the bog. We wanted the same kind of height for the house.

On our trip west in January we had stopped to visit long-time friends in Portland, Oregon, June and Jerry. We talked about our decision to begin building. They showed and then loaned us a book filled with great insight, *A Pattern Language: Towns, Buildings, Construction,* by Christopher Alexander and others. Its argument, in many short chapters, is that the purpose of architecture today should be to attempt to bring wholeness to a multiply fragmented world. In wholeness is harmony and beauty. Which sounds a little corny as I write it now, but the theory makes great sense when adapted to the process of creating a building or a community. The parts of a town should interact peaceably with each other. Similarly, the sections of a house should recognize and live with each other, bringing a sense of harmony to those inside. The entrance of a house should be designed to greet those coming in. The views from the windows should take in distinct areas of the world outside, rather than expose vast panoramas; discrete glimpses implicate the one who looks out, panoramas overwhelm. Christopher calls these glimpses "Zen views."

We mentioned *A Pattern Language* to Judith. She said it was her bible.

In my sketches the first floor was a long rectangle, the second a shorter rectangle. A solid, well-proportioned house. From the side, with smokestacks rising from the roof, it looked a bit like an old-fashioned steamship. I had incorporated into the sketches segments of houses we had lived in over the years, our house in southern California, the house in Montreal that we'd gutted and rebuilt, a house I'd enjoyed in Mexico. Judith said when I showed her the sketches, "You've done a lot of work on these." She asked if she could take my sketches with her because she'd like to study them further. Of course. We asked about her fee. She said we had to first let her try to figure out what she could do for us.

She returned a week later. In our minds we'd already chosen her. We simply enjoyed being with her and figured she did understand our requirements, desires, and needs. On the table she unrolled three large sheets of architectural drawings. Kit and I stared at them, both of us admitting afterwards we were horrified. My tidy rectangles were bent out of shape, right angles had been all but eliminated, the shape of my ship gone, the sides of the house set off from the centre at angles of one hundred and thirty-five degrees. My walls had been torn away. If Judith had understood what we hoped for, where did all this come from?

But then, no, as we began to look more closely inside the outline, we realized all we hoped for was in place. And more. And far more aesthetically pleasing than my rectangles.

I had told Judith at the previous meeting that one of my pleasures in the Mexico house I'd loved was the lack of corners, that walls met in curves; all simple to do if one is building with adobe but far more difficult to construct out of wood. She had taken that notion as one of her cues and designed my Mexican house as it might come into being on a gulf island in the Georgia Strait. And because the two major corners facing the strait couldn't be rounded, she'd extruded them, turning them into window seats. And many more such details. Quickly the shape began to grow on us. She had listened hard the week before. Quickly we became passionate about her design. And we agreed to go ahead.

A digression, to make a comparison. It was a March too, in 1968, that I met Welton, the theatre critic at the *San Diego Union*. I was in my second quarter of teaching at the University of California, San Diego (UCSD), in the Literature Department, where I'd been hired in part because of my experience with theatre—when I was a PHD student at Harvard I'd written and directed three plays that were produced at the experimental theatre of the Loeb Drama Center. UCSD was then a new university, its first cohort of students having been taken in only in 1966, and I was the first so-called expert in theatre. I'd been invited to take part in a post-performance discussion at the Old Globe Theatre in downtown San Diego about T.S. Eliot's *The Cocktail Party*. I made some comments that the audience seemed to think were witty (they laughed), perhaps even intelligent (they applauded). The next day I got a phone call from Welton. He had been at the play, had heard my critique, but needed to leave immediately after to write his review. He suggested we meet. We did. Over a period of time we got to know each other and each other's families. We became close friends.

Welton listened to me complain about theatre at UCSD— when I'd been offered my job, one of the lures was learning that Michael Langham of the Guthrie Theater in Minneapolis was coming to the university to head up the Theatre Department. This excited me, since my fantasy was to become a world-famous playwright. Langham would direct my plays, work out the creaks, and take them to New York. But Langham never arrived. He sent his assistant. His assistant lacked the insight and the imagination that blessed Langham. Also, the assistant didn't much like my plays. Suddenly my playwriting career was on hold. But Welton had read a couple of my plays and liked them. One day he suggested we start a theatre company. A great idea that panicked me. What would we do for money? For space? For actors? But Welton knew how to find these necessities. And actors were the least problem; many Hollywood actors lived in San Diego (much cheaper housing than LA, much less stress), and most of them would kill to do live theatre, for many of them their first love, Welton said. He would produce and direct, I would find the plays and produce as well. We called ourselves New Heritage Theatre. We created a logo, two arrows, the top one pointing left, the bottom one to the right.

Now all we needed was a play. Which, for our debut, had to be the right play. We talked about *The Threepenny Opera*, usually a winner. But it had been done so often, everyone was familiar with it, nothing new there. We talked about borrowing Brecht's own process, finding an old play as he had done with Gay's *Beggar's Opera*. And what should it be? First, it needed to be American—San Diego with its massive naval base was purely American. Second, it should have music and it should be funny—so, a musical comedy, a genre I had loved. What, then? Welton wondered if we might think about going back to the start of American musical comedy. Did I know *The Black Crook* by Charles M. Barras (yes, really his name)?

I did not. I found it, read it. Its language was arcane, its songs silly, and as written the whole of it would run half a day. For all that, a perfect project. First produced in 1866, it had come into being when a large French touring company alive with dancing girls arrived in New York to enlighten the masses. But a fire destroyed their sets and costumes, so the producer looked around wildly for a new vehicle that could be produced with American sets. He came into contact with Barras, who had been pushing his *Crook* for years. Something in it caught the producer's attention. He agreed to take it on. *The Black Crook* is the tale of an evil sorcerer who has made a deal with the devil for eternal life on the condition that the sorcerer provide the devil with one pure soul a year. The Crook finds a handsome, naive village lad, Rodolphe, whom he tricks into going on a long search for gold and riches, so that he can return wealthy and marry his beloved Amina. Everything works out well for the good guys in the end. That first night in New York was, even with the full nine hours it took, a roaring success, not least because the legs of the French dancing girls could be seen right to the tops of their thighs.

First I gutted the play, much like we did for our house in downtown Montreal. Then I wrote new songs. Then I stripped down the scenes, reducing the length by more than a half, and modernized much of the language. Then we had a reading. Which ran more than four hours. A critique followed. The most painful critique of my work that I'd ever had came from a man I didn't then know, Milton. He had worked with the San Francisco Mime Troupe. He went on for more than half an hour about what I'd done wrong. And all in public, before the members of the cast. The worst of his critique came from my realization that he was ninety-eight percent on the nose, the best encapsulated playwriting education I'd ever had. So I went home and cut some more. And more. And rewrote the songs and politicized the language. Finally we went into rehearsal, Welton and me producing, me rewriting as we went, Milton acting as key grip and stage manager and master carpenter. In the end it was a modest success, both critical and financial— we made enough money to go on to the next project. Which I wrote with Milton.

Why the digression? Because when Kit and I started, with Judith, thinking in a somewhat organized fashion about house building, I discovered the process was in many ways similar to running a theatre company, from the moment a play is first envisioned till it goes into production. Kit and I, the original conceiver-writers; Judith with her broad and deep understanding of how, à la Christopher Alexander, a house works, revising over the months she and we spent together, a version of the directorial Welton with his broad grasp of the theatre world. Stuart the builder would stand in for Welton the producer, and Kit and I stood in for me—at least me in the rewriting part of it all. We also doubled as costume master and costume mistress, and to some extent grips numbers one and two. Oh yes, and set designers as well. Many a dress rehearsal and tech rehearsal, not to mention yet more rescripting, and the usual tensions between the technical and the creative side. The play would open, everything in place. And when it did, when the house was built, we would also be the lead actors, living on this set year in and year out, acting through the scenes of our lives from opening day on.

For weeks the central questions related to sightlines: the frame of what we'd see when looking out. What would the view from the windows be: how large, where to cut the image, when to break it into parts, when to allow the full view head on; and the doors, for all our entrances and exits. Questions of vinyl versus wood or aluminum for the window frames become serious issues, not only in the nature of the framing but also regarding the upkeep of the set over the years—we would not have an ongoing stage manager to handle those details, and we'd prefer to do as little managing as possible. The question of expense was central as well. We needed to come in more or less on budget, so that operating costs would more or less hold firm. We couldn't afford to lose money on this production.

Then for weeks more we dealt with issues of harmony. How to choose the wood for the kitchen cabinets and the cupboard doors to heighten and blend rather than clash with the wood of the flooring? Would all the lighting fixtures be properly placed to highlight aspects of, and to create intimacy at places on, the set? Will all the physical bits gibe with the drama being acted out by the lead actors, and the walk-ons as well? And in the process, we wondered, how much would we, Kit and I, have to function not simply as producers writ large, but also as hand-holders to all the minor players and techies who'd need to be sweet-talked to make sure their contribution was in place and appreciated, their appearance perfectly timed, so that it all would come together at the moment of performance.

These comparisons are broad equivalents. But they helped me clarify the hugely important role played by Judith as director, and Stuart as the producer whose knowledge and expertise we needed in order to pull the largest and the smallest elements together. I knew nothing of, for example, what's legit in terms of stress and quality and what's not, nor any of the all-encompassing rules and bylaws and codes that control the way this building process works. Stuart did, Judith too.

3.

Dad learned to fish in Northern Ireland. Mr. Gilfillan, my father's boss, taught him. My parents, Miklos and Dora Szanto—they later became Mike and Dorothy—had come to live in Northern Ireland after a dramatic escape from Nazi Austria in 1938.

Mum, born in 1907, had lived in Vienna all her life. Dad was born Budapest in 1901, but his family had moved to Vienna in 1902. They both considered themselves fully Viennese. Dad lived in his long-widowed mother Ottilie's home until his wedding, thereafter moving in with Mum's family. Dad's father, Franz, had died in the early 1920s. Miklos married Dora Zollschan in 1933, the year Hitler took power in Germany, his eye already on Austria, in German called Österreich, the Eastern Reich. My parents, like so many others, didn't at that time believe there was any danger from this upstart German leader, who was himself Austrian-born. Any number of incidents might have finally convinced them to leave Austria, but it was the *Anschluss*—the annexation—of Austria to Germany in March 1938 that added special fear to their need to get out. Quickly Vienna was riddled with Nazis, the SS as well as regular soldiers. One evening, coming home from work, Dad came across an SS officer standing over a man on his knees, the man's fingernails scraping dirt out of the cracks between paving stones. Dad recognized the man as someone he'd seen at the synagogue. In the same instant the man recognized Dad and shouted at the SS officer, "Him! Make him do this! He's a Jew too!" The SS officer kicked the man in the side and told him to get back to work. But the man kept insisting, "Make him do this, leave me alone, he's a Jew too!" Dad remembered that the Nazi looked confused for a moment. Then he kicked the man again and said, "Get on with your work! I'll decide who's a Jew around here." Dad, terrified, walked quietly away. Years later he told me of the heart-gripping horror and the sense of betrayal he'd felt, in equal parts. Time to leave Vienna.

Which was easier to hope for than to do. Three things were needed to leave: a job in another country, entry visas to that country, and exit visas from Austria. The job wasn't a major problem. As a fashion designer, Dad would be able to find work in many places around the world. My parents' first choice of destination was the United States, where the largest number of their exiled relatives had already settled. But immigration to the United States was decided on a quota basis, the quota determined by ratio: if two percent of American citizens were of Austrian heritage, then two percent of America's annual immigrants could come from Austria. Mum, on the Austrian quota, would have no difficulty getting a US visa. But Dad, born in Budapest, had to qualify on the Hungarian quota. Since only a tiny fraction of one percent of Americans were of Hungarian origin, obtaining an American visa was next to impossible. They tried for months, each time with a new strategy, and each time they failed. Their second choice was Canada. At the embassy they were told at every visit that a visa for them was completely impossible. No explanation, just an ongoing "No."

They could not have known the basis for Canada's policy on Jewish immigration in 1938. Frederick Charles Blair, Prime Minister Mackenzie King's immigration minister, was thoroughly opposed to Jews entering Canada. He wasn't alone in this. King concurred with the policy, as did Vincent Massey, Canada's High Commissioner to Great Britain, together with most of Canada's leaders in both anglophone and francophone industry and society. Between 1933 and 1948 only five thousand Jews were allowed to immigrate into Canada. One of Blair's immigration officials, when asked how many Jews should be admitted to Canada, replied, "None is too many." This phrase became the title of a well-researched book dealing with Canadian immigration policy as regards Jews.

My parents understood only that Canada was unwelcoming. They could not have known that Vincent Massey would be, as soon as Kit was born, her great-uncle. That irony remained for the future. Another irony: Massey's niece, Charity Grant, is singled out in the book as one of the very Canadians who, working with the United Nations Refugee Relief Agency (UNRRA), are cited positively on their attitude about Jews. Her work was to help settle displaced concentration camp victims.

Miklos and Dora sought out other possible countries that would take immigrants. Chile, where my mother's sister and her husband had fled to several years earlier, seemed an option, but they believed that by moving to South America they'd never again see any other of their family members. Then they learned that Great Britain was desperate for men with expertise in knitwear. Through his trade paper Dad applied for and got a job in Londonderry; the job description called for someone who could design bathing suits for oversized women. The British visa followed. Only the Austrian exit visas remained. Mum lined up every day for two weeks at the appropriate department. Each time when she reached the Nazi official in charge she would hand him the job offer and the British entry visa in which exit visas would be stamped. Each time she'd be told, No, not possible. Finally she resorted to placing a large bill inside the covers of the British visa. She felt brave, but fearful as well—would she be put in jail for bribery? The Nazi slipped the bill into his pocket and smiled, telling her, "But we didn't mean to have such lovely women as yourself leave us, Fräulein." In half an hour she had two exit visas.

Over these months, incidents of violence against Jews were increasing in Vienna and throughout Austria, and tales of deportations were beginning to be heard. Dad's brother Leopold, my Uncle Poldi, a jeweller, was taken to one of the camps and held for months until, by some miracle, his wife, Elly, managed to get him released. (She made a tape of her experiences for Steven Spielberg's series *Shoah*, where she explains their ordeal. They escaped and went to live in Chicago.)

In October 1938, Dad and Mum departed for Northern Ireland. They left behind both Dad's mother, Ottilie, and Mum's mother, Anna-Netty, as well as most of their possessions. The mothers would follow when all their papers had been set in order. My parents' possessions would be shipped to them—Mum had for many years been a trilingual secretary with Schenker & Co., a large export-import company in Vienna, and was well appreciated by the management there. They would arrange shipping furniture, clothing, dishes, even the piano Dad had given Mum, to Londonderry. Getting the mothers out would be easier to organize from England, Mum was told.

Mum and Dad had all their own papers but feared having to cross borders—some low-level official might still stop them. So they developed a strategy I still find stunningly daring. They flew from Vienna to Berlin, their skis with them. No Jew, they figured, would think of flying into the heart of Nazi Germany, so there'd be no suspicions. From Berlin they caught a train to Munich, as if going on a skiing holiday, from Munich a local train into the Bavarian Alps, where they stayed the night at a ski lodge, and in the morning, their only luggage their rucksacks, they climbed high into the mountains on the German side and skied down into Switzerland. From there they flew to London, took the train to Liverpool, ferry to Belfast, and a train to Londonderry.

On arrival Dad met his new boss, Mr. Gilfillan—whom I have only recently learned had a first name, David. I'd always known him only as Mister Gilfillan, as if that was what his parents had named him. Mr. Gilfillan brought Dad to the factory. There he learned he would not be designing bathing suits for fat ladies, rather he'd be working on uniforms for the upcoming war effort. Dad was thirty-seven, Mum thirty-one. They were starting a new life with nothing but their talents, their love for each other, and whatever could be shipped to them.

Back in Vienna my mother's mother oversaw the packing of my parents' possessions, with an SS officer standing by. When the SS officer tried to stop my grandmother from including the silver candlesticks, my grandmother apparently said, "Surely you wouldn't begrudge my daughter these? Surely you would want your own daughter to have her candlesticks." The candlesticks got packed up. Kit and I still have them.

But in Londonderry, organizing the grandmothers' papers proved far more difficult than my parents had been led to believe. Twice Mum had travelled to London to go through the necessary bureaucratic processes, and both times thought all was well until another letter arrived in Londonderry asking for yet more information, which had to be delivered in person. After the second trip all seemed to be in order until my parents were told that back in Vienna the German officials could find only one of the mothers. In London again, my mother, hysterical, learned that all this time the papers were being made out for "the Szanto mothers," as they had been called throughout the process. The German officials had papers in hand for two women named Szanto. Mum finally cleared this up, making the trip to London, her third, just before Passover 1939.

(Both my grandmothers did get out. They lived with us in Londonderry, where, according to several of Mum's stories, they bickered with each other ceaselessly. Then in 1943 Dad's mother received, inexplicably, a visa to go to the United States. She travelled by boat at the height of the war and arrived safely, to live with her other surviving son in Chicago. My mother's mother left soon after the end of the war and lived out her years with a daughter in New York.)

So during Passover 1939 Dad was alone. He was about to leave for the synagogue when Mr. Gilfillan came by. Would Dad like to go fishing? My father explained he had to go to the synagogue service because of Passover. Mr. Gilfillan said he understood and drove Dad to the synagogue. But for some reason the synagogue was locked, no one there. So Mr. Gilfillan again asked, Would Mike, already Mike by this time, like to go fishing? Dad explained he had never been fishing before. Mr. G. told him not to worry, he had everything necessary and would show Dad all he needed to fish properly. So Mr. G. drove Dad home to change, then to a stream in the nearby countryside. Mr. G. provided Dad with a rod and reel, a box of worms, and told him to go downstream, letting his line out, and if a trout bit, to raise the rod tip, set the hook, and pull it in. Mr. G. would go upstream. They would meet back in the same place in a couple of hours.

Dad fished, even caught a couple of trout, and enjoyed himself immensely. As long as he lived he would say that on that day he, much like the trout, had been deeply hooked. Two hours later he reported back to the starting point. Mr. G. had unpacked a lunch for himself and handed Dad a package: lunch. Dad knew he had to refuse, the special dietary laws for Passover determined what he would eat. But he also had to be polite. Dad unpacked the package. It contained matzo sandwiches Mr. G. had made up, hard-boiled eggs, and fresh salad. Dad continued to fish his life long, loved being next to or on water, and years later, as I've explained, taught me to fish as well—one of the greatest gifts I have ever been given. A recent novel of mine is dedicated: *In memory of my father, who taught me that water too has a language.*

Many years later, when Dad turned fifty-nine, he suddenly lost most of the vision in his right eye. This panicked him. Fifty-nine had been a dangerous age for the male side of his family. His grandfather, father, and two uncles had died when they reached that age, of various causes: shot in the First World War, heart attack, cancer, heart attack. Loss of vision could only mean that something was killing him. Degeneration of some part of his eye? A brain tumour? The doctors searched, found nothing. In the end they did find a tumour, but not in his brain. Though it was benign, it had been growing for a long while, and had so severely pressed against the bundle of his right eye's optic nerves that it had destroyed the cells. Nothing could be done about it. He didn't die that year, so considered merely losing ninety percent of the vision in one eye his great good luck, his victory over death. He lived with vision in just the one eye for another twenty-five years; in the five following years, the dead nerve made no difference since he'd developed macular degeneration and could see little with either eye. But for those twenty-five years he had continued working, he travelled, and, scarily for us, he drove his car. Safely.

Which puts my complaints about my eyes in a different context. Two days ago I returned to the outpatient clinic of the Nanaimo Regional General Hospital for my second cataract operation. I still had little depth perception; I occasionally saw double with my left eye. They had given me a reasonable hour for an appointment, 11:20. I was kept waiting only long enough for my eyes to dilate properly and for the antibiotic drops to do their work. Someone wheeled me in. I had a chatty give-and-take with Dr. Spencer, and he went to work on me. My brother had asked me if, the previous time, I had been able to see the knife coming down on my lens. I couldn't remember, so this time I watched as carefully as I dared. Again the immense bright light, white mostly but with the blues and reds at its edges, stabbed down at my eyeball. And when Dr. Spencer started the actual procedure, yes, I could see the knife. But so close, obviously, that the knife was all blur. And then no discernible object as the lens came out, only light hitting my retina. It was over as quickly as the first time. I'd been a little worried, after speaking with the anaesthesiologist and learning my eye was Spencer's fifteenth procedure of the morning, that there'd be some palpable differences. What if he were getting tired? But it was I who felt tired and wanted to go back to Gabriola. We'd be coming to the big island again the next day, to Parksville this time, about twenty miles up-island, where Spencer has another office, to have my plastic patch removed, for him to examine my eye.

Which he did. Immediately, even in the little office, I could tell something substantial had shifted. He examined me, said it looked fine, and sent me off—four minutes and I was out. The day had gone grey, the most brilliant grey I can remember seeing, ever. All the edges were sharp and when I looked over and up I could see the tiny branches, the needles even, of a fir tree eighty yards away. Kit drove back to Nanaimo, as we had to do some errands. All the way I was taking immense pleasure in reading aloud signs along the road and, Kit says, giggling to myself. *Euphoria* would not be too strong a term; euphoria it remains today, in a more muted way. Thinking back, I had not seen that clearly even with glasses for perhaps twenty years—and without glasses, sixty. I don't know whether or not I was in fact giggling, but I do know I could feel a foolish little grin refusing to leave my lips. Still now, beyond the giddiness, it feels like somebody's faking all this new clarity of vision for my momentary benefit and can take away the fakery with equal ease. As if I were flying across a frozen bog, unsure of the forces keeping me high in the air.

Today the colours here by the bog are gallant and bright, green iris shafts sharply outlined, sporting a bolder green than I have seen in a long time, and there's a serious warm sun in a big blue sky. The yellow-brown road across the bog shines like polished gold, and at the shoreline I can see little tadpoles scuttling; hard to believe they hadn't yet become frogs searching for a mate. Later I took the truck to the village. All the depth vision has returned, or been reinvented. I felt as if I were driving with authority, which made me realize what I had previously not admitted to myself, that for the last few years my driving had become increasingly tentative.

On the other hand . . . When I put a log on the fire I have to sit back. The heat against my eyes, once protected from direct waves by glasses, is too great. No question now, when bucking up wood, goggles are an absolute necessity.

There's an amusing side to it all too. I don't mind wearing the dollar store magnifying glasses I bought for reading. Back when my eyesight was in decline I had no problem reading. But my eyes have been corrected only for distance viewing, so now I need these glasses to mince garlic, to keep from slicing thin bits of finger skin in the garlic, to keep it from going red. Or eating: we were invited out to dinner last night. The first course was escargots, deep in the shell. I could not see the escargot well enough to get it out, couldn't get the prongs to hold the shell properly, and when I did and stuck the little fork in, it was as if the snail were still alive and trying to hide. But with my reading glasses on, no problem either holding or skewering.

When I walk down stairs, I no longer need the handrail. I can see where the riser on the stair below stops, and I can put my foot in the right place. Before, it sometimes felt as if I were stepping into space hoping that some solid object would rise to support the sole of my shoe.

And this morning coming across the bog I could see blackbirds, many of them, those sitting on the tops of high stalks, keeping a watch on the brood in the nest below, and those sitting up in the bare high alders on the far side of the bog, the sentinels, their glance protecting all the new families down close to water level. And it made me wonder, had they been there all month but I hadn't been able to see them?

They are a bird I take a lot of pleasure in watching. They'll fly from the bog around to the back of the house, where our bird feeders are set up. They steal easily from the platform feeder, scaring away the smaller birds, white-capped and other sparrows, towhees, juncos, pine siskins, chickadees, goldfinches, nuthatches. They have a harder time on the hanging feeders since their necks are too long; they're too big altogether. But I've seen them stand on as-it-were tiptoes, and crane their necks so that, while perching on a lower foothold, they manage to grab seeds from an upper entry hole. The difference between the male and female is dramatic: the male is fully black and has epaulettes of bright red, the red sometimes bordered in yellow; the female has a brown and white back, with a brown-white streaked belly, something like an oversized sparrow. The juvenile of whatever sex looks similar to the female. Ours are about seven inches long; there are bigger and smaller versions elsewhere in North America, environment helping to control differences in their appearance. (In an experiment where redwing nestlings were shifted from one population to another, when the babies reached adulthood they looked more like their foster parents than their actual ones.) They roost year-round but in different locales—ours had arrived in January, unseen by me, and will be gone by midsummer. I've read that both males and females are polygamous, and a single male may service a dozen or more females in a given territory, while in many of the nests he considers his property there'll be some chicks of other male parentage.

It's grand to see them with such clarity. I keep myself from exclaiming aloud some of the phrases that run through my head: "Oh I was blind, but now I see," or worse, "The blind man picked up his hammer and saw." Never so blind as Dad in that one eye; but not for a long time have I had such full, pure sight.

Yesterday as I walked along the bog road under the big blue sky I noticed a fine rain precipitate, dropping from a single small cloud. It fell over the bog on my right, the west, not over the bog on my left, the east. I was walking at the edge of the little storm, each tiny droplet in sharp outline. I stuck out my right hand. It got wet. I stuck out my left. It stayed dry in sunlight. I followed the dividing point till the woods at the south of the road. I'd passed through a marvel.

And two days later the snow came, dumping five inches on the bog road.

But the day after that, by late afternoon, all had melted.

APRIL

I.

New on the bog this April Fool's Day: the skunk cabbage is showing, bull lily pads are starting to emerge, and pond skaters are back on the water.

Skunk cabbage, also known as swamp lantern, a prettier name, is the first of the spring's native wildflowers; it must have already stuck its tip out of the water a week ago, but I haven't noticed till today. We've had forsythia out for a couple of weeks (from Chinese friends I learned the word for forsythia in Chinese, translated to English, is welcome spring). The forsythia begins yellowing just as the first daffodils open; the earlier snowdrops and crocuses have already departed, but these are introduced plants, not native to West Coast gardens. Swamp lantern, however, is indigenous to many parts of North America, including Gabriola Island. In places where there's still snow when the skunk cabbage emerges, it gives off enough heat to melt the snow above and around it. The plant reaches a temperature up to twenty degrees Fahrenheit higher than the air surrounding it, day or night; as the air cools off, so does the skunk cabbage. That sheath-like yellow outer segment with long, thin maroon lines one sees first is a modified leaf, looking like a cape or a hood, to protect the yellow spike at the centre. The yellow appears fuzzy. On closer examination, the fuzz is made up of hundreds of very small flowers. It does in fact give off a pungent odour, but only some find it repugnant. Bees and gnats love it, which the skunk cabbage appreciates—these are the insects it needs for pollination.

We have only one skunk cabbage, transplanted to the bog by us eight years ago. (Strictly speaking it's not indigenous to the bog—just to a place half a mile from the house.) There's a springtime stream along a dirt road there where skunk cabbage grows in abundance. Kit and I had pulled on our gumboots and brought along the shovels. We figured if we dug up half a dozen, they'd reproduce over the years and we'd have a small colony.

Good idea, but difficult to carry out. We stepped into the muddy stream edge and started to dig at a plant maybe a foot high. We quickly discovered that the skunk cabbage's root system is complex, and prodigious. We'd gone two feet into the mud and still hadn't found the bottom of the root. We eventually dug up three plants, all smaller than our first attempt, brought them back and buried the roots at the edge of the bog pond, deep as we could. All three bloomed the first year, two in the second; only one has survived since. And it hasn't reproduced. But it's there, and when it emerges each year it seems to shout out, like the Chinese forsythia, Welcome spring!

The flower of the bull lily, as we call it—it's also known as cow lily, or spatterdock—looks a lot like the yellow water lily but can grow three times as large. The flower curves up from the stem, its seven or eight petals making a shape like the bowl for a glass for good red wine. Unlike the water lily's flower, which floats on the water's surface or rises a little above, the bull lily's flower sticks up into the air, with as much as six inches of stem visible. Its leaves at first rise from the water curled and pointed, like darts; this is happening now. When mature they open up and lie flat on the water surface. They're heart-shaped and big, as much as a foot long and seven inches wide. How the plants got into the bog we have no idea, because until Gordie dug the pond there was no water deep enough for them to rise from. Now we have bull lilies in three separate parts of the bog. Small invertebrates hide under the leaves, which are what the ducks come for. I've fished in many ponds, and my first draw is usually to the edges of lily pads, the weed beds where small fish also search, to gorge themselves with the little insects; larger fish, my quarry, hunt the little fish. So it's appropriate that, when the lily pads die off in the fall, their decomposing ghosts become food for the invertebrates themselves. Right now, however, the lilies are at the start of their annual life, rising up from the muck.

Of today's three new signs of spring, it's the pond skaters that fascinate me the most. They've spent the winter along some protected part of the bank, some covered and secluded place. They are the first obvious, visible biological sign of spring in the bog. The first auditory living things are the frogs, but they're nocturnal. I've only heard them, have seen very few since I've been here. Our skaters—twenty species exist in North America—are about three-quarters of an inch long. They have six legs and move along the top of the water with a kind of rowing motion carried out by the middle set of legs. With their rear legs they steer themselves in their wanted direction. They don't sink into the water because their bodies, including the tips of their feet, are coated with a waxy substance that resists the water. They literally float along the surface tension. They have excellent eyesight and hunt by watching for prey. I could see half a dozen of them from the bank. Yesterday I watched one tack in what seemed arbitrary directions until for some other non-obvious reason it headed back close to where I was standing. Then I saw its goal—a tiny bug had landed in the water and, trying to rise again, was making minuscule splashes. The skater hovered next to the fly for maybe half a minute, possibly trying to figure out if this was a threat or should it attack? Then it struck out with its mouth, held on to the little bug, and skated into the hardhack where I lost sight of it. Back at the cottage I Googled "water skater." The mouth, called a rostrum, is modified for what I had just seen; much like a mosquito, the skater had pierced its prey and was injecting saliva and enzymes into the bug. These would already have been breaking down the bug's tissues, turning them into a kind of broth which, like the mosquito drinking diluted human blood, it then sucked up through the rostrum. Dinner.

Also new for us this spring, an uncertainty about the septic tanks. Is it time to get them cleaned out? Neither the one at the cottage nor the one at the house have been dealt with since they were put in, fifteen and eight years ago, respectively. I contacted Vic, who knows better than most whom to call for such services. David, was the answer. David (not our son) has the suction equipment and a tank truck. I called. His first question: did I know where the tanks were buried? For the house, yes; the cottage one I had to guess at. David told me I would have to locate them both, and then dig away any soil that covered them so his man could get at the lids.

Armed with shovel and pickaxe, Kit and I laid bare the top of the tank behind the house—easily located because in the summer the grass growing above it goes brown the earliest, the soil below holding no water. I wanted to lift the top off and look in. Maybe all was okay and I didn't need to hire David. But the cement cap must weigh a hundred pounds. So David's man would have to come after all.

At the cottage we slammed a steel rod into the ground where we figured the tank should be and found it quickly. But here the grass stays green all summer because the twelve inches of soil and sand hold water expertly. Exposing the tank turned into heavy work. We did finally lay bare one of the lids but were too weary to dig for the second. Money would do the job: David's man could finish the digging. I called David back and we set a day for the job. Floyd would show up at nine, two mornings hence.

Floyd arrived. I took him to the tank behind the house. He backed his truck down the drive and brought out his hoses, sixty feet long, six inches in diameter, with a screening device at the service end, to keep from sucking up anything that might plug the pipe. He then pulled open the first compartment's lid, all upper back strength. He explained to me how a septic tank works. At the house all toilets flush toward a single pipe. The pipe's contents flow downhill—at our house, anyway (if the septic tank and field are higher than the house, Floyd said, one needs a pump, and that's much more complicated). The pipe from the house ends inside the first tank, where it enters the side of another pipe, a foot long, making a T lying on its side. The T is open at the bottom, allowing the effluent to drop into the tank, and at the top, so that if the bottom becomes plugged there's another escape route. He probed the muck and nodded. "Looks fine to me, nothing down there that shouldn't be." I told him it had been only Kit and I and our guests who'd been depositing anything into the tank. We've placed notes in all the bathrooms urging guests to dump only soiled toilet paper into the toilet. "Good." Floyd nodded. "Don't put anything down the drain that hasn't gone through you first."

Floyd lowered the vacuum end into the muck, which did stink but far less than I'd have thought, and slowly sucked it out, constantly hosing water in to thin down the contents, and to wash the sides. When it was empty and clean he opened the second lid. In the first compartment, he explained, the heavy matter drops to the bottom, where bacteria constantly break it up, while the liquid stays at the top and overflows into the second compartment. In the second the particulate matter is far finer, but it too settles out. More bacteria. At the far end of the second tank, high in the wall, there's another opening, with a pipe leading out which branches into two pipes, each of these also branching. These pipes as they run farther from the tank have holes in their sides allowing the liquid to leach into the ground. This is the septic field.

Our house stands on a slope. The only flat part of the land is the terrain above the septic field. When we first moved in, I spotted that area and claimed it for our boules court, boules (also called pétanque) being a game played in the south of France, somewhat like bocce in Italy. Now we play there every summer. The court has only one problem: despite our best efforts the ground still retains a bit of a slant. This allows the heavy metal boules balls to roll a little, or a lot. But that's an advantage in this game because it keeps the role of skill to a minimum; some of the best-placed balls tend to roll down the slope, so no one can be an expert. Men, women, children, the old, the young, the athletic, the clumsy, all are under the dominion of the slope. Ian, who plays here often, once said of our boules court: "It's not very level, but it's very levelling."

I asked Floyd, as he finished off the second compartment, "What's the weirdest thing you ever found in a tank?"

"I haven't found anything all that weird," he said, "but David once had to open up a tank so that a Mountie in a wet suit, a forensic investigator, could go down in to look for some kind of evidence."

We headed over to the cottage, where Floyd dug through the dirt over the second compartment. I told him this one might be messier because we'd rented the cottage out while we still lived half the year in Montreal and had no idea what they might have dumped into the toilet.

"That's one of the three dangerous tees," he said. "Teens, townies, and tenants. Teens don't think, townies don't know, and tenants don't care."

Wisdom from the muck-evacuater. Luckily he found only organic sewage.

We had spent three months, the winter and early spring of 1997, in the south of France, the Charente, beside the Bordeaux and

Cognac regions, with Mamane, our friend Bruno's grandmother. That year spring had come to the area in January and February, unnaturally warm, daffodils blooming, leaves on trees sprouting early. All to the dour delight of those there: "We'll have to pay for this in April." They were right, as we heard after we reached Gabriola: cold and grey since our departure. So that year we had two springs. Spring on Gabriola had blossomed before we arrived. Not so warm as to be able to sit outside and read, that would come a month or so later, but a slow slow swelling into green, a delicate evolution. Our neighbour Alan says spring arrives here in February, then takes six months to fully unfold. Unlike Montreal, where spring tends to explode into brilliant existence as one wakes on a certain late April morning, and then becomes, all too soon, humid summer.

I've wondered at times, why this fascination with spring, for me and many others? On Gabriola I enjoy each of the seasons in turn. But spring has its own quality. It doesn't flow naturally out of winter but arrives in spurts and bursts. Spring easily dissolves into summer, summer is reduced by fall, fall is closed down by winter. But spring is new and I'm delighted to see it again, like an old friend. I'm enchanted to know some things aren't lost, like places or people I've cared about over the years, rediscovered through chance or travel or email. Spring is that kind of friend, too long taken for granted. I have no reason to believe I won't see a good many more springs. But I also know I paid too little attention to spring when I was younger, living in it or in spite of it; squandering spring. I know, too, that I've lived through far more springs than I'll see again. So each spring becomes more rare, more to be savoured, appreciated.

My first-rate double spring of 1997.

This year, as in the past, the mating of birds. The bog is ongoingly alive with the red-winged blackbirds. They're again coming to our feeder, the tray straddling the deck railing. The females are the first to show, daring to land on the tray, pecking carefully at the sunflower seeds. Then comes a male, and another. Initially they are all wary—if they see us move, even behind window glass, they whisk away. But if the pattern of previous years is repeated, soon I'll be standing by the porch rail, listening to half a dozen different bird songs, and the blackbirds, suddenly brazen, will land a few feet away to nibble happily.

The ravens are courting again. We have constant transients; a couple of years ago we had a resident couple. They called to each other, the male letting the female know where he's perching, the female acknowledging, one or the other flying off to join the potential partner. There the couple sat, up in their treetop, in one of the hundred-plus-foot firs around the house. They billed and squawked and necked. Literally. They caressed each other's necks, she his neck with hers, he her neck similarly, each making soft cooing sounds. They groomed each other with their beaks. All of this was accompanied by a range of other sound, some private, some mimicking: the basic, raucous *kaaaw*; the popping of a wine bottle being uncorked; a rich melodic belch; the clap of two branches of arbutus tapping against each other.

Mallards too. Not those we'd fed sunflower seeds, new ones. Early April a few years ago a pair had nested at the edge of the bog pond. They would waddle along the road, sunning themselves, as if they were late-middle-aged long-time partners. Since we didn't want to frighten them away from the general area of their nest we followed them slowly, at their pace. They set the example, we mimicked them, happy to project our anthropomorphic notions onto them. One time another pair of mallards flew low overhead. Our pair began a loud squawk-bark, responded to by the newcomers, a quick, brash, insistent squawking. And suddenly our two took off after the newcomers. Friends getting together, I thought, wondering if they had migrated from the same pond somewhere in southern California. But not at all. Our ducks were chasing the interlopers away from their/our bog. Here was nesting space for the first arrivals only. Our lady duck returned first, landing in the small patch of open water. After a few minutes the male came back, setting himself down in shallow water on the other side of the road. A minute later her squawking began again, but more softly, more in control, as if saying, No, dummy, over here, this is our side. He returned her cry, more relaxed than she, and finally she flew the fifty yards to join him. Then all went silent.

2.

Yesterday I got my potatoes planted. The last of last year's crop have only just come out of the ground; since they need to be stored in the dark I leave them under the earth over the winter. This keeps them cool. They don't freeze because two inches underground the temperature never goes below zero Celsius. I dig up a dozen or so at a time from September to March as we need them for dinner. Once the ground begins to warm I harvest the rest because I don't want them to sprout uncontrollably. The only trouble with using the vegetable garden itself as cold storage site is that the green potato leaves brown and crumple away; unless I mark each bed carefully I'm likely to forget where they lie buried. I do manage to find most of them as needed, and most of the rest show up when the bed gets turned over to prepare it for its next residents. A few stay in the ground, appearing sometime in May in an inappropriate bed: volunteers. I vary the beds for potatoes annually, keeping charts of what I've planted where in past years; rotation keeps down disease and blight.

This year I've planted four varieties. Most of my seed potatoes are saved from last year's crop, Yukon Gold, Red Chieftain, Andean Blue. The fourth kind I don't know the name of, and I had only two whole potatoes, given to me by Lucy, a friend and gardener of the highest order, who was experimenting with them; they have very thin skin. I had four from her, two of which we ate, and they were so delicious we practised restraint and I kept the other two for seed. When I do dig up a dozen, I store them in the basement, under sheets of newspaper. They should be out of the light so their eyes don't sprout before the ground is warm enough to be ready for them, and until I've gotten myself organized into preparing their beds.

After the planting Kit and I went for a walk along the fence behind our parking area. Since this is spring, we decreed, the yellow violets have to be appearing. There's usually a small patch of them back up there, and another down at the bottom of the garden. By the fence the ground is exceptionally dry, very little soil above the sandstone ridge—why violets would choose to grow there we've never been able to figure.

Before we reached the violet site we spotted a garter snake sidling through the undergrowth. We have a number of them on the land. In the summer I spot them sunning themselves at the edge of the bog road, gathering in the warmth of the day because they can't produce any of their own. To spot one in April is unusual around here—out of hibernation and looking for feed with weather nowhere near warm enough means he guessed wrong. I usually let them be, but I have in the past picked up a few. Once, as I was holding one as he wiggled to get away, he turned to me and hissed some smelly substance my way, his forked tongue wiggling. Doug, the first handyman we hired, back in 1995 when we lived in the cottage, educated me about garter snakes. Good for gardens, he said, because they eat slugs. Their skin is comprised of dry scales made of keratin, the same material as makes up human fingernails. A garter snake doesn't have an outer ear, but hears with the skin at the sides of his head, which sends sound waves to an inner ear bone by way of the jawbone. He can't move backwards, he can only curve the front of his body around, dragging his tail behind him. And most fascinating, he uses his tongue to smell what's going on in the outer world. He flicks it out to pick up odour as particulate matter. Back in, the tongue slides along the roof of his mouth, the forks slip into an opening, the particles he has gathered filled with information that is sent to an organ designed for making sense of the smell: food, danger, disappear, search.

We found the yellow violets just where they'd been last year. Because they face downward they're often hard to spot. The first bits of them one notices are the basal leaves, lying near to flat on the ground. They take the shape of a rosette of four or five leaves, each a couple of inches long. From the middle of the rosette rises a stem, for our violets none higher than its leaves at their longest. The flowers are bright yellow, maybe half an inch across, five roundish petals. The lower petal has bright purple stripes, like veins, beginning at its base and rising toward the lip for a quarter-inch. Some of the violets also had similar stripes, one or two, on the right and the left of the lower petal. We'd wanted to have some in the garden and tried to transplant a few, but they never took, not even with much of their own soil around the roots. They apparently don't do well in humanly concocted areas.

We had hired Doug that spring to open up a bit of land near the bog so we could put in a small vegetable garden. He would build an enclosure to keep out deer, and some raised beds. Doug was a philosophical kind of gardener, beginning many sentences with, "Well now, what I think is . . ." He's clear on a great deal, relating to the island, to land, down on pesticides, knows logging is necessary for wood to build with and for attractive places to live but objects to wood being used to make toilet paper—there's lots of other stuff for toilet paper, in Japan they grow thistles for junk paper and for pulp, easy enough to do that anywhere, friend of his tried to start a thistle farm to make paper but there were so many governmental regulations it couldn't work, too many regulations all over the place. He was heavily irritated at all the slag fires on the island, stupid to burn all that out there, waste it; all you need are half a dozen little steam generators that can turn heat into storable energy, electricity, all these slag fires could keep the whole island warm all winter. Very irritated with Quebec, too much money spent on all those referendums, why does anybody want more than English anyway, the language that's taking over the world, everybody should know English. Well, Doug works well and fast, and has a respect for our land, so the rest is necessary chaff. As we talked, the mother and father mallard and their ducklings walked along the road, he with a handsome, multicoloured strut, she a large, round, brown shape, five little feather-balls trailing. The parents led them into the bog. Doug laughed. "Supper for somebody."

3.

That spring we also made one of our first permanent purchases. We went over to Nanaimo. Sandy came along, shopping as entertainment. We bought curtaining material for the upstairs bedroom so that we can't be seen from the neighbour's drive. These would be the only curtains in the cottage; we have one slatted shade, which at night keeps us from being seen if someone comes down our own driveway. All the other windows are unprotected, which brings a great deal of light into the house; looking out we have grand views in every direction. At a nursery, Buckerfields', Kit fell in love with the shape and the bright pink-white blossoms of an apple tree. It was on sale, late season, fourteen dollars. So we brought it across on the ferry, a five-foot tree lying partly on its side on the rear seat and sticking out the window, Kit back there cradling it for protection, all but talking to it, and feeling most content. We left it on the porch, awaiting the completion of the garden and its deer-protection fence. The tree was found immediately by hummingbirds, and by a couple of juncos that played bend-the-branch on it.

The next day I went to pay for the various pieces Doug needed for the garden fence—poles, wiring, clips, and nails. I had to do this myself because Doug doesn't want to get involved in what he calls all the GST bullshit: "The government doesn't pay me ten thousand a year to collect money for them, so why should I bother? I'll just stay under the line." He is deeply opposed to government of all sorts. He sees it as a techno-bureaucratic conspiracy. He and I didn't go far in these discussions. How did he want to be paid, cheque or cash? Oh, a cheque; he pays his fair share of taxes, won't pay more than his share, but his share he has no objection to.

He took me to see Mike, who runs a portable mill at his place back in the woods a couple of miles from here. I'd been thinking it would be valuable to use some of our own lumber for building parts of the house when we reached that point. Having our logs milled could be both satisfying and cheaper, what with wood costing much and the price for logs being low. I learned about turning trees into lumber: all done according to the requirements of the house: X number of two-by-sixes, Y of one-by-fours, and so on, milled up at thirty cents a board foot. A thousand feet of two-by-sixes or fifteen hundred feet of two-by-fours or a thousand of one-by-twelves are each three hundred dollars. As opposed to seven hundred dollars per thousand board feet if bought at the lumberyard. For now, I paid for wood for the garden fence and raised beds, fifty dollars, brought it back and left it for Doug. The raised beds seemed small, one four-by-six, two four-by-four, and one four-by-eight. And the job was taking him way longer than he had figured. The mallard adults did their elegant couple-waddle down the road. No ducklings in sight. Not a good sign. The next day I bought soil for the garden. Four cubic yards, one hundred and eighty-three dollars. We'd be eating the world's most expensive vegetables.

Friday, April 18, presented itself as a fine, clean, bright spring day, the sky a cloudless blue, the air a chilly but windfree four degrees Celsius. As I exercised with my weights I stared out over the back deck at the garden, falling away below. Directly in front of me the large forsythia glowed a golden yellow, side-lit by the low sun from the east. Beside it to the left, the dangling bird feeders, and to the left of them, one of our flowering plums, the single blossoms light pink, most of the branches still bare of leaves; in the summer the green leaves will go bronze. The advantage of a nearly bare tree is one can watch the dozens of birds flitting from branches to the feeders: pine siskins with their sharply lined wings, black-bibbed juncos, purple finches with ruddy heads, the first of the chickadees, towhees strutting on the ground as if they owned the place. And, just arrived for the season, the goldfinches. They bounce from the tree to the feeder and back to the tree, glowing yellow amid pink blossoms, an impossible combination as a fashion statement but that morning embodying the glory of new life. At one point I counted fifteen birds of differing feathers pecking away at the sunflower seeds we fill the feeders with. Beyond the feeders, the next level down, the double-blossomed flowering plum glows a pink so outrageous it too would have been crass as a dress colour, but here it lights the garden with its over-the-top opulence. To one side, a volunteer: a bright red flowering currant. We have been trying to grow them from transplants since arriving here, and have failed three times; they simply died. Now suddenly one has appeared. It's the blossoms of these shrubs that mark the return of hummingbirds.

Below the flowering plum's pink, more bright yellow forsythia. And, near the bottom of the garden, two fruit plum trees which last year together produced three mature plums. Now, decked in innocent white, they look as if they're begging our forgiveness; no more such chicanery this year. The vegetable garden shows the first burst of broad beans, the overwintered lettuce and arugula in neat rows of green and ruddy purple, the annually meagre leeks tall but thin, the garlic in its serried ranks. The grass, already spring-high the previous morning, was cut eighteen hours ago and now lies lush and smooth, emerald in streaks of sunlight. Altogether a garden lavish with bird life and luxuriant colour. And at the front of the house, two more flowering plums, one given us by Judith, our architect, when we took possession of the house, each of them also double-blossomed and so thick with blooms we can't, from below, see the sky through them.

We woke the next morning and stared out the window in disbelief. White white white. An utterly unannounced snowstorm had passed through overnight. And the power was out. We got dressed without pleasure to start the generator and, as important, to pack the feeders with more bird food; dozens of birds were perching on the snow-covered branches of the upper plum tree, flying off and circling the vacant plastic containers, landing on the feeding rods to check, in disbelief, the empty chambers: how could these people abandon us precisely when any other seeds lay buried under a foot of snow? The generator started only after some coaxing, but at least Kit could now grind coffee, essential for a civilized morning, and we could run water. As little as possible. It's a small generator, attached only to the pump, the refrigerator, an outlet in the kitchen and another in the living room, but it does its job: plug the grinder into the kitchen outlet, grind, unplug, plug in the coffee maker, wait for the coffee to gurgle to a stop, unplug, cover the pot with a cozy, plug in the kettle for my tea, and so on.

Armed with hot drinks we headed outside. On the deck, twelve inches of wet snow. I began to fill the feeders when I heard a groan from Kit. The lower plum tree had paid the price for its outlandish pulchritude: more than half of its upper branches had broken off, caught by lower branches or lying on the ground. A version of this had happened to the same tree four years ago, so we knew it would grow back, but still. We agreed later we'd cut a few of the branches, bring them into the house. And me thinking, Yeah, so we could watch them die from close up.

We continued the morning chores, mainly bringing in wood for the fireplace and stove. We decided to walk up the long drive, across the bog road, up to the cottage and the road, to see what other damages had occurred, and found only one, a long, skinny pecker-pole fir, its trunk barely four inches in diameter. But it would keep a car from passing—not that one would try without chains in the ten-inch iced-over wet snow. I would take it out later with a chainsaw. Usually we have word of snow threats, so we can drive the car to within a few feet of the road to keep from being snowbound. This time, no warning. We learned only later there had in fact not been any forecast of the extent of precipitation; the wet weather had crossed Vancouver Island eastward in a narrow band and met a sluice of the cold air that had made the earlier day bright and clear. The combined system had selectively dumped heavy snow on the south end of Nanaimo, very little on the north. Then the system crossed from the big island to Gabriola, where it ditched its load at the centre of the island, our twelve inches, while at the south end very little fell, three or four inches, and on the north barely two.

The snow was destroying our plans for the day. Kit had museum duty in the afternoon, selling admissions and guiding visitors. I'd wanted to spend the morning writing, then get my beans into the garden in the afternoon, and in the evening we were invited to a birthday party for Phyllis at a restaurant at the north end with a grand view of Georgia Strait and the mainland coastal range. But not likely we'd get out today.

No other trees down between the bog and Chernoff, which, however, wasn't yet plowed. We trudged back, the foot of snow on the bog road melting, now turned into eight inches of slush. We would circle the house to see if, hoping not, there was further damage.

We found it. Both the flowering plums in the front were shattered, the weight of the snow on the thick blossoms having broken not just the branches but even the trunks of the trees, just above where the first branches appeared, snapping the trunks in two, the twenty-foot one at six feet, the slightly shorter at eight feet. Branches with tens of thousands of pink flowers lay and leaned on the ground, covered in snow. We both felt smitten, oddly heartsick. Many worse things in the world that can happen, but these beautiful trees so smithereened seemed unfair.

Kit called her museum colleagues to say she would not be in that afternoon. As it turned out the museum's power too was dead, so no issue. We then thought to call friends, Nick and Jenni, who live down at the bottom of the hill to ask if we could get a ride to the party with them—if our road had been plowed. Yes, they would pick us up. With nothing productive to be done we built a fire in the living room fireplace and sat around reading, warm and contented. When not looking out windows at mutilated trees.

In the late afternoon we trudged back up to Chernoff to discover the road was partially plowed, so our friends could indeed come by for us. Their car, with four-wheel drive, appeared. "Oh, no problem here," said Nick. "It's the slalom course down Ferne that's the real fun." So it turned out, what with power and cable lines down in—I counted—fourteen places, some hanging so low across the road a car a foot taller couldn't have passed underneath. Most lines had been snapped by trees, several of which were still hung up in the wiring. But by the time we reached the Village at the north end the snow had all but vanished, and from there to the restaurant the roads had already dried out. At the end of the road, a first-class party.

The next morning I glanced through the glass of the sliding door at the front of the living room. The ground remained white, but a rhododendron beyond the pergola had thrown off its snow and a single flower at its crown was preparing to open, all its bright red blooms rising separate, the other blossoms still closed. The small victories of spring.

Kit suggested we hack away at some of the snow on the slope between the cottage and the road so that the sun could melt it more easily. After a few minutes I noted a slight pain in my chest. I've had angina for eight years, have rarely felt it, this only the third time it's given me any difficulty. In each instance I'd been overexerting myself. So I stopped. Kit walked me slowly back to the house. I sprayed some nitro under my tongue. The pain disappeared. I hate having to carry the nitro with me wherever I go (or sometimes not, like when shovelling the drive). In fact it irritates me that I might need it, as much for health reasons as for the fact that its strength expires after a year, so I have to buy a new one annually. I've never taken more than a single squirt from any one bottle, and not even once from five of them, but they still need replacing.

When I was first diagnosed with angina I did substantial research on the Internet, then had a long consultation with a heart specialist. He suggested I have the artery stented, so as to open it up to a better blood flow. But I'd read about stents. The procedure is invasive and can even, very rarely, be fatal. Also, stents don't last well and often need to be replaced, and sometimes they slip, so the procedure has to be repeated. "Then why use them in the first place?" I asked the specialist.

"It eliminates the pain," he said.

"But do stents increase one's lifespan?"

He didn't know the answer. Strange, I thought. He checked a

couple of books. "No," he answered, "there's no obvious evidence of that."

Which was the moment I knew I'd have nothing to do with stents. Pain if it came would tell me to discontinue whatever it was I'd been doing. If I felt no pain I still might be stressing myself but wouldn't know about it. But if pain was to be my alarm clock, I wanted to hear it. And stop doing whatever had caused it. Which that afternoon I did, returning to the fireplace, reading my book, pain-free.

It's the third morning after the storm and virtually all the snow has melted. By the side of the bog, not present before the storm, small bluish flowers have appeared: veronica. Each blossom is about a third of an inch in diameter. We have them aplenty in the garden growing with the grass; they get mowed slightly, a haircut, when the grass is cut. But this is the first time I've seen them in the hundreds between the road and the bog. They are most welcome. The female name, Veronica, comes from the Latin *vera icon*, meaning the true image. How the name carried over to the flower I have not been able to learn. It can grow in little clumps like ours, or rise up in spikes. Ours are a complex blue, four petals, the lower one a purplish blue with thin, darker purple rays leading out from the central ovary to the rim of the petal. The lateral petals on the side near the lower one are a lighter purple-blue, the side away white tinged with the same blue, also with rays. The ovary is yellow, the eighth-of-an-inch filament white, and the anther, smaller than a pinhead, black. They make little impression unless one sees a field of them, many set against deep green grass. Then they delight the eye. As, suddenly, when crossing the bog road in April after a freak snowstorm.

Late afternoon brought on the job I was dreading, taking the chainsaw to the branches of the downed flowering plums. The one at the base of the entry path was the most painful. It had literally snapped in two. I climbed a ladder to reach the break and cut it cleanly across, then lopped off several of the larger branch stubs. I felt like the crassest of First World War surgeons, cutting limbs from trunks to save whatever was left of a once whole and living being. Several lonely, unbalanced branches remained. Then the same job for the other two. We smeared tar on the raw stubs, to keep disease from attacking the tree. The stubs might scar over, but we weren't taking the chance.

The job done, I felt better. Staring at the mutilated trees gave me only a sense of devastation and loss. Now, with luck, healing and growth could begin. We cut two dozen branches down to size and brought them into the house in several immense bouquets; the flowers produced a wonderful sweet scent that filled the living room for over a week.

Yesterday evening, after having written the above, I crossed the bog to return to the house and do my self-hypnosis. I stopped to watch two ravens in a low tree on the far shore surveying the scene below, including no doubt the eggs in the red-winged blackbird nests. And suddenly, a black swarm, fifteen or twenty male blackbirds, took off from the hardhack and attacked the ravens from all sides, above, below: dive-bombing, side-swiping, individually or in groups of three of four. The ravens sat, unmoved. The attack died back, only to start again, though fewer attackers this time. And so on, for maybe fifteen minutes, while I watched, till one of the ravens flew down to the ground. A couple of blackbirds attacked him there. Was the raven stealing eggs? I couldn't see. The attack stopped. Finally the two ravens flew off.

This is why I came to Gabriola.

MAY

I.

May Day. Not as in mayday, no ship or plane or me in distress, but as in the best of affirming certainties, all spring festival, coronation of a May queen, merry dancing. This because my visit to the cataract surgeon Spencer happened yesterday, for his final check. The right eye is perfect, 20/20, not a hint of macular edema in sight. The left eye is 20/30, doesn't need a corrective lens, get bifocals only if I want to move back and forth quickly between reading and distance seeing. Or I could live my life without prescription lenses and, for reading or chopping garlic, those dollar store items are all I need.

I bought many dollar glasses. Five pairs. Because of the irritation of being in a room or any other specific place and needing to read when my glasses are elsewhere, I splurged and bought a pair for my studio at the cottage, another for the car, one more for the truck, and two for the house, one for downstairs and one for upstairs. I may need still one more for the basement. Walking upstairs once again just to bring the glasses down had been irking me. Driving to the village to buy flour and marmalade, cereal and vodka, not having glasses with me to read the small print—on canned goods, so I know what percentage of my daily requirement for sodium I'm getting from one fifty-gram serving—irritates me. So, glasses in the glove compartment of the car. Then I need only to remember to take them into the market. I find I let these reading glasses slide along the bridge of my nose so that glancing down I can read and looking straight ahead I can see into the distance. A bifocal experience.

Seeing details on the bodies of birds is a pleasure. Before the two cataract procedures each bird was little more than a blob, then a patch of flight. Only the most brilliant and sharpest colours came through to my retinas. I could differentiate size easily enough, which only led to greater frustration. All this is the more important now, when many varieties of birds come feathering through. Earlier today a small flock, eight by count, of black-headed grosbeaks. I'd never seen any before. They are close cousins of the rose-breasted grosbeak, of which we had a good number at the cabin in the Laurentians, same strong, thick bill, same plump shape, but larger, seven-plus inches. A great difference in colouring: on the male the black head, sharp delineated black and white tail and wings, white belly and orangey-brown back, and a bright gold-brown breast; the female's head is brown with a white strip for a crown, and its breast and belly are deep yellow-tan. Peterson's *Field Guide to Western Birds* notes that the black-headed occasionally crossbreed with the rose-breasted where their territories overlap. I'm fairly sure they are travelling through, not nesting nearby. Their nests, I've read, are so thin it's possible to make out the eggs when one looks up from below, and the male spends about the same amount of time on the eggs as the female. Both are highly attractive, and I can see them so clearly.

Impressive, too, how tame our regular birds have become, the chickadees, and especially the pine siskins. This morning one was feeding at the platform feeder, but I could see it was struggling to find a sunflower seed that was more than a husk. So I brought out more seed, stored in an ex-yoghurt container. I walked slowly to the feeder, the container open. The bird looked up at me as I approached and went back to the task at hand. I touched the lip of the container to the edge of the platform, the bird glanced my way and backed off slightly. I poured a small pile of seeds onto the feeder and stepped away. The bird hopped over to the new seeds and crunched away happily.

The hummingbirds, too, have become downright sociable, unusual for them—aggressive hostility is more their style. Often when I'm sitting on the deck with a book one will perch on the backrest and look over my shoulder to watch me read; once I had two sharing the bench, rare for them because they can be as antagonistic to each other as to humans who don't keep their feeders filled with sugar water. They feel no compunction about making eye contact before roaring off. There are, so far, fewer of them this year; last summer we sometimes had as many as ten feeding at the same time, with others hovering behind their fellows awaiting their turn, sometimes buzzing the feeding birds to chase them away, taking their place. We had so large a number that often Kit had to refill the feeders every day—a quart of liquid in each. Ours are rufous hummers, so called because of the golden-reddish colour of their backs; the female's back glows green. The male's throat is a dazzling red, as brilliant as a ruby-throated hummingbird. The female's is a more ordinary white. With their swooping badinage, they provide constant entertainment. As I am writing this in the cottage, no feeder nearby, a rufous has appeared at the large side window, hovering and staring in. It is making its way laterally to the corner of the house, constantly watching me. Now it's around the corner, at the equally large front window, still checking me out, edging sideways, now at the sliding glass door, its beak near to touching the glass. And now it's gone, having swerved out across the bog. A full minute of being watched. Strange and lovely.

Later in the afternoon as I was filling the bird feeders I saw a complex hummer display. A female was buzzing her wings loudly on the left side of the rosemary bush, flying in place. She kept this up for perhaps five seconds, then darted to the right side of the bush and, facing where she had been previously flying, repeated the loud in-place buzz for about as long. Then back to the left of the rosemary, and again over to the right. She repeated this half a dozen times, like an actor in a one-woman show playing both sides of an antagonistic conversation. Then suddenly she flew closer to the bush, low to the ground. From out of the bush roared a male, blazing red, and shot away into the garden—with her immediately behind him. They disappeared into the trees. Ah, courtship.

May of 1962 contained no hummingbirds, but it was a month that set the basis for dramatic changes in my life. I was about to graduate from Dartmouth College in New Hampshire—too cold for hummingbirds—and had received large fellowships to work on my PHD from the German departments at Brown and at the University of Southern California. How large? Enough for me to consider buying a three- or four-year-old TR3. Thousands and thousands of dollars from monies that were then being doled out to American colleges by the National Defence Education Act. Especially money for language education—in 1957 the United States discovered its population could speak little other than English, and American scholars weren't keeping up with scientific advances in foreign countries, most notably in the Soviet Union. That slap of reality had come in the form of the Soviets putting a satellite into space before the United States could. *Sputnik* was circling the globe and, thanks to it, I and many other about-to-be graduates were finding large amounts of scholarship money thrust in our direction. I was ready to accept. Then one day in early May I returned to the house where I was living and found a thick envelope from the US government. It contained a letter telling me I had been awarded a Fulbright Scholarship for a year's study in Germany, specifically at the Goethe Universität in Frankfurt. My stipend would be a hundred and ten dollars a month, about a fifth of the value of an NDEA scholarship. I remember only a brief moment of regret—no TR3 in my immediate future.

I consulted with my professors, who strongly suggested that, though my German was quite good, I spend a couple of months before starting the university at a Goethe Institute for intensive German lessons. I would begin in July. I consulted with my parents, who felt both proud of me and sad that I would be going abroad for a year—they wouldn't see me for a long time and, in its own way worse, I was going to Germany, the country that had produced the monster and the party that had driven them from Europe. Mum talked then about one eye laughing and the other crying. But they would not stand in my way. We tried to organize a berth on a ship from New York for early June so I could tour around a bit before starting my summer course, but it seemed everyone was travelling to Europe that summer and all the ships were full. Alternatively I could sail from Montreal; I got a reservation for a bunk in a room I'd share with three others.

So Mum and Dad drove me to Montreal, my first time there even though I had lived only three hours away while at Dartmouth. Being American, I had no knowledge of or particular interest in Canada. We spent one night in Montreal, and the next day I boarded the ship. By mid-afternoon we were sailing down the St. Lawrence River. I met my bunkmates; today I have a bare memory of only one of them, and even he became unimportant. But it seemed he had a couple of female friends on board, he and they were bridge players and they needed a fourth, so he asked me. I joined them and now have memories of only one of the women, a beautiful, blue-eyed blonde from Vancouver named Alison. She would be living and working in Europe for a year, specifically in London and Paris. We became bridge partners. The day was warm and sunny, so we played out on the deck. At one point the other male in the group said he was too hot and took off his shirt. I made some teasing comment to the effect, How rude. He became flustered and put his shirt back on. Alison found the exchange humorous and, after the game—we won—she and I laughed about it.

We spent the afternoon together walking the length of the ship and talking. When the call came for dinner I decided I wanted to eat with her—except that we had all been assigned our tables. Her table was four women, mine four men. That seemed to me inappropriate, and I said so. In my best debating manner I convinced one of the women at her table to take my place at mine. She was delighted to do this, now a solitary woman among three men. I had three women that I would share meals with but was interested in one only, both of us more or less ignoring the other two. We spent the rest of the trip, another four days, together.

One afternoon we decided to see a movie, Hitchcock's *North by Northwest*. We arrived at the theatre a few minutes in advance but could tell we wouldn't get in, the lineup was too long. I had an idea. I led Alison around to the back door of the theatre and turned the door handle. The door opened. We walked into the dimly lit theatre. The front dozen rows were full—no way would we have gotten in by way of the lineup. But seats in the five back rows, for first-class passengers, were barely half occupied. We sat quietly and chatted. Time for the film to begin, but it didn't. At last a man in a coat and tie came onto the small front stage and asked for silence, which he got. It had been brought to his attention, he announced in a high, prissy voice, that a number of seats in the first-class section of the theatre were occupied by tourist passengers, and would they please get up and leave. Alison turned to me and would have stood, but I grabbed her wrist and whispered that we should stay. Half a dozen tourist passengers did get up and walk out. We sat still. Prissy-voice stared out at first class, waited a few more moments, and left. The house went dark and the film began.

At one point, a particularly scary moment, Alison grabbed my arm and let out a terrified little scream. I whispered to her, "That was a first-class scream," and we both began to giggle uncontrollably. People stared at us. We finally contained ourselves but couldn't look at each other for fear of laughter again taking us over. When at the end we left the hall we each knew we'd wandered into a new intimacy.

We agreed to meet before dawn of our last day on board, to watch our arrival in Southampton. We stood at the rail and talked little—she would be disembarking there, while I'd continue on to Le Havre and Paris beyond, staying there for about a week before heading on to the Goethe Institut near Munich. I planned to leave my baggage there, then tour Germany on my own for a couple of weeks, heading back to the Goethe Institut in time for courses to begin. Would we ever see each other again? To plan on it suggested a kind of commitment, and neither of us, having not talked about an after-the-crossing time, were prepared to take that on. She didn't know her precise goals, where she was going after London. She might be heading to Geneva to visit friends. At the last moment we agreed that if the Geneva trip did take place soon after her arrival she would have to pass through Paris, and we might meet up. But I had no base in Paris, no idea what hotel I'd be staying at. Well, if she went to Geneva she would send me a telegram at American Express. Would AmEx take telegrams? No idea. We never thought to exchange home addresses because neither of us would be back across the Atlantic for a year. We left it at that: American Express at the Place de l'Opéra in Paris.

I reached Paris, found a hotel, walked the streets, tested the museums. Went to American Express. No telegram. More streets, more museums. American Express. Three times a day I went to American Express. No telegram. I could not believe my stupidity, to leave our meeting again to such chance. A telegram at American Express? So thin a thread. For three days I planned my itinerary to check for held mail first thing in the morning, late morning, and late afternoon. Then, fourth day in the morning, a telegram. Alison would be arriving the next day on the boat train in the early afternoon. Deep relief. I remember my legs wobbled.

I got to the train station two hours early. The train did not arrive ahead of time. At last it pulled in, and there she was. We would spend the afternoon with my showing her what I liked best about Paris. Her train left at eight in the evening. She had checked her luggage through. We were together in Paris, and for each other. We walked miles and talked non-stop, we didn't want to see art because it would be distracting. We talked and walked and ate, and walked and talked some more. At a certain moment I glanced at my watch. Aarrgh! Eight-fifteen. I said, "Look! You've missed your train." She smiled and said, "I know." She contacted her hosts, told them she'd arrive on the morning train instead. But what would we do, where would we go? I knew I couldn't get her past the nosy concierge at my hotel. No one would rent us another hotel room, not when passports had different names on them—this was 1962—not even in Paris. So we would have to continue doing what we'd discovered we did best: we walked and talked through the night, and often held each other. Paris never closed down. Now I can only marvel at how much we found to say. Among the things she told me was that, though her name was Alison, since earliest childhood her family and closest friends called her Kit. Would I too call her Kit? No question. We realized we were giggling again, like at the Hitchcock film.

Around five-thirty we found ourselves at Les Halles, the huge outdoor market at the centre of the city, the vendors long in place, restaurateurs buying produce for their daily meals. We found a small café and ate a thick, hearty onion soup heavy with cheese and the whole of a fresh baguette. At seven we slowly worked our way to the station for her train to Geneva. And now we knew we had to see each other again, and soon. Would I come and visit her at the home of her friends in the little town where she'd be staying? I would indeed. First to Munich, deposit my trunk, and turn around and on to Switzerland! All plans altered, as necessary. And this was very necessary. Freedom.

I spent two weeks with Kit in Hérmance, the home of her friends, then headed back for my courses. She had told me that as she boarded ship in Montreal her cousin had called to her, "People you meet on boats can be very nice during the voyage, but you don't want to have anything to do with them afterwards!" Now we were writing each other every day, and three times we spoke on the phone. Twice in July and once in August I got on the autobahn and hitched to London, where Kit was now staying. One of those times I missed the ferry so sat in a bar in Ostend, drinking wine and bemoaning my fate—so little time, to waste a half-day till the morning ferry—to a congenial man who let me rant. At one point he said, "The Channel is very pleasant at night. We can take my boat and I'll get you across in a few hours." An offer I couldn't refuse. So in effect I hitched across from mainland Europe to England.

Kit and I also spent September and October together, the time between the end of my Goethe Institute courses and the beginning of the fall/winter term in Frankfurt, hitchhiking throughout England and Scotland. I took a brief trip to Londonderry/Derry, where I was born and had lived my first three years, but I remembered nothing of that time. I met some people who'd been friends of my parents, and they shared their memories. I tried to locate Mister Gilfillan, Dad's fishing teacher, and learned he had died some years before. Then four months at the university, where I took my courses and wrote my first play, *A Play and a Half*. It would be produced the following year. Kit was by then living in Paris with her aunt and uncle, and later as an au pair for a Canadian family. I would hitch from Frankfurt to Paris every other weekend. We knew by this time we were intensely committed to each other, and very much in love, and that she would join me wherever I'd be doing my PHD work. Also, in the two months between the end of the winter and the beginning of the summer semester in Frankfurt we would travel together, hitching to Athens, then taking a ferry to Israel.

We decided to get married. I know Mum and Dad were shocked and hurt, and Kit's parents were, well, surprised. Kit's mother, Margaret, decided to come to Paris for the wedding. It would be a simple affair, held at the town hall, the *mairie*, of the sixteenth arrondissement, since Kit's aunt and uncle, also named George and Alison (their chauffeur was Georges as well), lived there.

At that point I knew no Canadians other than Kit, and had no inkling of her extended family's role in Canadian life. I had visited Kit in France and met the aunt and uncle several times. I became very fond of them as people, as Kit's kin. The uncle was George Ignatieff, then Canadian ambassador to NATO, the aunt Alison Ignatieff, Kit's mother's sister, both of them sisters of George Grant, the philosopher. He had come to visit as well, so we were four Georges in the apartment. At our wedding ceremony, George Ignatieff served as my best man.

For an American to marry in Paris, he or she needed to find an American lawyer who would swear that the American bride or groom could legally marry in the state in which she or he lived, New Hampshire for me. Finding such a lawyer in Paris proved only a small problem; the amount of cash he asked for his services was a considerably larger one.

In addition, we had to post bans publicly, minimum of three weeks before the wedding, on the bulletin board of the *mairie*. Within three days of the posting we began to receive mail from merchants around the city, inviting us to drop by for a free gift so that they could show us their wares—from bedding and furniture to utensils and cars and wedding rings. We ignored most of these but would need rings. At the shop they took finger measurements and showed us a variety of rings, all costing far more than the money I had left over for the rest of my stay in Germany. We said we'd think about the rings, we had to visit the other shops that had contacted us. As we left they gave us two slim silver rings, *bandes d'alliance* they were called, to be used by those who are intending to marry, pre-engagement rings. They fit perfectly on our pre-measured fingers. And these we used at the *mairie* for the wedding ceremony. These are what we still wear, no other rings, nearly five decades later. Another slender, but this time powerful, thread.

We had no bog in mind, no southern Gulf island off the coast of Vancouver Island. We had nothing but the packs on our backs and enough money plus tickets to get back to Canada and the United States. I didn't know where or even if I'd be going to grad school in the fall, and neither of us had any sense of how we'd be earning a living back home—and where would home be anyway? It didn't bother us. We had an immense love for each other, nothing could faze us, and we've been exceptionally lucky. We've built off that foundation: owned houses, lived careers, produced two remarkable children. A home, increasingly so every day, overlooking Georgia Strait and dozens of little islands. A vegetable garden, a road across a bog.

2.

Last week the garden took a huge turn for the better. A couple of months ago we stumbled into the service of a local gardener, Kimm, in her other lives a plastic artist and line-dance teacher. She breaks the back of any problem that's been facing us. In earlier years—earlier months—we might see a problem somewhere in the garden but couldn't figure out how to solve it. It needed to be taken care of because, till it was out of the way, we couldn't get on to what lay beyond. Tasks seemed too complex so were postponed, and postponed.

Example: Taking out a dozen alders and arbutus that grew taller each month. They had to go because they were beginning to hover over the electric, phone, and cable lines; one messy storm could wipe out our power and more. How to remove them without their dropping onto the very lines we wanted to protect? It took Kimm, with Kit and me as assistants, half her four-hour weekly session to dispatch the trees.

Example: The daisies had gone rampant, covering small rose bushes, the pasque flowers, the lavender, even the thyme. What to do? They're daisies, a real sign of spring. So is the rest of it, says Kimm. Sure, we say, and in an hour the flower beds regain their diversity and a new brightness, not daisies alone at the expense of all others.

Example: My vegetable beds. I built them as mounds, horizontal against the slope of the land, a method of planting I'd discovered in Mexico, used as far back as Aztec times. Between the mounds are gutters for walking along to plant and weed, and for catching water as it runs downhill. The trouble was, the downhill side of the mounds was heaped four or five inches higher than the uphill side, providing a less than perfect surface for planting, and water tended to erode the downhill side of the heap, washing it into the gutter below. What to do? Create raised beds, suggested Kimm, supported with bricks or lumber on the downhill side. Yes, well, expensive, lots of work, and so on. We let it go for the moment. But before she returned the following week I'd been working in the high-ceilinged crawl space under the house and my eye, which hadn't been thinking let alone seeing right, found, yes, lumber.

Years ago, when the lot had been cleared, a large number of logs remained. Some of them became firewood. Some were solid fir, possibly useful for later building. We brought in Mike with his portable mill, and he milled up hundreds of feet of four-by-eights, three-by-eights, two-by-eights, three-by-sixes, whatever could be gotten out of any given log. We'd left these outside over two winters and two summers, to let them dry. Then it seemed like a good idea to store them away. If they weren't covered, we'd lose them. But tarps over them for another winter could bring in mould, no tarp and they'd warp and crack. So we wrestled them into the basement and laid them on racks, on top of each other. And forgot they were there—or if I noticed them, I'd wonder what I could possibly do with them. Not about to build an addition onto the house or even a large shed. Now, years later, I saw the planks again and my mind's eye suddenly transformed them into soil-support material. When Kimm arrived we unstacked and wrangled them out of the crawl space. She comes once a week, four hours, so the job took three weeks. I cut a couple of dozen stakes, to support the mound walls. Like a jigsaw puzzle she worked their various lengths along the downhill side of the vegetable beds, I smoothed the soil in place, and, lo! my mounds metamorphosed into raised beds. Now the garden not only produces better, it looks far neater.

I don't work any less hard in the garden with its new beds. But the board supports provide control, making life in the garden just that much easier both physically, because I can sit on the boards as I work, and psychologically, since the sense of work overload has departed.

All this is less bog tending, more tending the ecology near the bog. Part of the ongoing process.

Kimm has been a find. Over the years we've had an assortment of garden help, some good, some less so. Kimm does everything, including bucking up logs with the chainsaw. This year we had only one tree come down on the bog road, and she took on the job of reducing it to a manageable size. Two winters ago we also had help. Eight trees came down during three killer winter storms. We had them bucked up and hired two young men, one a handsome, smart, and strong fellow named Everest, the other a bear of a man, big around as fifty-year fir, muscled, sturdy, with tattoos over whatever part of his body I could see, including up his throat and nape to his bottom lip. In his ears he had rings, his lobes having been cut and widened and two plastic circles placed inside so that there are three-quarter-inch holes in his ears. His name, as given him by his parents: Tree. He worked hard. When I commented on how quickly he got the work done, he said he had to, a satisfied customer is a repeat customer, and he's got a new baby at home and the mortgage, that's what he's working for now. All very Gabriolan. Tree and Everest moved on. And now we have, and are very happy with, Kimm.

A week after Tree and Everest's work, our son, David, arrived. He was here for three weeks, getting himself organized for a new job. He had decided to return to Montreal, using the city as a base for the job, consultant to the University of Gastronomic Sciences in Pollenzo, Italy, just outside Bra, the hub of the Slow Food movement. The purpose of the job was to help them set up a strong North American base. He'd earned his master's degree from this Italian university. Immediately on graduation they turned around and hired him. As a consultant he would be able to do his work via the Internet wherever he lived, and could be available for additional special projects that would draw him back to Italy. His contract would be for six months, to be re-evaluated in the fall. He's a wanderer, Elisabeth is not. David: a dozen different careers in twenty years, in Toronto, New York, Los Angeles, Portland in Maine, living here, there, and many another place. Elisabeth: one job in twenty-five years, a union organizer, forever based in Cambridge, Massachusetts. They joke they must have had different parents.

While David was here we experimented with another new presence, a recent toy, an electric log-splitter. A total pleasure. Gone are the days of long, soaking baths and back exercises to return my weary body to a point where I can live inside it. Now a simple push of the button and a press on the lever, the log is pushed forward to the steel wedge and voilà! the log is split. David helped us fill two woodshed bays to overflowing. And we still have many a round of wood up on the ridge where we park the truck and the boat, drying out for future fires. Over the coming summer we'll refill the last of the bays.

Several years ago, another May, Kit and I spent a few days with our Portland friends, June and Jerry, at a rustic resort ranch on the eastern slope of the Cascade range, the Flying M—flying because some of their patrons flew in, landing on their small airstrip. The four of us rented a cabin in the woods, away from the resort, which was given over mostly to trail rides and overnight camping trips on horseback. Abutting the ranch was a tract of woodland destined to be cut down in 2028. It was posted PRIVATE PROPERTY. No one from the ranch went back out there. But it didn't say NO TRESPASSING. A stream flowed through the ranch, rising high up the woodland's slope, ten or twelve miles away. So with rod in hand I followed the stream into the wilderness. It was clear no one had been along this route since spring runoff, the water as close to pure as any I've ever fished, a classically beautiful trout stream. It made me think of Norman Maclean's novel *A River Runs Through It*, which was transformed into a film true to the original.

Since I'd started making my own wine soon after coming to Gabriola, I wanted to try some of Oregon's highly sophisticated wines. So we took a half-day off to tour the growing region. We made some fine discoveries. But none proved as entertaining as our mini-sophisticated wine experience at the lodge. We ate dinner there twice. The first night our waiter— "Hi, I'm Matt"—didn't seem to understand his role, possibly one of the ranch's stable hands doubling in the dining room in the evening, his body language desperately uncomfortable as he waitered. I asked to see what wines they had. "No wine list is available," said Matt.

"But you do have wine," I said.

"Oh yes."

"What kind?"

"Red and white."

A pause while we tried to figure out if this was intended as an amusing line. But, no, he was serious.

I said, "I saw a wine list earlier in the day."

Matt said, "The list is obsolete."

I tried a different approach: perhaps I could see a list with the various kinds of wine they did have. Matt repeated that there were red and white wines. But wasn't there a list?

He went back to what must have been his new phrase of the day: "It's obsolete."

To our decreasingly unrepressed amusement he repeated the phrase two more times. At last I persuaded him to go to the kitchen and ask for the names of the red and white wines that were in fact available. He returned and recited the names of two reds and three whites. No list available for us to look at. The last of the wines was "peenot greese." That took me a couple of seconds to decode. So I ordered the "peenot gree-(pause)-se." I found it hard to speak aloud both the t and the s. Matt went off, came back with a bottle. It was in fact a very pleasant Pinot Gris. Each sip brought forth a new pun about peanuts and grease, enough bad jokes to keep us amused all evening, yet feeling a little bad for poor Matt. We all looked forward to a second dinner with Matt as server, but alas, next time we ate there, he wasn't on duty.

It's now approaching the middle of the month. Yesterday, as I was racking a batch of wine from the clarifying carboy, my eye caught, on the deck, a bit of movement. There, handsomely striding from west to east, an elegant raccoon was making his way to the tray bird feeder. I say elegant because he had a fine pointed nose, more like a fox than his usually round-snouted brethren. I stared at him; he caught my eye and stared back. Casually he turned and began to climb up the railing to the feeder. I rushed to the door and slid it open. He stopped in mid-climb, looked at me with a glance that could have been saying, Well, I tried. Then he dropped to the deck. I shouted at him, "Get out of here!" He leapt lightly into the herb garden, jumped to the ground, and headed down the slope to the little path around the pond. I followed. He sat by the pond, again catching my stare. He didn't move as I approached. Only when I was fifteen or so feet from him did he again turn away and amble to the wire fence. I'd never noticed before that the bottom of the fence had at this point lifted from the dirt. He'd found the spot, or created it, slipped beneath, and away. He or his friends must often come at night to steal seed from the tray feeder—we know if they've been around when the feeder has been knocked to the ground. One more of the local animals. Attractive in his place—not on the bird feeder—but with a vacuum cleaner appetite.

When we were first coming to Gabriola we introduced another animal to the island—our cat, Daisy. Daisy was short for Lesser Daisy Fleabane, a wildflower prevalent in the Laurentians, where we'd taken her the day we'd acquired her. Daisy, yes; fleabane no: she was covered with fleas. We drowned them. For a couple of hours she was an unhappy, sodden cat. Over time we grew very fond of her. She'd always be there to greet either Kit or me when we returned to our otherwise empty house. Once, one winter, she'd somehow gotten out of our downtown Montreal row house and disappeared. For eight days we believed her to be dead. Then one afternoon a neighbour knocked on the door and reported seeing her huddled under some steps a dozen houses away. We never did learn where she'd been.

When we started spending half the year on Gabriola we'd drive across the country and, once we'd arrived, a Montreal friend would crate her in her box and she'd fly across the country. Then as we were leaving we'd ship her back and she'd be picked up in Montreal. After a while we found a cat-sitter for her here on the island. She was getting old but still enjoyed crouching in the herb garden, her eyes following juncos and towhees bopping around for seeds, she possibly thinking dim but stealthy feline thoughts brought up from the depths of some atavistic prey-stalking memory. The embodied Daisy was never a threat to birds.

A warm May day, 1998. The vegetable garden was in. Time to go fishing. Time to get out on the ocean. Time to look for a boat. Off to Nanaimo.

At the first three places we checked it was made clear that we were into the twelve- to fifteen-thousand-dollar range at the very least. The danger of going with anything cheaper was stressed by all: we wouldn't want a boat filled with dry rot, we wouldn't want a motor that wasn't totally trustworthy. In fact no motor could be fully trusted, so after buying an eighty-horsepower engine we'd need to get a little six or nine-point-nine back-up system. Even a small, solid aluminum boat would go for twenty-five hundred dollars, plus a motor for three thousand. We headed back to the ferry. But had forgotten it was Friday late afternoon, always a ferry overload time. We didn't get on. We watched it sail away, so pulled out of line—we'd go check out just one more boat-sales place. Nothing to suit our needs. And on return half an hour later found the waiting line already so long there'd be no chance of getting on that ferry either. So we had another hour's wait, returned to the island weary, and collapsed. Nothing moving forward on a boat and the chance to go fishing.

3.

Back in a May even longer ago, 1967, I invested my time heavily in the politics of the day. I had finished and defended my PHD thesis at the end of March. In June and July I'd be heading up the freshman composition program in the summer school at Harvard, teaching one course. In September my job at the University of California, San Diego (UCSD), awaited me—that is if the governor of California, Ronald Reagan, elected the previous November, hadn't closed the system down by then. For more than a month I had no university responsibilities, first time in nine years. We were footloose and happily pregnant, our second child due over the summer. With new responsibilities soon arriving, time for a brief holiday. My mother, always eager to spend time with her beloved granddaughter, her golden child, agreed to look after Elisabeth. We borrowed Mum's car and drove down to Washington, DC, where Kit had never been. It seemed important to visit the belly of the power that was fighting a demented war in Vietnam. We toured the city, visiting the memorials, many of them impressive, rich with important ideals. Where had those values gone? we wondered.

Back in Cambridge I realized I needed to participate in some way in the opposition to the war. An anti-war play I'd written, *Time and Again*, had been produced the previous fall, again at the Loeb Experimental Theater, then in April as a reading by the Theater Company of Boston, so I'd made my statement; but it felt like much too little. Anti-war coalitions across the country had decided there must be a large consciousness-raising push: June, July, and August 1967 would be Vietnam Summer, a concerted effort to bring pressure on the government to get out of Southeast Asia. I learned that the Cambridge headquarters for Vietnam Summer were in the basement of Memorial Hall, an immense, squat, cathedral-like structure on the Harvard campus. It had many uses, the one I'd mainly encountered being the hall in which one took exams, a thousand desks in many rows each the site of someone's impending success or failure. The basement, on the other hand, was a rabbit warren of criss-crossing aisles and offices. The splendid-sounding Vietnam Summer HQ turned out to be one of the larger rooms, central so without windows, sparsely filled with boxes of leaflets, folding chairs, three card tables, anti-war posters on the walls. And one man hunched over a typewriter, possibly a priest: black shirt, blue jeans, dog collar lying open on the table. He was deep in concentration and only turned when I coughed and said, "Excuse me?"

He pulled himself slowly from the typewriter and swung around on his chair. He looked at me hard for a moment before saying, "Yes?"

"This the headquarters for Vietnam Summer, is it?"

He nodded. "What can I do for you?"

"Well," I said, "I have some time this summer and I'd like to help out."

Another nod. "Where do you live?"

I told him I had an apartment in Somerville. Somerville is a mostly working-class town adjacent to Cambridge, a community unto itself though part of greater Boston.

"Good," he said. "Very good." He got up and walked toward me. He extended his hand, and I brought mine up to shake his. He said, with great solemnity, "Congratulations. You are now the Chairman of Vietnam Summer in Somerville."

"No, no," I said. "I just want to help out."

"We have no one in Somerville yet. You'll be organizing locally."

"But—but—but—" I heard my stammering and hated myself for it. "I don't know anything about organizing."

He nodded. He was generous with his nods. "None of us do," he said. "We're all on a steep learning curve."

"What—what do I do?"

"Find others in Somerville who are opposed to the war, get together with them, figure your strategies and tactics."

Great. Finding people in Somerville who were against the war was like finding a Kennedy who'd become a Republican. Somerville, a working-class, heavily Catholic town, was a supplier of sons and some daughters to the Vietnam gristmill, soldiers and sailors who had joined the services because they provided the best jobs around. Their parents were proud of their brave offspring and loyal to their government, a government headed by President Johnson, who had been the selected vice-president of their native son John Kennedy. Organize these people into war resisters? I said to the priest, "You have to be kidding. Do you know what kind of people live in Somerville?"

This time he didn't nod. He looked me kindly in the eye. "The sort of people we have to convince," he said. He gave me a thin "organizing kit," as he called it—two sheets of suggestions for getting started—and returned to his typewriter. As he sat down he said, "Good luck."

This was ridiculous. I felt a number of reactions come bur-bling to my brain. I hadn't signed a contract, I could just walk away from this, he didn't even know my name. Or, somehow, did he? Okay, I'd talk to the two other Harvard people I knew in Somerville; I'd never spoken to them about the war, how should I know where they stood on it? What had I thought, Vietnam Summer was going to send me to organize among the converted? I went back to our apartment, exhausted, my good intentions void of content.

Well, I'd said A, so maybe I should figure out what B might be. I reported to Kit and she found it all humorous. She said we should call a meeting, a small meeting. So over a three-week period we did indeed bring together six people who wanted to participate. Our next job, figure out what to do. None of us had ever organized something out of nothing before. We brainstormed. Rent a space, call a meeting, see who showed up? We had no budget. We could invite people to our apartments, but who? Some of us didn't like the idea of posting flyers with our home addresses on them, letting the public know just where the radicals lived. Then someone sug-gested we should work through present ongoing organizations. What, businesses with bottom lines that they didn't want to jeopardize? Non-governmental organizations? No, they all had agendas of their own and were always overworked. Someone suggested the churches of Somerville. Church leaders who might be approachable, possibly holding values that didn't include the killing of Southeast Asians, forums at which we might be heard. We got out a phone book and began making lists, making calls.

We had to decide, too, what precisely it was we wanted to do. Simply to convince people they should be against the war would leave them as powerless as we already felt ourselves to be. Then an idea began to germinate: we would bring together a groundswell of Somerville citizens who would try to convince our member of the House of Representatives that he should oppose the war. If we could add one voter in the House who wanted the war to end, we would have done our local job. If other Vietnam Summer teams did the same . . . We had a goal.

Over the summer we talked at dozens of churches, Catholic and various Protestant denominations. Often we had an audience of three, or five. We went back when people told us they knew of a few others who might be interested in hearing what we had to tell them. So the summer passed. I had to leave the group behind, which I did with regret—I'd learned to enjoy the project, maybe doing some good, as well as working with the some excellent people. They promised to keep in touch, let me know what was happening back in Somerville.

In mid-August David was born, an easy birth, two hours of labour, a happy child. At the end of the month we flew to San Diego. Our first view of the city was from high above as we realized we were circling, sometimes over the inland desert, sometimes over the sea. Twenty minutes after we'd been told to prepare for our descent the captain's voice came on: "Folks, sorry about this circling, we've been told by the tower down there that they can't see our landing gear. But sit tight, they've got fire trucks at the ready and they're going to spray the landing strips with foam."

Wonderful. Kit and I stared at each other, made sure Elisabeth between us was buckled in, I reached over and grasped Kit's armrest as a secondary support for Elisabeth, and Kit clutched David tight. This was not a good way for him to begin life.

We descended, and descended. Our wheels were in fact in place, and we landed. Without foam, without fanfare. Except from the passengers who gave the captain a relieved round of applause. Welcome to San Diego.

From a member of the department on leave we had sublet a little house in La Jolla, close to the UCSD campus, and began life anew. I had done my PHD in comparative literature, my fields of study being French and English literature from 1750 to present, and all of German literature from the Middle Ages on. So naturally the first course I'd been given to teach was a humanities course, the Renaissance, emphasis on Italy. Which was fine, providing me with one of my early pedagogical principles: If you want to learn certain subject matter, teach it.

I made it through my first quarter, which ended at Christmas, then my second, ending in mid-March, with both success and relief. One day late in the third quarter the phone rang. It was one of the people in the Vietnam Summer group. He was all but shouting over the phone: "We did it! We did it! We turned him!"

They had indeed. That morning the representative for Somerville and several neighbouring towns had come out against US involvement in the war in Vietnam. His name was Thomas P. "Tip" O'Neill, one of the highest-ranking Democratic House members. In a very few years he would become Speaker of the House. The event made me, for a period of time, a believer in the ability of the active citizen to bring about real political change.

Vietnam Summer was a long time before the warm May day on Gabriola when we heard that Vic, whom we were getting to know and like, had a boat for sale, a twelve-foot, wide-beam, aluminum runabout. It came with an eight-horsepower, four-cycle Honda engine. Sounded very good. We'd take a look.

Vic had bought the boat eight years before and no longer used it, so it was in very good condition—nothing less to be expected from Vic. If there were ever a person who would have done the homework before buying, this man was it. He'd paid thirty-two hundred for the boat and motor six years earlier and would sell it for half the price. We were tempted. I was the hesitant one—though sixteen hundred was a great price, it still seemed a lot of money. Kit was insistent; she knew how much I wanted to fish, and she planned to be very happy out on the water. So we finally said yes. Excellent condition, great price. And safe. Of course we would buy the very best in life jackets. And no, we would not go far from shore, we'd just tootle around the islands. We were both pleased and excited. We would put it in the water in two days, with Vic's help.

Vic taught us how to work the motor: set it in neutral, open the vent in the gas can—important, he'd once forgotten and stalled out—open the choke, prime it with the hand pump on the gas feed, pull the cord, close the choke when it starts, push off, and put it in gear. Then he drove the boat in the bed of his truck to Silva Bay Marina and a ramp we could roll the boat down on. We followed with the car, the motor in the trunk. He brought his truck to the water's edge, we pulled the boat from the truck bed and slid it into the water. It floated nicely. Kit rowed it over to Page's dock while Vic and I drove our vehicles around. He showed us how to put the motor on—obvious enough, but we had to remember to slide a thin piece of ply-wood between the clamps and the metal stern for a better grasp and to avoid wearing away the stern plate. But then, the stern heavy with the motor on, the boat began to leak. There's a bung plug made of rubber inserted just above the waterline in the stern that had dried and cracked while the boat was in storage for the nearly four years since Vic had last used it. Now water was trickling in. He tried to tighten it, but the whole gizmo broke. Quickly we pulled the motor off and lifted the boat out onto the dock. Vic tried to repair the plug but didn't have the needed tools along, so he took off for home and brought back a new plug. He screwed the plug in, we lowered the boat into water again. Ready to go fishing. Well, soon.

A few days later Kit and I were at last on the water in our trustworthy boat. We trolled along happily on the relatively calm sea, the little waves lapping the side of the boat, close to some cliffs near the shore, catching nothing. Then the motor died. Try as we might, we couldn't get it going. I pulled at the starting cord, over and over, while Kit rowed like crazy against increasing wind and current, heavy going with one human-power, barely moving the boat away from rocks. I removed the casing and poked at the engine. She worked us through kelp beds and past a huge floating log. Ten minutes of rowing had moved us about seventy-five feet toward a somewhat sheltered shallow bay. And still I was diddling with the engine, fifteen, twenty, thirty, sixty pulls of the starting cord, fiddling with the choke, halfway, full choke, close choke, and flooding it, and waiting for it to unflood. Night wasn't exactly coming on, but early evening had arrived. Then a wind came up and the cute little waves that had been breaking lightly took to crashing, just a bit, yet more than before. Seventy pulls, seventy-one— And it started! Slowly, carefully, we pulled through the bay, through the kelp, past the log, out into open water, then full throttle holding our breaths much of the time, back the whole fifteen minutes to the harbour and our mooring. We were clearly a bit shaken, mostly because our wonderful motor had not in fact proven trustworthy.

At last, tied to the dock, I again opened the motor up, played around with it, having only a minimal idea of what I was doing. Nothing seemed obviously broken. I closed it up, tried it again, it started nicely. But did we dare take it out into open water again? Very bothersome. So we packed up the tackle and the life vests and ourselves, tightened the gas tank's air valve— But it was already tight! Which meant the engine was trying to suck gas out of a mostly airless gas container. It would run on open throttle, sucking hard for air, but stalled out when trolling, when the gasoline flow was just a trickle. We felt foolish—stupid, actually—because Vic had told us he, too, had committed precisely the same non-act, forgetting to open the air valve. We returned home, tired but relieved, two fisherfolk who had caught nothing, feeling very lucky, having learned an unforgettable lesson.

JUNE

I.

Last year at the beginning of June, two major adventures. Kit's brother Ed and his wife, Donna, came to visit. We'd do some fishing together.

The first adventure took place on a boat just off Gabriola. We'd gone out for salmon with Bob, skipper of the *Silva Blue*. He'd shown us how a serious guide attracts salmon: bribe them. He came equipped with a pocket full of copper pennies. When the fishing was slow he threw a pair of pennies into the ocean, one to starboard, another to port, equal donations for each of the rods we were running. It would turn into a successful strategy, all the more so as we heard reports on the ship's radio that none of the other boats out that day were catching. We were fishing the same area of water as Kit and I cover when we go out in our little boat, but Bob's is equipped with downriggers that take the lure deeper than I can get when trolling—a hundred to a hundred-and-twenty feet and more rather than my thirty to forty. And deep down is where one finds the fish.

We'd been on the water for maybe half an hour when I hooked a salmon. Keep the tension on the line, I told myself over and over; the hook has no barbs, allow any slack and the fish can throw the lure with ease. From the fight it gave I could tell it was a fair size. It ran hard. I played it back in, it ran again, and suddenly it took off as if it had multiplied ten times in strength. Bob knew instantly what had happened, an unfortunate development. I now had both a salmon and a seal at the end of my line, the seal stealing my salmon! Bob roared the boat after the speeding seal, which was stripping line from my reel so rapidly I was in danger of losing it all. And then the line went slack, seal and salmon both gone, the seal's onward thrust tearing the hook from the salmon's mouth.

We fished some more, and I brought in a seven-pounder, Ed an eight-pounder. Then Ed lost another salmon to a seal, then Kit got a nine-pounder. After about three hours on the water I hooked another fish that from the start made me feel I had a seal on again, a smaller seal but still a thief. The fish took off, I worked it in a little, it fought again and ran, I teased back inches of line, sometimes a few feet, it ran again. After about twenty-five minutes I'd at last brought it to the boat. Bob grabbed the net, swooped it through the water and had it in place. But when he tried to lug it up Ed had to grab the net's rim to hoist the fish over the gunwale. It lay on the deck, the largest salmon I've ever caught. Thirty-eight pounds. Thirty-seven inches long. Twenty-two inches in girth. A remarkable fish.

Afterwards I learned it was the biggest fish taken so far that season off Gabriola. I wanted to keep it whole, frozen, until an occasion for a large-scale celebration came along. But we had no way of cooking such a thing—its length was near to double the width of our oven. After many photographs I agreed to have it filleted. We gave away one of the smaller salmon, had another smoked, and cooked the third that evening. Four of us were able to manage barely a quarter of the fish. A wonderful failure.

The second adventure proved less than wonderful. A couple of days after the salmon fishing we drove to Corbett Lake, about three hours east of Vancouver. We had rooms in the lodge, and would be taking breakfast and supper there as well. We arrived around five and went out fishing immediately, Ed and Donna in one boat, Kit and I in another. We caught nothing, came back in for supper at six-thirty, and headed out again around eight, all of us in heavy, flat-bottomed wooden rowboats, no motors allowed. Kit and I fished sometimes in sight of Ed and Donna's boat, sometimes not. Around ten-fifteen—it was a couple of days before solstice, long evenings—Kit and I decided we'd had enough, and dark was coming on. We didn't see Ed and Donna anywhere so figured they'd already gone back. We headed for the dock, maybe half a mile away. We'd gone a short distance when we thought we heard, faintly, someone calling, "George!" It sounded like Ed. We listened hard. The call came again.

I said to Kit, "I'm sure that's Ed wanting to taunt me with the large fish he's just caught." But I wasn't about to row to the far end of the lake to let him brag. We continued on toward the dock. Then the next call wasn't "George!" It sounded more like "Help!" So we turned around and charged heavily toward the far end, frustrating, slow work as our tub of a rowboat was built for slow trolling, not for gliding through water. The post-sunset light was fading. We finally saw the shape of their boat. And no one in it. Then there was Ed in the water some thirty feet from a heavily water-bushed shore, dog-paddling, hanging on to an oar. At last we spotted Donna, fingers barely grasping the gunwale of the rowboat. The back of her head was under water, her face visible only from chin to brow. Did I mention she doesn't swim? Did I mention she wasn't wearing a life vest? I could see a vest on the seat of their boat, another float-ing a dozen feet away. We jammed our boat over to Ed first, he fiercely calling, "Get Donna first!" But we were already by him and he caught on to the stern. We sogged over to Donna, Ed's fully clothed weight in the water a hefty extra burden. I took off my shoes and stepped across to the boat Donna barely held on to. It was half full of water. I grabbed her arms while Kit continued to work her boat closer to Donna, and the shore—not really a shore, the water-rooted bushes so thick it was impossible to manoeuvre the boat through them. And the lake bottom was a foot of mud. Finally we reached a place where Ed could stand, his shoed feet sinking slowly into the mire below. Together, Kit from her boat, I from theirs, Ed in the water, heaved Donna, one leg, then the other, rolled her body over the stern, till at last she was in our dry boat.

The next trick, get Ed at two hundred and ten pounds plus his water-laden clothes into the boat. A wonder that his fishing hat remained perched on his head. His fly line had wrapped itself around his body, had caught on the oar, and was snagged in a bush.

I said, "I'm going to cut the line."

He growled at me, "Don't cut the effing line!" (This is when I knew he had every plan to survive—he was damn well going fishing with that line in the morning.) But his shouts did contain more than a little panic, a new stance from him; while the job was getting Donna into the boat he had maintained a controlled calm. With her safe if shivering, the water about fifteen Celsius, his composure fell away. But I managed to work Ed free of line and shrubbery.

Kit and I, with a physical strength neither of us could reproduce in a calmer time, tugged and dragged and somehow elevated him into Kit's boat. Mine, the one they had swamped, was no haven for him, the water five inches deep.

So Kit rowed with newfound power back to the dock, a fifteen-minute journey (felt like forty-five) in the by-now-deep dark, Ed and Donna shivering all the way, Ed urging Kit to row, harder, till Donna in a small but clearly enunciated voice whispered, "Ed, she's going as fast as she can." They finally made their way to the dock and up the longish slope to their room. They both stood in a steaming shower till they ran out of hot water. Then Ed rushed into our room rumble-whispering, "I've got to get into your shower." Kit checked on Donna, who was in the bed under all the blankets in the room. I got a bit of whisky into them. We brought them half our blankets.

When we could finally ask what happened, we learned Donna had hooked a good trout and fought it. When Ed tried to net it, the fish dove under the boat and came up the other side. They both switched to the fish side and the boat spilled them out. They'd been in the water for more than half an hour. Ed did say he believed that if we'd not come they wouldn't have made it—he could possibly have saved himself, but not Donna, and he wasn't about to leave her. In fact he had saved her by pushing her toward the boat when they first got dumped. I, too, had a whisky. A double. Even now I still sometimes see Donna's face, white and bloodless from chin to brow, just above the waterline.

For the next two and a half days we fished happily. They both wore life vests at all times. My biggest, and only, rainbow was two and a half pounds. But Ed did catch the largest rainbow of his life, more than ten pounds. He felt the trip had been worth it. And I'd rescued his fly line.

Leaving the house and bog behind, and the garden, is always hard. Especially in June. Especially this June when my vegetables and herbs were not behaving, not germinating, or germinating ultra-slowly, growing slowly. Every gardener on the island agrees: slowest spring they could remember. But we had committed ourselves to the Yukon and Alaska, Helena our guide, and we were going.

2.

The Alaska holiday proved to be grand—I caught my first graylings—but far from the bog. In the morning after our return we found ourselves surrounded by a partial reversal of the garden we'd left behind: much thick new growth, not all of it for the good, as well as some plants as scrawny as when we'd left. The lettuces and arugula, lush, vigorous plants at the beginning of the month, had bolted, now two and three feet high, pieces of an ill-weeded garden going to seed. Parsley, broad beans, and potatoes were crowding out each other, as well as their fellow plants. I'd planted more than a hundred and fifty big, healthy green beans from my last year's seed crop and protected them under white poly-cotton ground cover. Now three had sprouted from the earth, and these were chewed by bugs; first year ever that I won't have any. My basil, which had been tiny at the beginning of June, three weeks later remained tiny, half an inch at best. Gabriola had had its wettest June in decades.

On the other hand, the bog had attained a kind of glory. The hardhack glowed with acres' worth of light green blush. The volunteer willows on the banks on both sides of the road had grown a foot and filled in densely. In the fall I'm going to have to cut them back, to allow space for cars to pass without being brushed. Ditto the crabapple, which threatens to take off side mirrors and door handles. Tall daisies grow along the length of the road, as well as hundreds of tiny alders. In an earlier year our gardener–helper Everest took out more than two hundred of them. To be repeated. Most impressively, a section of the road is chock-full of horsetail, a long, skinny hollow stem of a plant that, after protruding phallically from the ground for a month or so, grows thin, green, hairy branches that reach upward, much like the stem. It's jointed every half-inch or so, and pulls apart easily at these points. Less attractive are some of the grasses that feature the froth of spit bugs, produced when the nymph stage of a bug called the froghopper sucks sap from whatever plant and spews it out to create a hiding place for itself and for protection against heat, cold, and drying out. All intriguing but, as grandson Jake said, kinda yucky.

Running the middle of the bog road is a ribbon of green—grasses, weeds, and flowers that have been pretty much undisturbed by the undersides of cars for a couple of weeks. In past years I've given the ribbon one or two summer haircuts to control its raggedness. On the other hand, not mowing has its own advantage, as it gives the undercarriages of passing cars a regular scrubbing. This is fine for us but often bothers visiting drivers. So I brought out the grass cutter—no mere lawnmower this, rather the world's mightiest weed eater on wheels, which we had to buy because the grass and dandelions that came up at the back of the house grew on terrain so rocky and uneven it could destroy the blades of regular mowers—and lopped the tops and middles off hundreds of the intruders. We had returned to a bog and garden more robust than tender.

Robust, too, are the foxgloves, on the bog's peninsula down from the cottage deck. Four feet high, the white cones are up to an inch and a half long, the inside of the cone riddled with multi-sized purple patterning, from tiny to a quarter-inch in diameter. As I passed by earlier this morning, three bumble-bees had crawled into a larger bloom, scraping about, covering themselves with pollen. I watched till they flew away, heading for further flowers. By the cottage the foxgloves are purple on the outside, the inside a lighter purple fading to a tinted white that in turn is a backdrop for mottled patterning in the same purple. More bee activity, more honey manufacturing.

Also healthier than before departure are our humming-birds. They'd been lying low in May, presumably on their nests. When, coming back, we'd put the feeders up again, the babies had hatched and fledged, and were hungry. Though the feeders had been down for two weeks, the hummers, likely including many of the new generation, reclaimed their sugar-water source immediately. Already they're doing battle with each other, one at the feeder, another suddenly buzzing the one drinking, scaring him away, taking off after him, and as these two fight, a third, fourth, and fifth take over the feeding. We, sitting six feet away, hope they don't mistake the direction of their fighter-pilot bursts and dives and plow into one of us. Those mighty beaks could do a bit of damage at what seems like spurts of sixty miles an hour.

Last year was our best for hummingbirds. We'd had some people at the house for a dinner party when the season was at its peak—often more than a half-dozen birds at each of the two feeders. One of our guests spends a day every couple of weeks as a member of a team that bands hummingbirds. She asked if her group could come by and band some of ours. We set a date. They arrived around nine-thirty in the morning, five of them, and set up on the deck to work, taking down one of the feeders so all the birds would gather around the other and setting up a drop net above it. Usually the team arrives at their banding place before dawn; the birds feed most heavily in the early morning after waking. Also in the evening, before sleeping, since they need heavy-duty energy to make it through the night. During the day their hearts beat about twelve hundred times a minute; at night the rate plummets down to sixty.

Each member of the team had a prescribed job: the man who released the net so it fell down, trapping the bird; the woman who reached into the net to grasp the bird; the woman who placed the bird in a kind of heavyweight paper-towel straitjacket to keep its wings from flapping about; the man who took the measurements; and the woman who recorded the evidence. The net is about two feet in diameter, stretched on circular frames top and bottom. The bottom of the net can be drawn up, bunching it like a curtain. When a bird comes to the feeder beneath the open net, the man holding the rope to release the draped net lets go and the bird is caught inside. (About half the birds escape in that tenth of a second it takes the net to fall.) Then comes the straitjacket, and the measuring and weighing begins. The birds are also checked for parasites, and are relieved of one tail feather, which is sent to a researcher in Oregon who can tell from the DNA of the feather where the bird last molted, providing a record of its migration pattern. Then comes the band, a tiny thing coded with numbers and letters, which are recorded. At last it gets fed a large drink of sugar water and is released.

Kit asked, "Do the birds ever get stressed out?"

"Sometimes," was the response. "There are several signs of stress, the most obvious being its tongue hanging out of its beak."

A hummingbird's tongue is as long as its beak and extremely thin. It literally droops out forward. During the banding we had three birds that did get stressed. They were immediately released. Most intriguing piece of information about the hummers: a bird drinks about half an ounce of nectar or sugar water every twenty-four hours. Each of our feeders holds a quart of liquid, which is thirty-two ounces. At the height of the feeding season both feeders could be emptied in a day. If those figures are correct they mean that some days we had at least one hundred and twenty-eight different birds feeding here. Or more, since some of them would get part of their sugar from real flower nectar.

We've had to reconcile ourselves to the fact that this will be the first year that we haven't put the boat into the water. It usually spends the summer at Page's Marina from end of June till early October. But the next few months will be filled with a number of responsibilities and complications, so we've decided, reluctantly, not to use it this year. I'm much divided about the decision, but last year we went out in it only four times over the three summer months. We were either busy, or, when it might have been possible, the sea was too rough.

We don't go out when there are whitecaps or swells greater than two and a half feet, as the rear gunwales of our little boat rise little more than a foot above water and the stern about six inches. It's a shame, especially since we both have our fishing licences, good till the end of next March.

So we won't be taking any ling cod this season. We discovered ling the first summer we had the boat. I was learning to mooch, a form of fishing using live or frozen herring or herring strips, sent to the bottom with enough weight to keep it in place, reducing the drift in the current. For my birthday, from Kit, I'd gotten my beautifully balanced saltwater spinning rod and reel. It was the first time out in several days—it'd been too windy for us to try, not heavy winds but strong enough to produce whitecaps scary for us—and I mooched, maybe seventy feet down, looking for salmon. Yes, the motor was working well; we'd been letting it have its necessary supply of oxygen. Suddenly a mighty tug, the whole of the bottom of the ocean pulling my line down. It took over ten minutes to bring the bottom up, working it, it running away, stripping line, till it finally came to the surface. I saw it, it saw me and dived hard. A large ling cod. Which isn't a cod, just as most fish called bass or perch aren't bass or perch. Ling is the fish preferred to salmon by many here for the taste; I enjoy having to decide which I like better, and will keep from a decision as long as I can keep tasting. At fish markets ling cod is often more expensive than salmon. The regulations say that to keep a ling it has to be sixty-five centimetres (nearly twenty-six inches). These days one is allowed only a single fish per day; Chinook salmon have to be the same length but one can keep four. So, a much-appreciated fish, which made me feel pleased. And worried I might lose my ling as it took off again for the bottom. I did finally land it. It measured seventy-two centimetres (just over twenty-eight inches) and weighed seven and a half pounds. Its immense mouth, when wide open, made a circle six inches in diameter. The inside of its cheeks and its tongue were a brilliant aquamarine.

In landing the ling we'd drifted maybe half a mile away from where I'd caught it. We headed back to where I thought that place was, I let out line, found we were in about thirty feet of water, too shallow. I reeled in and as the herring rose to maybe five feet under water, had a massive strike. The fish, which must have been following the herring, suddenly dove hard, ran wide, and played games with me for again ten minutes or so. I worked it back to the boat, it ran off again. Finally we netted it, another ling, this time sixty-nine centimetres, just a little fellow, and five and a half pounds. I had caught my limit, so released it, fished some more, another huge strike, a different sort of battle, the fish heading off in jerks and yanks rather than a mighty-muscled run (maybe a salmon, finally? or a large dogfish), and then I lost it. We headed in around eight, and I spent the rest of the evening cleaning ling cod. The fish gave us five fat steaks and two ten-inch filets. By nine-forty-five I was ready to have a drink and eat supper. I fillet slowly. One of many grand evenings of fishing. Which this year we won't be repeating.

We do have another use for our licences, though. They are obligatory for taking oysters and clams, both of which are profusely available at selected points around the island, the best site being about two miles from the house. At low tide the oysters lie sometimes as much as three deep, waiting to be picked up. These are wild oysters, not farmed. They grow larger than north Atlantic oysters, and are less delicate—the size of the oysters used in the southern United States for making po' boy sandwiches. In fact they are so big I find it impossible to shuck them, so have to steam them open. Usually they are not eaten raw. After steaming, the shells have parted sufficiently so that with the oyster knife I can pry them open the rest of the way.

They are then almost cooked. We reheat them in a variety of sauces, spicy or savoury, or they can be breaded and fried.

We take our clams from this same beach; they need to be dug. One can tell where they're hidden in two ways: by watching for an arc of water spouting up from the sand and by noting the number of old clam shells in the area. Since the tides move the shells about, one can find shell everywhere, but the greater agglomerations of shell say, Dig here. One is allowed seventy-five littleneck and/or manila clams per licence. Mature ones are between an inch and a half and two inches in width. Though they are buried in the sand, a couple of inches or so below the surface, their shells often come in brilliant colours—slashes of blue, green, orange, sometimes purple, dependent on the minerals in the sand used to build their shell homes. We rinse the clams several times, then keep them overnight in cool salted water with a little oatmeal added to de-sand them. Then we steam them with white wine, garlic, and parsley—very satisfactory when it's our homemade wine, the garlic and parsley are from the garden, the clams hand-plucked from the sand. Their shells open, they release their juices, and the broth is succulent, tangy, and smooth—and even richer if one dips my whole-wheat bread into it.

When we first arrived here, before we'd learned about this shellfish treasure horde, another June, we'd gone over to Nanaimo to buy some oysters in the shell as a birthday treat for me. We had no shucking knife, so I went in search of one. And found what I wanted in a kitchen do-dads store. The pleasant clerk said, "Ah, having oysters tonight."

"Yes," I said. "We've just bought some, realized we had no knife, so needed this."

"Right. You don't want to be using a paring knife for that."

I agreed, and told her I'd seen some nasty hand wounds from just that sort of thing.

She laughed. "A few years ago, you know what the most common accidents were around here that people went to emergency rooms for? Deep cuts in the palm."

I was puzzled. "From oyster shucking?"

"No, back in '92, '93, this was about the time the West Coast got introduced to bagels." I laughed, and she went on, "Since then one of my biggest sellers here has been the bagel knife with its protective sheath."

3·

Another fishing story. One June when we still lived in Montreal, Kit and I brought young friends, met by way of a friend of our daughter, Elisabeth, up to our cottage in the Laurentians. They were waiting for us in front of their apartment building. This would be their first trip out of Montreal since they'd met some months before. Junco had arrived in Canada from mainland China barely a year earlier. Wendy, a year and half out of China, was doing a PHD in oncology, Junco the same in chemistry, both of them at McGill. Six days a week they worked fourteen hours. On the seventh they went briefly to their labs, just to check the progress of their experiments. But today, a sunny early June Saturday afternoon, they were taking an overnight holiday.

Each carried a small pack and Junco clutched a fishing rod, a Zebco outfit, rod, reel, and incidentals, still encased in its Canadian Tire plastic package. We put their gear in the trunk. "I didn't know you liked fishing," I said to him.

"I like fishing more than anything else," he said, grinning broadly.

Junco, then in his mid-twenties, is short and slightly stocky. The pleasure of his grin makes others happier. His colleagues and teachers said he was already a first-class chemist.

We drove north. I told him not to expect too much, all pretty much low-level fishing at the lake, mostly filled with perch and bluegills, recently stocked with small trout. Junco sounded delighted.

We'd known Wendy first. She comes from a family of intellectuals, her parents both medical doctors who had suffered badly during the Cultural Revolution. She met Junco at McGill; even in the busiest of schedules it seemed there was time to fall in love. As they were becoming a couple she had brought him around, to make sure we approved; in only partial jest she had come to refer to Kit and me as her Canadian parents. We liked Junco immediately.

Since we couldn't get to the cottage by road, we took our boat, which, while we were in Montreal, lived at the landing a few feet from where we'd parked the car. For us the boat ride was, every time we came to the lake, a satisfying recognition we'd finally left the city. Wendy was delighted, Junco even more—the farther the boat got from the car, the greater the breadth of his grin. At our dock he was first out, eager to be helpful. He pushed himself up a little harder than necessary. The boat rocked sharply. Wendy lost her balance. Junco apologized, embarrassed but undaunted.

Both Kit and I liked the arrival rituals—unloading, stashing food and clean clothes, opening windows, filling the bird feeders, laying a fire. But this time Kit had sensed another agenda. She gestured to me, pay attention. Junco was kneeling on the deck that overlooked the lake. He'd unpacked his rod, had half-threaded the line, and was now staring out at the quiet water, hypnotized by it—more, eager to be out on it. Understandable, since he'd not been fishing since coming to Canada.

So while Wendy and Kit prepared supper, he and I went fishing. The best tactics I've found for the lake involve a slow troll trailing a wet fly—the muddler minnow or one of its imitations, barb of the hook squeezed flat to allow easy release. I rigged up Junco's Zebco with one of these. He watched carefully as I tied a clinch knot and nodded in understanding. I wondered if he knew this as a Chinese knot or some kind of chemistry knot.

He let out about eighty feet of line, a good guess for this water. He looked pleased, but at moments troubled.

"Something wrong?" I asked.

He hesitated, then said slowly, "You . . . don't use worms?"

I laughed. "Not necessary." I started to explain just as his rod tip twitched. He struck, the fish was on, and he began cranking as if he were drilling for oil. He had the fish at the boat in seconds. I tried to grab the line, release it, but with great elation he swung it aboard. A five-inch bluegill. Following in my footsteps. It fell from the barbless hook and flopped along the bottom of the boat. I picked it up, to show him.

He stared at it, grinned broadly, and said, "We will eat it. Tonight." And argue as I might, he insisted on bringing the fish back to the cottage. "My first Canadian fish." And he had to show it to Wendy.

Getting dark. We headed in. Ashore, he scaled and gutted it, providing about two tablespoons of meat. He cooked it up for us in a little butter. We shared it four ways.

I'd not eaten bluegill since I was a kid and Dad and I used to catch big ones, ten or eleven inches, in that stream near our house. This evening at the cottage Junco's tiny fish was a suddenly remembered taste, and for a few seconds I was yanked back to a time when Dad and I were a team, spending hours of shared silence by the side of a brook or on a little dinghy, each trusting the other completely, each waiting for a fish, on my line, on his line, it didn't matter which, both were *our* lines.

"When you were a kid," I asked Junco, "did you fish with your father?"

He laughed. "In China, fishing is not for grown men. Unless they are fishermen." Junco and his friends caught their first fish in the pond near the collective farm his family worked on.

Already back then he was by far the brightest of the bunch, excelling in his village school. At nine he was one of eleven who were shipped off to the district middle school, to continue studying. He came home weekends. From there he was one of the select to go on to high school, a dormitory living situation. After, to Beijing University, as one of the true select. And from there to Canada, to McGill, for his doctorate. An immense passage.

During those early graduate school days he'd had almost no contact with his parents. It did little good to write them; like the others in the village, they couldn't read. And the nearest phone was eight miles away. So he'd send pictures of himself, of Wendy, together with a few words that one day his sister, who lives seventy miles away and visits their parents occasionally, would read to them.

Early the next morning Junco and I went out fishing again. He caught his first perch, and his second, and his tenth. He kept one. He needed to know how it tasted, the scientific imagination at play. We shared it, a nibble a person. Yes, there'd been a time when I caught perch to eat. But I dealt with our lake differently now; its fish life is too precarious. I imagined, one day, the successful chemist Junco buying a cottage on a lake, and fishing, and releasing what he caught. Lakes insist on changing us.

After breakfast he found his camera and shot a roll of photos—the cottage, views of the water from the shore, the shore from the boat. Pictures of us, of Wendy, and we took shots of them in the boat. A few weeks later these images would turn up in a hamlet in rural China.

I had to finish some work before Monday morning, so withdrew. Junco went by himself to the dock, casting his fly, using a float for weight. After an hour I joined him. He'd caught nothing but was smiling, totally content.

Up the hill from the cottage a couple of trees had come

down during the winter. I wanted to cut them up for firewood before the brush got too thick. Junco asked if he could help.

"Sure. Ever use a chainsaw?"

"No, but I can learn."

He did. From holding the blade too high or too angled, he mastered the skill. Over half an hour he learned how to notch, to rock the blade, to judge the downhill roll of separated logs. I took this part of cottage life as a necessity: Want to be warm in winter? Cut wood in spring. My satisfaction came when the work was done. But that afternoon I was watching pleasure in action, the whole of Junco's body, all his concentration, given over to the job, and the job gave him joy.

As did splitting logs. I took a few swings with the axe. He watched barely a minute before asking, "Can I do that for you?" I set a log on end and gave him the axe. He raised it high over his head and brought it down, shaving away half an inch of wood and bark. He glanced at me, not quite asking what he'd done wrong, yet wanting to know. I acted it out for him in slow motion, the handle-roll back over the shoulder, the blade at one o'clock, the forward rotation, working the blade's energy down, not to the top of the log but into its centre. Till explaining this to Junco I'd not realized how well I grasped what I did when I split wood. Teaching the technique felt good; I knew more than I knew I knew.

Junco learned quickly. Ten minutes and twenty logs later he ran his hand over his forehead, to wipe away the sweat. He saw me watching. "I like to sweat," he said and grinned again. "In the lab I don't sweat very much."

Neither Wendy nor Junco had ever been in a canoe. After a three-minute lesson on how to handle a paddle, Kit took them out. As they glided away I hinted, gently, that a canoe was way more likely to tip than a boat. They agreed, yes, they would be careful. Back after an hour, Kit reported they both had excellent strokes and had manoeuvred with great precision in the shallows out beyond the island where the great blue heron sometimes fished; Junco paddled in back, steering, Wendy paddled in front, Kit the esteemed passenger. "We moved so quickly and quietly," Wendy said, a touch of awe in her voice. Junco added, "There is a lot of peace here."

In the afternoon, before heading back to Montreal, he and I went fishing once more. The water had become choppy, and the wind more cold than pleasant. Junco let out line, and more line. At about a hundred feet I hinted that might be enough. He agreed but in the next fifteen minutes let out another thirty or forty feet. I was about to impose a little of my expertise on him when suddenly his little rod curved back sharply. "George—" he said, and I turned quickly to look back. A good little rainbow cleared the water, then rushed away hard. Junco played it far more slowly than the first bluegill, with care, now taking pleasure in the process. A few minutes later his first trout was in the boat, gleaming even in the dim light.

"Very nice," I said.

"Should we let it go?" he asked carefully.

"If you like."

He looked at it for a few seconds. "No, I've never eaten a trout I caught."

The last two pictures on the roll were flash shots, devoted to an eleven-inch rainbow trout.

We drove back to Montreal in the dark.

"Before today," I asked, "when was the last time you went fishing?"

"Oh, it was in my village, before I left home."

"Before you came to Canada?"

He laughed. "No, no, before I first went away to school. When I was nine years old."

"Nine?"

"They never let us. I always had to study. But many, many times, when I was alone, I thought about catching fish in the pond near the village. To remember about fishing, it helped me work harder. And working harder, that was a big responsibility."

I see them both, but particularly Junco, watching the lake, listening to the wind in the trees. I try to think myself into a Chinese village, in my mind's projection looking at the quiet water of a Laurentian lake, and the fish below. I knew it well. So did Junco.

JULY

I.

The weather has turned hot and much of the bog has gone dry. Not a lot of tending to do at this time of the year. The bog road is baked hard, and the hundreds of tiny alder lining it grow taller and bushier, happy in the strong sunlight. The heat started two days ago, end of June, after a grey and damp few weeks. David has been here with us for nearly a week, doing much good work around the house and garden, cutting the grass, using the machine with me to split logs, fixing a wire gate some animal, likely our raccoon, had plowed its way through. That piece of repair David finished yesterday; today by the gate an animal, likely the same, in its irritation at not being able to get through had, as a special present for us, dumped a load of excrement.

Animal life here varies from summer to summer. Some years we get a plethora of wasps, as three years ago when every hardware store on Gabriola and in Nanaimo ran out of traps. On the deck the wasps enjoy participating in our lives, especially when we have a picnic that features fresh salmon. The scent of the fish calls sweetly to them and they arrive by the busload. They aren't interested in people, the fish alone is their pleasure. So old salmon turns out to be the best bait in the traps. But one still has to be careful around wasps. That year when they were so plentiful we heard the story of a man eating a barbecued salmon burger on the deck of one of the pubs. Deep in conversation, or a beer, he took a chomp of his burger, not having noticed the wasp that had crept into the bun. A wasp sting on the palate is an unsettling experience.

Last year almost no wasps, and I've not seen many so far this year. Four years back it was tent caterpillars, and none since. We do have that all-but-live-in raccoon who parks himself beneath the bird feeder and snorts sunflower seeds the finches and pine siskins flick down as if in league with him. He remains a handsome fellow, still undaunted. His sharp snout gives him an aristocratic elegance. His eyes are clear and look intelligent. I say this with certainty because I've stared at him and he at me several times from as close as five feet. We'd tolerate him more readily if he would only stop climbing up to the flat bird feeder, which is only notched in place, and knocking it down. We keep it there, unsafely, in order to be able to watch from up close birds that are primarily ground feeders, like the juncos and towhees that find it hard to perch on hanging feeders. Though they try.

This is a rich summer for red squirrels. We figure we've noted five or six separate individuals; usually we have one, rarely two. These fellows enjoy sunflower seeds too, and will clamber up to the deck feeder, sit on the flat wood plate, and gorge themselves. And, of course, they frighten the birds away. Mostly. Last week I watched a towhee defending his turf as a squirrel tried to snatch a seed already in the towhee's beak. We attempt to scare the squirrels off, but they have no fear. When here, grandson Jake pronounced himself head squirrel chaser. He was good at it. While I could go out on the deck and come within a foot of a squirrel, stare it squarely in its fearless eye, ask what it thought it was doing, Jake could merely appear at the door and the squirrel would scoot. Jake took to sneaking out the long way because he dearly wanted to pick up the hose to blast the beast off the feeder. But he never had the chance. The squirrel regularly noted his presence and disappeared into the herb garden. After Jake left, the squirrels were mine, I the lesser squirrel chaser.

One of the squirrels may be in oestrus because her behaviour is stranger than most. Squirrels can mate twice a year, in March/April and in June/July, so now would be her second time. We watched her perching on the thin branch of an arbutus, scolding with hundreds of rapid *tsk-tsk-tsk* sounds at something in the bushes below, then going into a kind of yoga position, her forefeet on the branch, her hind feet up above her head grasping the tree's trunk. Finally she scampered down the trunk and rushed in the direction she'd sent her chiding. Later I saw her, I think it was the same one, up a tree out in back of the house, now staring down at me, producing a series of sounds that began with a sharp click and segued into a hiss as a tomcat might make, dozens of these a minute. But with no interpreter I couldn't make sense of what she was telling me. I saw her again on the standing feeder, and let her be; she needs about three ounces of seeds a day and seemed to be tucking down half that much in a single sitting. I wondered if she had in fact mated and was eating for six, the normal size of a litter. Good thing only a quarter of the little ones make it past year one or we'd be overrun by them. They can live from three to seven years; about half of what's left of any annual production serves as supper for someone else. Luckily for them they're promiscuous, both males and females, so reproduction does go on.

Yesterday, July 1, the national holiday, we spent part of the afternoon down at the beach at False Narrows, the stretch of water between Gabriola and Mudge Island, watching that annual local ritual, the Potato Cannon Contest. With nearly twenty contestants, the competition was tough. Each participant brought his or her own homemade cannon, metal tubes ranging five to twelve feet in length, and the propellant, hairspray from a canister. Potatoes, the ammunition, are supplied by the Ratepayers' Society. The idea is to stuff a potato down the barrel of the cannon with a ramrod as one might shove shot into an eighteenth-century breech-loader, open the cannon at its other end, or base, spray in the propellant, seal the base, aim across the water, ignite the hairspray, and fire. Sometimes nothing happens—the firing apparatus malfunctions. Sometimes there's a *pssst!* sound as the potato travels thirty feet and plops onto the beach. But more often there's the solid *crack!* of hairspray igniting and the potato shoots out across the water, possibly more than two hundred feet. Whether it's a dud or a deep shot, everyone applauds.

This time the tide, incoming, refused to work for the contest. The distance signs, first the 200, then the 150, at last the 100, slowly disappeared under the deepening water. Winners were decided by the best-guess method. But this year the competition, which has been going on for a number of summers, may have seen its final moment. We were told that the cost of liability insurance has risen so high it's now out of reach for the Ratepayers; the Rod and Gun Club may take it over, someone else hoped.

A few years back, after a couple of competitors had fired far across the Narrows, three little boats were launched from Mudge, their owners waving wildly toward the Gabriola side, then flying white flags, shouting, "We give up! We give up!"

A variety of rules and regulations are eliminating many of the island's little traditions; last year the health inspector came over from Nanaimo and closed down the chowder cook-off, an annual fundraising event for People for a Healthy Community, because the contributed chowders were cooked in people's homes; after all, there's no way to tell if the private kitchens are sanitary. In much the same way the inspector is trying to crack down on free-range eggs that are sold directly from farm locations; who can know what condition the chicken coops might be in? We've been buying our eggs from a certain place, freshest and richest eggs we've ever found, and remain completely healthy. But for the authorities, this is proof of nothing.

I had gone down to watch the cannon competition wearing, as I regularly do, my belly pack, which contains a small device I try always to keep with me, an epipen. This is because of an unpleasant incident that occurred in an earlier June. I had driven from the house to the cottage, something I rarely do, because I was transporting a couple of heavy flowerpots filled with soil and geraniums to give the deck some colour. I took the first pot from the trunk, brought it around to the front of the car, turned to the steps—and heard, probably for less than a quarter of a second, a whirring sound, followed immediately by something smacking into the back of my head, just behind my left ear. A pellet? More to the point I felt instant pain, as if my scalp had been gouged. I swatted at the intruder and knocked off something black, elongated. From whir to swat to seeing the black projectile fall to the ground took less than a second.

Now, immediately, the left side of my head ached, and the point of impact felt tender. I had, I guessed, been stung by something. Well, it wouldn't last long. I carried the flowerpot to the deck and set it down. Now my whole skull was aching. But the pain would surely go away; it felt no worse than if I'd bashed my head against an overhead beam. I brought up the other pot, bent to set it down, felt dizzy as I straightened up. This wasn't good. Better get into the car, couple of hundred yards to the house, lie down. I drove, growing dizzier, parked in the carport, went in and told Kit what had happened. She looked for the bite. A tiny puncture wound, virtually no blood. No, didn't seem to be a stinger stuck there. But I had trouble standing. I sat, feet up, head back. We applied ice. I took an antihistamine. I felt weak, my head hot. Then tiny ants seemed to be crawling under the skin of my forehead and the top of my head. Should Kit call a doctor? She phoned a friend for advice. The friend reminded us it was the Sunday of the July long weekend. Any doctor's recorded message would send us to Emergency. We applied more ice. I drank a little water.

The friend called back. She had spoken to her sister, a nurse. Call 911 immediately!

Kit did. Now my lips had gone numb, my eyelids felt puffy, and my tongue had increased in size by maybe fifty percent. We waited for the First Responders. Now I felt alternatively hot and cold. Quickly it became difficult to swallow saliva. Then it became hard to breathe—my throat was constricting—

A pounding on the door. Three large men arrived, immense in full paramedic regalia. They were, I remember, very calm. They asked what had happened. I told them, my voice jaggedly weak. They said it sounded like a hornet, and when one of them described hornets that sounded right—no yellow and black here, all dark grey and vicious. They checked vital signs, but to this point I'd not been given any treatment. Minutes later a paramedic arrived, heard the story, and injected me with epinephrine. I felt a kind of absurd shame—all these large and worthy people, to deal with one tiny insect bite. But they were taking care of me, treating the situation seriously, and I wasn't about to suggest they were overdoing all this.

An ambulance arrived. Two more people, a man and a woman, wheeled in a stretcher. I said I thought I could walk. A rash statement: my legs wouldn't hold me up the two steps to the stretcher even with their help. They laid me flat, rolled me through the house, carried the stretcher down the steps to the ambulance, lifted and slid me in. I lay still, head slightly raised, while they ministered to me—blood pressure, pulse monitor, now some kind of intravenous drip. With my arm bare I saw it had become covered with hives. When I whispered this the paramedic pulled back my shirt. Hives all over my skin.

The ambulance drove off. On my back I stared out the back window. A strange sensation, watching as the world receded behind me. A road I've driven on more than a thousand times, now a thoroughly unfamiliar stretch as I, in effect seeing it upside down, watched it move away backwards. The siren wailed the whole way. I felt an ongoing embarrassment, causing so much commotion, so much trouble. We turned corners I must have known but now didn't recognize, we drove down hills I had a perverse inverse familiarity with. It was even hard to ask questions, or answer any, my mouth so swollen, my tongue so large, my throat so tight. Though the breathing had become a little easier.

And all the time the siren's ululation. I've often wondered what was happening inside when an ambulance wailed by. Now I had an inkling.

At last, the ferry. A new paramedic, Sandy (not my writing partner-in-crime), a neighbour whom I hadn't met before. The ferry had been held for twenty-five minutes to the displeasure of a full load of cars and vans (often my take, too, when I'd been delayed; never ever again), all starting early to leave the island at the end of the long weekend. More administrations of drips and tests along the way, crossing over, the twenty minutes passing faster than on any other remembered trip. On the Nanaimo side I was shifted, on my back the whole time, to a big-island hospital ambulance. Suddenly I realized Kit was in the ambulance too. New driver, new paramedic; he had all the paperwork about me but asked the same questions nonetheless. One new question: "Do you know which hospital we're going to?" Which for an instant seemed like a truly dumb question—and then I understood its intent. I said, "To the Nanaimo hospital, I hope." I tried to grin but my mouth wouldn't move that way.

Finally, the emergency room. An hour and a half from sting to hospital. I was still badly swollen about the face, deep drooping sacs under my eyes, tongue still huge, hives ongoing, brain numb. But I was recovering. They continued to monitor my blood pressure. It bounced about, 154/45, 110/90, 165/55. Almost as bad, after a couple of hours of lying on the emergency bed I sat up, and I found myself staring at my feet. At my right sock. My big toe stuck through a hole down there. Whenever you leave the house make sure your underwear's not torn, as many mothers have many times said.

Before I left the hospital I was told about hornets. Their stings come in three categories: local, where the reaction is limited to the area hit; secondary, where the venom spreads a small distance; and general, where the venom travels throughout the body. My reaction was category three, already well advanced. And it's not the venom that causes such great harm. The internal reaction is a function of one's own immune system, protecting the body, overcompensating.

My head still ached as they released me. Directions on taking Benadryl. I was warned, "Buy yourself an epipen, a self-administrable shot of epinephrine, and carry it with you at all times. It's fully loaded. Just set it against your upper thigh right on the pant leg, press the little button on the top, shoot yourself through the cloth, you'll be fine." We took a taxi back to the ferry dock. While I waited, Kit bought an epipen at the pharmacy across the street. The ferry arrived only a few minutes late—there'd been an ambulance run, they told us, but they'd made up some of the time—and we were home by seven, very happy to be back. We stopped at the cottage to see if we could find the body of whatever had stung me. Nothing. Back to the house. The thing I wanted most, a Scotch, I was not allowed—no alcohol after all the drugs. Our insect guide made it even clearer what had stung me. Hornets attack when they feel threatened, the book said. But I was only carrying a flowerpot! I could visualize the thing as I swatted it away, as it fell to the ground: black, and long. I remembered the whir and thought of the old radio serial *The Green Hornet*. Only he was the good guy. I slept a sedative-induced sleep.

The next day we went back to the cottage, heavily swathed in toques, goggles, scarves, gloves, solid jackets, and jeans. In July. We needed to find the nest, to destroy it. We looked under the deck, on the posts. Nothing. Then I thought I heard a whir again and looked up. Directly above the front door, which I'd been going in and out of for many previous weeks, hung the nest. All my entries and exits must have been far more threatening than the pot I'd been carrying. But not in the mind of that hornet. Now three or four of the insects were buzzing around the nest, landing on it, entering through the gateway on the underside. We would return after dark when, the insect guidebook had informed us, all the members of the colony would be inside.

Actually, the nest is impressive. Ovoid, about six inches in diameter, maybe seven long, it's constructed out of a kind of papery material. I researched the process. The hornets make the nest by chewing wood, at first the queen, then the workers she produces. The hornets wrap this paper material around the centre in increasingly larger dark grey layers, more or less hornet-coloured. Cleverly designed. Graceful. But its inhabitants had to go.

In the evening, again fully armoured, we came back with Raid and a ladder. I dislike the use of chemicals, but . . . The entryway's angle was difficult to get at. We approached—and the motion detector light came on. We waited for the light to turn itself off; since a couple of hornets had appeared, maybe they thought morning had already arrived? We set up the ladder and firmed it in place. I blasted the nest with death, and with the pleasure of revenge.

The nest still hangs above the door, both as a war memorial and to keep other flying, biting things from building there. Even wasps fear hornets.

Afterwards came other people's stories. A friend's brother was stung by a hornet. No, they didn't call 911, his wife could just as easily drive him to hospital, he in immense discomfort, then barely able to breathe. Just as he arrived at emergency his heart stopped, he had no blood pressure. Fortunately the paramedics got him on a gurney and sped him down the hall, electro-shocked his heart, brought him back. He's been fine ever since, and never leaves home without his epipen.

In the old days one had to load the epinephrine into the epipen. A friend of a friend had been stung by a hornet. He'd always carried his epipen with him but died while loading it.

A doctor playing golf with three of his buddies was stung by a hornet. He knew he was allergic so always carried his epipen. Unfortunately the epinephrin in the epipen was two years old and had lost its potency. He died on the golf course.

My epipen is ever with me, including at potato cannon competitions, where perhaps there are no hornets . . .

2.

I have a history of minor but unpleasant incidents in July. In 1965, I was a graduate student in comparative literature at Harvard, studying for my comprehensives, the qualifying exams one takes after finishing all one's required courses, preliminary to writing a thesis. My fields of study, as I've mentioned, were German literature from high middle German (c. 1050–1350) to post-war fiction, theatre, and poetry, as well as English and French literature from 1750 to the present, the so-called modern period. The exams would be selective: identify and analyze four passages from my major field, two each from my minors. The written exams would take place in late August. I'd be defending them on September 14 because on September 15, Kit, Elisabeth, and I would be flying to France where we would live for a year, me to do thesis research and to write my first novel (never published). September 16 would be Elisabeth's second birthday. Before that day the cost of her ticket would be ten percent of the price of one of ours; on her birthday and after we'd have to pay fifty percent. I had only a Harvard Travelling Fellowship, so there was no money to waste.

But that July, days and evenings were spent reading the mass of material I'd not covered in my courses. I'd been deep in it the whole of that July day. At about ten I figured I'd call it an evening—wasn't taking in much, brain thick with disorganized information, stories, factoids, rhymes. Kit had put Elisabeth to bed a couple of hours earlier and was reading. We lived at the time in a basement apartment in Cambridge with low ceilings, probably not more than six and a half feet. I stood up from my desk, stretched to loosen tight shoulder muscles, and threw my arms up high. Unfortunately my right hand smashed into the cover of the ceiling lamp, one of those cheap glass plates ubiquitous to graduate student apartments. The sharp edge cut into flesh, severing I would later learn the major vein and artery, as well as the tendons and nerves, leading to my right index finger. Yes, blood everywhere. I remember Kit trying to apply pressure to the wound, I trying to wash it clean and succeeding only in flushing a substantial amount of blood down the sink. Kit finally ran to a neighbour with a car, to get her to drive me to the hospital, and found another neighbour to stay with Elisabeth while Kit came with me to the luckily close-by hospital. The neighbour with the car had some nursing experience and tied up the wound to keep most of my pulsing blood from messing up her car's interior.

In the emergency room I was well and quickly treated, lightly sedated, then told I'd have to wait till they could find a surgeon at that time of night to sew me up. This took the best part of two hours. My hand throbbed. I sat, Kit sat. I remember worrying about my upcoming exams, how I would write them, would my hand be up to it. But with the sedation, however light, I felt my concerns ebbing away. At last the surgeon arrived and I was wheeled into surgery. He explained to me what he'd be doing, trying to find anything in the wound that he could tie back together. I was struck by how remarkable this was, and I asked him questions about the size of needles, what kind of thread, and so on, all of which he answered clearly. He asked me, "Do you want full sedation for this, or local?"

"Local," I said. "I'd like to watch as you do this. Is there some way I can?"

I remember his scowl and squint as he looked at me, as if I were a bit weird. But I've always been curious about procedures of whatever sort, and when would I ever again get a chance to follow a surgeon's moves as he sewed human flesh back together?

A couple of nurses had appeared, and an anaesthesiologist. The surgeon told him I wanted only local sedation. I was laid flat on my back on the operating table. Now someone attached a level extension protruding at ninety degrees from the table itself. A nurse took my right arm, set it on the extension, and tied it in place, the wound pointing up. The anaesthesiologist poked my hand three times with a needle and the throbbing stopped, the whole hand numb. Then he inserted another needle into my arm below the elbow and hooked this up to a drip. I watched as some thin liquid flowed into my system.

The surgeon must have explained my desire to follow the operation because the other nurse now appeared with a small round mirror, maybe eight inches in diameter, which she fixed to the extension and angled about. "Can you see your hand?" she asked.

I couldn't, so she shifted the slant till my hand's reflection filled the mirror. "Great. Thank you."

The sedative must have made itself felt more than just locally. While I could watch and even concentrate, I felt literally no pain; probably one of the three shots was meant to instill general calm. Or maybe the drip did it. The anaesthesiologist was holding my head up slightly above the pillow it lay on, to give me a good line of sight. The surgeon went to work, with tiny instruments. His movements were slow and seemed precise. I asked questions but realized he wasn't answering, he must be concentrating hard. Suddenly his concentration became humorous. I knew I mustn't laugh. I could feel myself smiling, though, and suppressing a giggle. Then it came to me, what I had to do. If I didn't do it now, I'd never get another chance. I said to the anaesthesiologist, speaking very slowly, making certain I got all the words right, "Tell me, when this is over, will I be able to play the piano?"

The anaesthesiologist answered with great gentleness, "Of course, of course, not to worry."

"That's great," I said. "I've never been able to play the piano before." I had done it! One of the oldest jokes in the world, and I'd manipulated it perfectly.

The last thing I heard was the surgeon saying, "That's it. Put him under."

It took weeks for a bit of feeling to return to the finger, months before I could use it for something as simple as dialling a phone, and many years before it went straight again. In the cold it still aches. I took my exams as planned in late August and, because I couldn't write with a pen, revolutionized the department by being allowed to type my answers; prior to this every examinee had written by hand. I defended my answers on September 14, that evening we celebrated, and the three of us flew off to France on September 15.

For the last several days a few dragonflies have been around, the big-bodied, iridescent blue ones, a few of their cousin reds.

The days have regularly been warm, mid-twenties, and the sky a perfect clean blue. No rain in weeks. The dry heat is preferred dragonfly weather. And today, as I walked along the bog road, I spotted a different kind of dragonfly. It flitted ahead, alighting on the hard-baked sand, waiting till I approached, taking off again, repeating its broken flight several times. I've not seen the likes of it before, black head, white thorax and abdomen, its double wings clear close to the thorax, abruptly black on the extended half. An attractive insect. I watched it fly out over the bog and settle on a lily pad, as if expecting me to follow through the shallow water. Finally, perhaps tired of my inability to participate further in its game, it flew deeper into the bog and disappeared. I waited, watching the spot where I'd last seen it, hypnotized for minutes by its absence. When I got to the cottage I looked it up online: dragonfly black white. And found over a dozen species that answered to that description. I did narrow it down to two, from different sites: *Libellula pulchella* and male widow skimmer. *Libellula* means dragonfly, and *pulchella* means pretty. What widow skimmer means I have no idea. I preferred "pretty dragonfly" and took another good look at *Libellula*. Unfortunately the pretty dragonfly has only one set of wings, the widow skimmer two. I was not meant to be a bugologist.

Nor, as it turns out, any kind of scientist who deals with animals. Our handsome racoon is back. I watched him sneak onto the deck and head for the flat feeder on the railing. But he wasn't alone. And apparently he is not a he. Or raccoons are into co-parenting. Trailing her, two miniature racoons, certainly her kits, perfect tiny beasts. She had brought her new family to the deck, to teach them how to steal birdseed. First reaction, *This has to be stopped, we'll be bedevilled by them the whole summer!* Kit noted them first and called to me. We made noises, which deterred them not at all. Kit grabbed the hose. The mother recognized the weapon and leapt off the deck into the herb garden and disappeared. The kits followed. Kit sent a spray of water at the mother's point of entry. Something struggled under the growth—not the mother, she jumped down from the tangled herbs and sped down her escape path under the hanging bird feeders. There she turned and watched. One of the kits showed up beside her. It, too, stared at us. Finally the second kit appeared, still among the herbs, soaking wet. It looked ridiculous, it looked sad. We didn't send any more water blasting its way. It joined the other two and together they all stared at us, the kits seemingly confused, the mother angry, accusing.

I thought at that moment, we've been doing this wrong. Sure, raccoons steal a little birdseed. But they are graceful creatures whose ancestors lived on this land long before we built the house. We could at least share some of the space with them. So, yes, we have started actively feeding them. A special red bowl, placed under the hanging birdfeeders, only for them. And they have been taking our offering, salted pretzels gone in the morning, though we haven't seen any racoons since the time the mother brought her kits to visit.

We lived through a version of this story last year when the red squirrel was our major thief; I can put the animal in the singular here, because last summer we saw only the one. He'd been a regular pilfering guest in June. Then for a few weeks we didn't see him. When he reappeared in mid-July we could assume that either he'd had a sex-change operation, or we had mislabelled his sex. Because now she had swollen teats. "A nursing mother," Kit said. A nursing mother had to be allowed all the food she needed. We only chased her away when she made a pig of herself, stuffing her cheeks with seeds, but even then we remained far more lenient; likely the food was intended for her babes. Who obviously lived and grew fat and learned to filch in the far greater numbers now thriving about us.

In July 1999 we made a trip to France and Italy, three weeks, because *The Underside of Stones* was being published in Italian as *La Faccia nascosta delle pietre*. We flew out of Vancouver. The immediate problem we encountered was the substantial change in our sleep patterns. Six hours from the east, from Montreal, to Europe still had seemed viable. But nine from here in the west felt like we were sleeping on the back side of the clock.

At the launch we sat in warm, gentle air under the stars in the publisher's villa garden north of Rome. The proceedings were for the most part academic. A panel talking about *Stones*—uh, *Pietri*—and then a one-hour (sixty minutes, count 'em, sixty) academic analysis of the fiction. Remarkably I understood most of the Italian, in part because academic jargon translates easily, all those latinates, and in part because I'd written the book. I learned a great deal about my unconscious structuring. I learned too that one can have wine labels for any occasion, in this instance two cases of bottles saying, in Italian: Vintage 1996 Bottled for the Occasion of the Launch of *La Faccia nascosta delle pietre* by George Szanto. I was impressed. And the book looked good.

I spoke a few words, reading an Italian translation of the words in what I gathered was comprehensible Italian. At least people laughed in the right places and not at me. In the garden the air grew softer as evening came on, with the perfume of linden trees in blossom (*tiglio* in Italian, like *tilleul* in French, by whatever name a rich, hushed smell) and jasmine, as well as a dozen varieties of roses, and scores of other flowers whose names I didn't know even in English. Food was spread out in abundance, medium-size nibbles before the panel began, an ever-filling cornucopia after the panel ended, including a dozen kinds of olives, bruschetta, eight varieties of local salami, six different kinds of quiche, peppers sautéed in local olive oil, more and more large succulent delicacies. We ate and drank ourselves happily into oblivion, and assumed this was dinner. Wrong. Out came the whole roast suckling pig that had been turning on the coals in a pit for eighteen hours. I was asked to make the first ceremonial cut. With a sword that might have been a scimitar, I hacked off the head. Long thereafter, to bed.

A few days later, off to Amsterdam and our flight. It always impresses me that we could walk along the old canals in the morning, get on the plane at one in the afternoon, gain nine hours and arrive at two in Vancouver, and end the day by taking the ferry across the water of a different ocean to Gabriola that same night. True, we were awake for twenty hours, but still . . .

3.

Mid-July and the vegetable garden has reached the exploding stage. Peas are alive and well, the chard is demanding to be eaten, the tomatoes are just on their way. Beans are bushy and should be ready next week. The lettuces, even the ones that are bolting, range from semi-sweet to mildly bitter. Rhubarb is in its fifth bestowal, cilantro running wild wherever a seed was dropped by bird or spread by other chance in the early spring. The onions are slow but coming. Zucchinis are threatening to multiply, broad beans already have. The raspberries ripen daily, and the strawberries. If we don't pick black currants today or tomorrow, we'll lose them to the birds; the red currants will be ready next week. I'll be able to pull up my year's supply of garlic in a couple of weeks, and we've had our first round of young potatoes, both the local red and the blue from Peru. The basil, lacklustre till a week ago, is bushing into heavy green. Even one of my three artichokes is ready for the plucking.

As ever, my leeks did not do well. Katherine, another Gabriola writer, has recently produced a book, *The Garden That You Are*. She argues that there are so many agricultural sub-zones on the island one cannot predict what will grow well where. I have complained to her about my leeks, and she to me about her peas. She used that difference of growth potential at the launch of the book. The island newspaper, the *Gabriola Sounder*, made much of her argument but an unfortunate typo crept into the article, captioning a photo of her with the line, "George Szanto can't grow leeks, but he sure can't grow peas," the second *can* having become *can't*. She wrote a letter to the editor: "It is incumbent upon me to save the reputation of fellow Gabriola writer and gardener George Szanto. Let no man (or woman) ever malign his pea-growing reputation again. The photo caption implies incorrectly that Szanto cannot grow peas. In fact, he is a pea-grower of international stature. His peas are spoken of with reverence in vegetable circles worldwide. No peas can compare. His leeks, however, are, as stated, a disgrace." Katherine writes a pithy public letter.

The kale this year has been more plentiful than in the past, and we've taken full advantage. Using a good vegetarian cookbook, *Still Life with Menu*, yesterday we made pasta with shredded kale and feta—some extra virgin olive oil (sadly not produced locally), chopped onions, the kale, fusilli, the feta crumbled, some pepper. Simple and delicious. Broad beans sautéed with garlic are a daily staple, and salad greens are picked half an hour before eating. Rhubarb every morning with cereal. Much more of this to come, and we look forward to it each day. In the evening there's a beer or vodka-tonic as we sit talking on the deck in back overlooking the strait or on the pergola on the west side as the sun sinks lower. Then the meal, sometimes with guests, but most often we're alone.

We enjoy the casual visitor. (Most of the time; danger of generalization.) At one point, a warm July afternoon some twenty years ago when Kit and I were up at our cabin in the Laurentians sipping beer on the little deck between the house and the lake, a man we knew appeared in a small boat, trailing a fishing line. I'll call him Henri. He hailed us. For years at the start of each new season he would tune our outboard motor, readying it for the spring and summer. He was a convivial fellow, though given to an oversupply of chat when we were in a hurry. That afternoon we invited him to dock his boat and join us for a beer. He told us about his life as a mechanic for Trans-Canada, now Air Canada, which had given him and his wife and family the right, if seats were available, to travel anywhere Air Canada flew. So he'd seen a lot of the world, and took delight in discovering new places and people.

"You seem to like all the people you meet," I commented. "Are there any you don't?"

He thought about this for a couple of seconds and said, "Oh, yes, I don't like Jews."

Conversation stopped. Kit told me later she just barely kept herself from immediately putting him in his place. I had a different reaction, one akin to wanting to watch the surgeon stitch my hand together. In the 1920s and 1930s, Quebec had seen a major growth in anti-Semitism. I'd never met a Quebec anti-Semite; now I was drinking beer with one. So I asked, "Is it because of something a Jew, or the Jews, did to you?"

"Oh, no," he said, "I've never met a Jew."

I came very close to saying, Well you have now but held back. Instead I told him, "My father was a bit like that. He couldn't stand Parisians."

Henri nodded. "Me too," he said. "I really dislike Parisians."

I did not ask him if he'd ever met a Parisian. Nor did we offer him a second beer. He left soon after. The next spring we found someone else to tune our outboard.

But back to Gabriola. Growing well this year, the ten cedars at the bottom of the garden. We'd planted them soon after the house was finished, July 2001. We'd been given them by Phyllis;

they had been left over at the end of the annual summer tour of the garden club. Where we put them in the ground the space was bare dirt, having been the entry point onto the land from Alan and Sharon's property for excavators and backhoes. As a result we had a naked view of their house, as they did of ours. The cedar trees would one day provide a screen.

The day we put them in, Kit and I were in our sixty-first year. Each of the ten trees stood barely a foot tall. In a quarter of a century, we figured, they finally would block the view not only of Alan and Sharon's house but of the narrows, the strait, and the islands as well. Looking ahead, I figured when the time came we'd have to top them. Maybe Jake could help. He'd be twenty-six in a quarter of a century. But in fact this year they do provide that screen between the two houses. Over the years they have grown more than thirty feet.

It reminded me of the Moulin Sartier, Bruno and his wife, Christine, and Mamane's mill in the Charente. Christine told us the story of Bruno's grandfather, who, when Bruno was six years old, planted a line of poplar trees, *peupliers,* at the property line. His grandfather told Bruno that he'd put the trees into the ground right then so they could be cut in forty years. In forty years the barn would need a new roof, and the lumber milled from the trees would pay for the reroofing. That moment, says Christine, has now arrived. Forty years have passed. But Bruno refuses to have the trees cut down. He doesn't need the money from the trees to put up a new roof. People remind him that the trees reach their peak at forty years, soon they'll rot and be worthless. But Bruno won't cut. His unspoken reason? Bruno loved his grandfather, honours his memory, had worked on planting the trees with his grandfather. The trees are an ancient link.

I on the other hand have few such compunctions, as my links to cedars are much shorter—if they exist at all. We will have to take out several cedars that we planted close to the house, and two directly beside the railing on the cottage deck, as well as a couple of hemlocks; they crowd the space. And several days ago we did the necessary surgery on one of the large crabapples beside the bog road. It had stretched its branches beyond the edge of the passage of oncoming cars. Trucks arriving had to dodge away to keep from being scraped. So, chainsaw in hand, we hacked at the threatening branches, all of them covered with tiny green apples the size of half a fingernail. Not feeling good about the job, either of us, because in the early spring the tree is that explosion of tiny white blossoms, every branch alive with reborn virginity. Now, as I walk across the bog to the cottage, this crab, like its two sibling trees on the other side—these spreading out over the bog rather than across the road—glimmers in the morning light, a welcoming presence preliminary to my workday.

We dragged the branches to the burn pile, laying them apart. We'd leave them this way because the deer love the little apples. Mostly they're too high in the tree for the deer to reach, but if a branch breaks off or is hacked down, as now, the apples are quickly gone. One time several years ago I came around the corner from the cottage and saw a doe standing on her hind legs, her forelegs heavy on a crabapple branch, pulling it down, all the while moving her head to nibble away. We noted now, as we hauled the branches away, small bundles of the little apples, dull green clumps, had broken off and lay on the road. The deer will soon find them.

Today as I passed the tree I noted a few bunches, and some single apples, lying in the dirt. They were no longer green. In four days they have turned red, ripening without benefit of sap from the tree.

AUGUST

I.

Kit and I headed out for an afternoon walk across the neighbouring land on the west side, away from Alan and Sharon. When we first came to Gabriola it had been a hundred and sixty acres of forest, the firs like ours about fifty years old, standing over a hundred feet tall. But the winter after we bought our land, our neighbour Dave clear-cut a large part of it, including the area beside our house, leaving a broad expanse of bare earth spotted with fifteen-foot-high piles of branches and roots, purportedly to be burned; they never were. He also left standing some scraggly trees with no value as lumber. Grass and brambles grew on the burn piles, turning them into hillocks. After a couple of years grasses had grown up on the bare earth too, transforming it into a meadow. So Dave ran sheep on the meadow for a number of years. The sheep ate the grass down to stubble. Had this happened on common land in the old American West it could have been cause for warfare between cattlemen and sheep herders. Now the sheep too are gone, and the land has been subdivided. Zoning for such subdivision calls for lots no smaller than twenty acres. Dave asked for and received from the Islands Trust the right to divide the land into five lots of ten acres, and one of a hundred and ten. To do this he had to accede to a covenant on the land that says it cannot be further divided. He sold the lesser lots. They each have the same magnificent view as we do. On a section of the big lot, less than a hundred yards from the cottage where I'm writing, the same distance from the edge of the bog, Radio Gabriola wants to put a radio tower. I've been fighting this; the radiation from its electromagnetic field could well destabilize the birdshot on my retinas and neuter the frogs in the pond. But despite the covenant, Dave might lease to the radio station the necessary two and a half acres. More battles to come.

We stepped over the fence onto Dave's land. He had long ago told us he has no objection to our going for walks over there; mostly Dave is a decent man. Little pink flowers grew in every direction. Perhaps it's the openness of the field that brings about such ecological differences on Dave's land; one sees immediately a shift in the kinds of grass and flowers, and the difference in the insect life. Damselflies are the most obvious here—none for weeks on our side, on his many, steel blue needles flitting among the grasses. Likely this is because, at the edge of the bog, Dave and his excavator have dug out a pond, far larger than ours by the cottage and considerably deeper, ten to twelve feet down when full, about sixty feet in diameter: perfect breeding ground for damselfly nymphs. Now, at the beginning of August, the water level was down by at least three feet. It lay flat and black, dimpled every few seconds by tadpoles coming to the surface to grab some speck of food, a water spider, tiny larvae. I checked the near edge of the pond but saw no nymphs. That would be normal, as they'd have hatched in late June or early July. I've seen them, not here but years ago in Wyoming, scudding along under water from weed banks toward the shore, dragging themselves onto the mud at the waterline, thrashing about till their outer shell cracked, crawling their folded-up selves out of the old outer skin. It's then that the insect is at its most vulnerable, no longer an armoured nymph, not yet an insect that can fly away from hungry birds. Such transformations usually take place in the late morning or early afternoon, when the sun is at its highest point, so that the just-hatched damselfly's wings and body can dry out quickly and take to the air.

But Dave didn't dig out a pond for the benefit of damselflies or their nymphs. The island needs a controlled water supply in the eventuality of forest fire, and Dave has an arrangement with the Gabriola Fire Department that allows Rick, the fire chief, access to the water. There's a white eight-inch pipe that eases up a bank from the water. It leads to a pump-capacitor that can draw water up from the bog, pressurize it, and send it down to a fire hydrant. The line from capacitor to hydrant, down on Lockwood Road at the lower edge of our land and abutting Dave's, is buried. The hydrant is one of five on the island.

When the capacitor was first put in place, it had been painted a drab military green. Then a couple of Rick's fire-fighters painted it luminous white. Before the paint job it had blended in among the tall grass, salal, and scrub bushes. White, it looked like an obscene eight-foot-high marshmallow. When our son, David, came to visit us he found it an arresting eyesore. Something had to be done. I called Rick to ask if he minded if we repainted it; he had no objection. When I spoke with Dave, neither did he. So we bought paints that would withstand sun and ice, and Kit and David sketched a forest onto the side facing our house. Now the capacitor disappears into its surroundings. Camouflaged. More or less.

A few years after our arrival here, my cousin Carol and her husband, Jim, came to visit. They were enchanted by the island. After a couple of days Carol said, "All I've seen is beautiful places. Isn't there anything ugly on Gabriola?"

By this time the field beside the house had greened up and the marshmallow was not yet in place, but as we drove along I did point out to her, across the water on the Nanaimo side, the local paper mill, Harmac. "Not exactly on the island, but it lets out ongoing steam, which if you're downwind has its own unique stink. But luckily ninety-eight percent of the time the prevailing wind sends it south of Nanaimo. At night it's brightly lit, a mile of incandescent orange. Truly ugly."

Harmac is also central to Nanaimo's economy, providing a substantial proportion of the city's jobs and so its tax base. Without it many of our favourite restaurants and shops would have to shut down for lack of clientele, the hospital would be cut back, there'd be any number of school closures. So it's a necessary evil we have recently come to accept. Some time back it came to the edge of bankruptcy and went idle, laying off most of its workers. But then the BC Supreme Court ruled to allow an organization calling itself Nanaimo Forest Products (NFP) to take possession of Harmac. NFP, a combination of the mill's managers, workers, and several private investors, paid $13.2 million for this privilege. The workers, over 350 of them, invested up to $25,000 apiece for shares in the ownership of the mill. And so keep their jobs. I am impressed.

As Kit and I walked farther we came across what we already knew was there, Dave's most recent project. Several years ago, at the ridge with its magnificent view, Dave began quarrying. Using his excavator he has scraped away the surface of the land and hauled out many huge slabs of the sandstone and shale that lie beneath. These he loads onto trucks and ships off to house contractors and landscape gardeners. The slabs become the immense paving stones of verandas and garden steps of new homes. Using such stones in this part of the world is not unusual; our contractor also built outside staircases and raised flower and herb beds with such slabs. But ours had been dug up in the excavation of the house's foundation. More important, our monster excavation hole disappeared as the house was built over it. On Dave's land, the hole, the many holes, remain, their unusable slag dead hillocks standing at the peripheries, a possible movie set for a film to be called *Flanders 1917*. Beyond the peripheries, the grand vista. Proving it's possible to make a sow's ear out of a silk purse.

After the quarry we arrived at the fence to the first of the sold lots. We'd met the couple who bought the land, Bob and Lesley, when they were first building the house. We'd talked then but never since. We have admired both their handsome home and, even more, the acre of raspberries he's put in on the non-view side, a south-facing slope. He happened to be outside as we came by, so we chatted and renewed the acquaintanceship. He offered us a taste of his berries picked early this morning. Ambrosia. He and his wife take out between a dozen and fifteen flats a day, each flat containing nine pint containers. It's late in the season for raspberries, but the summer has been cool so the berries keep on coming. Bob sells them to the Village Market here, several restaurants on the island, half a dozen more in Nanaimo and beyond. Each flat costs, wholesale, twenty-five dollars. Having gone on our walk walletless, we came back later with cash. We immediately ate one pint, took another to a friend's home where we had dinner together, and froze the rest. Fresh local raspberries for the middle of winter. If they last that long.

Then we rounded the bog and headed across the field back to our house. Along the way we stopped to nibble black caps, wild berries much like raspberries in shape but smaller and darker, the field dotted with bushes of them. And, passing the occasional wild gooseberry bush, I stopped and took my share of these. The earth is bountiful, even on an ex-clear-cut. We reached the fence to our land at the precise point where, back in late February, we had deposited the dead deer. Or thought we had, because at first we found no trace of it. Then, closely examining the earth, I noted a scraggly tuft of fur. Nothing more. No deer skull for me. Nature had fully reclaimed its own, with the possible help of a dog.

In 1996 we spent a few summer weeks on Gabriola at the cottage. We went back to Montreal middle of August, back to our institutional responsibilities, me still at McGill, Kit teaching, at Vanier College, one of the English-language CEGEPs—like a community college. In a course on communications and urbanization, I planned to teach Lewis Mumford that year. In the city, Mumford explains, time becomes visible. Cities demand organization. Organization takes place in time.

I wrote about some of that in my notebooks, from which several of these memories derive. But I'd only started those notes in December, four months or so after we'd returned. During the fall we sold the Montreal house and prepared to leave for France come the end of December. Until then I had *no time* to write. *No time* because we had to plan the move from Montreal. The organization of time as I had known it was disrupted utterly. Time was now made visible by storage boxes labelled by years and places: materials to take to Gabriola, things to leave for the garage sales. And a few painfully basic decisions: what to keep, what to sell, what to give away, what to throw out. Among the items kept, which would we need in the apartment we had rented for the fall? which in January in France at the mill in the Charente where we'd spend those ten weeks? which should go to Gabriola in April on our return to Canada? which should remain till the end of 1999, when we finally moved to the island and the house we'd build across the bog? and more. Time made tactile.

The months before that summer in 1996 carried a sense of a mythical future. Off to Gabriola, where we'd one day live. While there I'd be able to reflect, make notes; two and a half weeks with nothing else to do. The Gabriola time came, with indeed some reflection. But over those weeks I wrote nothing in my notebook. I wrote nothing, I now realize, because on the island I was living in a different kind of time: an artificial time, an escape time, in another way a *no time*. I had, in a most positive way, *no time*. I was living outside of time.

Some who live on Gabriola might not feel it this way. They'd say something like, *island time*. Island time is a lightweight version of *no time*, time partway toward urban time, because living even on island time means responsibilities; people have associations with each other that have found some kind of structure. Yet *island time* remains a non-city time because it does not make the notion of today, right now, into the dominant category. If something doesn't get done today, it will (perhaps, perhaps not) get done tomorrow. It's all strongly reminiscent of the Mexican notion, revolutionary to northern minds, of *mañana*: not a laziness, simply an avoidance of the mechanical domination of ledger, clock, calendar.

I've brought some urban time with me to the island. I have a writing schedule. I again keep an agenda, for me, a necessity: without an agenda, I forget. I'm one of the few people I know on Gabriola who wears a watch.

In August 1993 we had come to Gabriola for a couple of weeks. It was the summer after we'd bought the Engineer's Challenge. We would have ourselves a bit of vacation, swim (well, Kit would swim), picnic, fish. We walked the land, both sides of the bog, to get a better feel for it. The previous months had been unusually dry, so we could make our way right through some parts of the bog, along deer trails between the hardhack. Both sides of the bog felt the right mix of privacy, away from others, and participation in a natural ease. Where to place the house? And then we would build a cottage as well, both as a studio for me to write in and to sleep the many visitors who had already promised to come out to see us on this strange new island where we'd chosen to hide. Or which, a notion I was feeling increasingly comfortable with, had chosen us.

The second or third afternoon at the village, I met our real estate agent. He asked me, "So what do you plan to do with your land?"

"Oh," I said, "we'll be retiring in about six years, and maybe a couple of years before then we'll get down to designing and building the house we want to live in. And after that we'll put up a guest cottage."

"Mmm," he said. "Remind me, how big's your land? Five acres, wasn't it?"

"Yeah, just a bit over."

"Well, you ought to know, the Trust is in the middle of changing some zoning bylaws."

"Oh?" And what did this have to do with building a house?

"New regulations coming in over the winter. You'll need at least ten acres to build two domiciles on a single piece of land."

"You mean we won't be able to put up a cottage?"

"Not if you do it the way you're planning." I remember him grinning.

"What else?"

"Well, see,"—I could feel he was trying to tell me something—"if there's already a little house on the land and you want to build a bigger house, then the little house sorta gets grand-fathered in. Like, nobody's going to make you tear it down."

"So if we build the cottage first—"

"First, and before they put in the new bylaws."

So our two weeks of summer calm and quiet took on new character. We consulted others regarding possible builders. We contacted banks in Nanaimo for possible mortgages. We asked three contractors to bid on the project—and later learned such things weren't done on the island: contractors don't compete with each other. I had made a sketch of a design for the cottage we wanted: two floors so it'd be high enough to overlook, from the balcony outside the bedroom, the whole of the bog.

Upstairs, only the one large bedroom, fifteen feet by twenty, and a tiny bathroom with sink and toilet—Stuart our builder's idea, and we learned to be glad of it. Downstairs a single large room, living room/dining room/kitchen, a tiny side room, the "guest bedroom"—two foam pads set side by side would cover the entire breadth of the floor—and a bathroom complete with tub and shower. Four hundred square feet. Even before the new bylaws came in, no second structure could be larger than seven hundred square feet.

I showed my sketch to the three contractors. Two told us to find an architect to draw up working plans so that they could give us a quote. In the week that remained? The third contractor, Stuart, came back the next day with a quote and complex drawings, not quite working plans but full sketches conscious of our intentions and hopes. We hired him on the spot.

Over the winter we stayed in telephone conversation with him, both Kit and I marvelling that such construction could be going on over on Gabriola while we in Montreal were locked into icy immobility. We followed the building process from the photos Sandy generously took and sent on to us. These gave us a bit of a visual sense of the process. I came out to the island in March, the frogs in full mating swing, and was still able to suggest some small changes. By June the cottage was finished, fridge and stove in place, ready to be inhabited.

We flew west again in August and for two weeks lived in the cottage. Alan next door loaned us two plastic chairs and we concocted a table with a stump and a board, from Barrie and Cathy we borrowed the two foam pads to lay on the floor as beds, and Kit had cleverly brought a pair of plates, bowls, glasses, mugs, knives and forks, a couple of pots, a frying pan, and the coffee grinder. We had a new home. We could feel the bog, the land, calling us. We felt we were playing house. We lay in bed in the morning staring out at clear sunlight in the top of high firs through large windows on all four sides and the two skylights above. We felt giddy.

Toward the end of our time on the island I once again ran into our one-time real estate agent and told him how glad we were that we'd been pushed into building the cottage. I thanked him for letting us know about the proposed changes to the bylaws.

For a moment he didn't respond. At last he said, "Well, maybe now you won't want to thank me."

"Oh?"

"You see, those bylaws never went through. They were defeated. So it wasn't really necessary for you to build right away."

I felt a moment, just of moment, of irritation. But then I shook my head and could sense myself grinning. "One of the best things we ever did, building that cottage. It's been great. It will be great."

It has been. The cottage, the bog, the house. I feel, for the first time in my life, that I've come home.

2.

As I've said, Kit and I feel privileged. We've felt privileged for a long time. And lucky. Buying the Engineer's Challenge, building the cottage, is only a recent version of our luck and privilege.

Our luck began when we met. That we met. It continued after we got married and spent six months hitching around Europe. However, for a short period of time that year we didn't feel so lucky. I had applied to only one graduate school, Harvard, in German literature. I'd been accepted the year before, Harvard was where I wanted to be, and I was sure they'd take me again. In June I learned that, yes, they had accepted me. But I'd been given only a small scholarship. I had applied for a non-university-based grant, a Woodrow Wilson Fellowship that, if received, would cover not only my tuition but also enough monthly income to support Kit, me, and the upcoming baby. Except to complete my application I needed an interview with a Wilson official. Usually interviews took place at one's home university or some site close by. If one were abroad at another university, a Wilson interviewer would travel to a central city to interview candidates. On this my brother, Jeff, was running interference for me, trying to set up the interview. But each time he let me know where the interviewer would be at a certain time—London, Paris, Munich, Athens—Kit and I were long and far away. At last Jeff arranged for me to be interviewed, when I returned, at Princeton, home of the fellowship.

We got back to the United States, Manchester, my parents' home, in the third week of August. Classes would begin in twenty days. I was irritated with the German Department for offering me such measly support. Furthermore, I had over my time in Europe realized that to do intellectual work in a single, narrow field, a national literature, could be suffocating. I called the Wilson Fellowship office and set the time for my interview. Then I arranged another interview with Professor Harry Levin, chair of Harvard's Comparative Literature Department, and drove down to Cambridge. We met. I told him I wanted to transfer out of German and into Comp Lit.

Levin, a serious man and a powerful scholar, looked at a little place just above the top of my head and said, "This year eighty-two candidates applied and we accepted eight for the PHD. Why should we take you in and not one of the other seventy-four?"

I will never know where I pulled the chutzpah from. I do remember leaning forward to catch his eye. I know I said, "Because I'm smarter than they are."

I clearly recall a tiny smile on his lips, lasting less than a second. We talked some more about my studies in Europe, what I hoped to work on if I were accepted to Comp Lit, and the meeting ended. I had no idea where I stood.

A couple of days later I flew, squandering money I didn't have, down to New York and took the train to Princeton. At the Woodrow Wilson Institute I met first with one of the three men who'd be interviewing me, a young assistant professor I immediately liked. We talked a little about our interests and our lives. Among the things I told him was that I'd met my wife on the boat going over to Europe. He laughed and said, "You know, I met my wife on a boat to Europe too." A good sign? The other two interviewers came in, a dour older German professor and a third man who has completely disappeared from my memory. The German professor grilled me on some aspects of nineteenth-century German drama, and with the assistant professor I'd met first I talked about theory and methodology. The third person said very little. The interview ended, they told me they'd be in touch soon, and I retraced my steps to Manchester.

Kit and I needed to find an apartment. We drove to Cambridge four days in a row before Labour Day and finally found a place, living room, kitchen, bathroom, bedroom, small study, for eighty-five dollars a month, just across the Cambridge line into Somerville. We moved in on September 1. It looked as if I would have to borrow a great deal of money that year. I could register in German beginning the day after Labour Day. I walked into the German Department. The secretary asked my name. I told her. "Oh," she said, "we transferred your file to Comparative Literature last week."

I walked over to the Comp Lit offices, my feet no less than fifteen inches above the floor. Bette Ann, Professor Levin's secretary, stood as I came in and said, "Congratulations, and welcome." We talked for a few minutes. I led the conversation around to the possibilities of getting a teaching fellowship, since I now didn't even have the German Department's minimal scholarship. She looked puzzled. "You probably won't need to teach this year."

"I'll need to get some money to live on, and—"

"But you have money."

"I do?"

"Didn't they tell you? You were awarded a Wilson Fellowship last week."

I have no memory of how I got back to our apartment.

So I felt overwhelmingly lucky that all of this had happened to me so quickly and just when it was most needed, my first year of graduate work—a full year. Looking back, I can't conceive of how I managed it. I took the required eight courses, and two more. I audited three other courses. I produced my first play, *A Play and a Half*. And I became the father of a baby girl, our daughter, Elisabeth. I do remember we always had time to see friends, and quite often we drove up to Manchester for a weekend. The young have that kind of energy.

The summer between the first and second year, Kit and I taught at a pre-prep school in north-central New Hampshire, the kind of place that prepares kids for getting into a prep school that will get them into a better college. We thought of it as a school for overprivileged boys. Three of them were flown to the school on their fathers' float planes, landing on the school's lake. I was the French master, Kit taught English. Months before at the interview, it was clear I also had to be in charge of some sport or other. I suggested tennis. But they already had a tennis master. What about sailing? Well, I'd sailed a couple of times with my friend Peter on his tiny sandpiper, he handling the sail the whole time, so I'd said—we needed the jobs desperately— No problem, I could be the sailing master.

Several weeks prior to the start of summer school, Kit bought me a little book, *How to Sail*. But exams were coming up, I had papers to finish, and besides I'd sailed before, hadn't I? No problem. We arrived at the school, settled in. I glanced through my book. No, it couldn't be as complicated as that.

The first evening, before the boys arrived, the school held a cocktail party for the masters. This seemed like an excellent time for me to try out one of the little sailboats. I dressed as if ready for drinks with the other teachers but headed over to the dock. I climbed down into one of the half-dozen boats and undid it from its clamp. A slight breeze drifted me away from the dock. Time to raise the sail. I thought I remembered how Peter had done this: plant feet firmly, pull the rope, and the sail slips up into place. I raised the sail. A small gust of wind caught it. I held tight. Suddenly the boat tipped, I was in the water, the boat upside down, the mast stuck in the mud twelve feet below. Disaster, on all levels. I swam back to the dock. My watch was full of water, my sunglasses at the bottom of the drink. Despite the cocktail hour, I had been observed. I was relieved of my duties as sailing master. What else could I do? the headmaster wondered, ungently. What did I know about diving? As much as anyone who swam. Okay, I was diving master. Since I never have much liked swimming I didn't get into the water all summer—just that one instance of falling in. I taught theoretical diving. I taught the boys how to do a racing dive: don't go deep, that slows you down. I showed them how to dive off the dock and merely skim across the water. Kit and I were not asked back for the following summer.

During my second year in Comp Lit I decided I'd had enough of courses and would ask to take my qualifying exams at the end of the summer. It was a year of heavy concentration, filling my head with narrative, poetry, and theory. I did take out time to produce my second play, *The Horrible Assassination of Lester Miserables*. Professor Levin had come to both my plays and told me he was impressed. I did have a scholarship but also taught that year, two courses in advanced composition. Because I wanted to spend the following year in Provence, where we'd be borrowing a tiny cottage, once the village *lavoir*, from Kit's aunt and uncle, I applied for and got a Harvard Travelling Scholarship. Kit had taught at a private grade school and we'd saved enough to buy a small French car, a Simca 1000, for eleven hundred dollars, to be picked up when we arrived in Paris. That was the summer I slashed my hand and got to come out with my great joke.

The year in Provence, in Les Martins par Gordes in the Vaucluse, transformed us both. And likely Elisabeth too. We had a house, our time was our own, we had a car and could go anywhere. Dreadful things were happening in Vietnam; though that was half a globe away, we began to follow the American involvement. We travelled to Spain, Italy, and Greece. We fell in love with Mediterranean culture. I wrote that never-published novel; completed my third play, *Time and Again*, an anti-war play; and read extensively about Samuel Beckett and Alain Robbe-Grillet, central to my thesis research. I went regularly to Aix-en-Provence on the other side of a low mountain range, the Luberon, where I was officially registered at the university. The Luberon is known in the literary world as the setting for Alphonse Daudet's *Lettres de mon moulin* and, on one of the narrow curving roads through the hills, the site of the car crash that a few years earlier had killed Albert Camus.

The university at Aix was in all ways provincial. With thirteen thousand students, its library held seventy thousand books, about 5.5 books per student; Harvard, by comparison, had more than ten million. At Aix one could take out only two books at a time. The stacks were closed; ancient little men took one's list of two titles and disappeared to search for the requested books. More often than not they reappeared after half an hour to announce the books were either loaned out or had disappeared. It was during this period, the mid-1960s, that French academics were beginning to write the obscure theoretical discourses that would be the bane of graduate students for decades to come. My own theory is that because so few books were available outside of Paris, academics at provincial universities had to invent literary theory out of whole, or sometimes patchwork, cloth.

My parents came to visit. My brother came too, after a year in Israel. We made pets of the trout in the small pond, feeding them table scraps. The field behind the house had been planted that year with spinach, which would be plowed back into the earth to enrich it; most days Kit and Elisabeth picked fresh spinach for a lunchtime salad. I read and wrote.

We came back in August. I reported in to Professor Levin. I told him I planned to finish my thesis that year and wanted to apply for teaching jobs. I explained that I'd had a fine year in France and now wanted to write fiction and plays as well as academic criticism. We had again lived on very little for the year, so what I'd really like to get, I told him, was a half-time job with naturally its commensurate half-pay. And if possible the job should be in Mediterranean Europe with its wonderful climate. He thought about this for a moment and said, "I've just come back from a semester at the University of California in San Diego. It has a Mediterranean climate."

I had no sense of where in California San Diego was. I kept my mouth shut.

He went on. "It's a very new campus. All the literatures are taught under the auspices of the Literature Department, which has its own Comparative Literature section. It's a highly progressive way to teach literature."

I made noises about how remarkable that was.

"And the teaching load is so light it's as if you're only teaching part-time."

He'd convinced me. "It sounds wonderful. How do I apply?"

He thought for a moment and then spoke words as clear to me today as in August 1966: "Let me make a phone call." A hugely different time from that which arrived only a very few years later, when new PHDs would make job applications to a couple of hundred universities.

A week or so after my conversation with Harry Levin, I had a letter from Claudio Guillén, head of the Comp Lit section at UCSD, describing the program as if he were selling it to me. He ended the letter, "Our chairman, Roy Harvey Pearce, will be in Cambridge next month. He would like you to interview him." Another remarkable phrase.

I did meet Roy, we had a long chat, he said I'd be hearing from him. For several weeks, no response. I was producing the play I'd written in France. Vietnam was coming closer to home. Norman Mailer spoke at Harvard, telling us to hang Lyndon Johnson's picture "Upside down!" I received a thick package from UCSD, the papers I needed to sign to become an assistant professor. Never a job offer. Only the assumption that I'd been hired, that I'd be there in the fall.

I spoke with Claudio several times over that year. The department was looking forward to meeting me and the five other assistant professors they'd hired. "And we will," Claudio said, "late in summer. Unless—you've heard of the governor we just elected, Ronald Reagan?"

I certainly had.

"Unless Governor Reagan decides to close down the university."

"Why would he do that?"

"Too many left-wing intellectuals here, he thinks."

I was getting ever more eager to be there.

The hiring policy at this brand new university had called for the provost, with many a consultant, to find a senior professor to be chair of a department at its inception. The chair would then hire a number of other full professors, leaders in their fields. This group would bring in one or two professors at the associate level but mainly would look for young academics who had just completed their doctorates. The older men and the young bucks. And male is the proper notion: when in September 1967 I arrived in San Diego, the twenty-seven members of the Literature Department were all men. The newly hired young would slowly change that.

So began my academic teaching career. The "as if . . . part-time" position became a full-time job. Until, that is, the year in Mexico, 1985–86, after which I did truly become a half-timer.

Until I retired, fifteen years later. And came here to the island, and the bog. And the garden, which keeps coming into more of its own. August is the month when we literally reap what we have sown. Fresh peas and beans every day, garlic, salad, potatoes, kale. Leeks—yes, I did manage to grow some this year, though not as large as Katherine's. My squash have never been as large, or as abundant. The figs will be ready in about a week, the grapes in three.

We had our first fig harvest in August 2005, thirteen of them, as well as a sweet black table grape harvest, about eighteen pounds, more than sixty bunches, much sweeter than those of the year before, when we had eight. The vines serve two purposes: to produce grape, and to provide shade under the long sunroof over the deck side of the kitchen. When the sun is directly overhead, the heat coming through those skylights would be insufferable were it not for the broad grape leaves covering it entirely. By the time autumn comes, when the sun is at a slant and we want its heat and light, the leaves are long gone. Another brilliant aspect of our architect Judith's design.

In 2004 we shared our eight grape bunches with the wasps. We'd left the island for a couple of days, the grapes nearly ripe; when we came back they had fully matured and the deck was abuzz with wasps. The wasps after sucking at the grapes lay prostrate on the deck below the vines, on their sides, their backs, drunk on the rich grape juice. Funny, and possibly dangerous, as we didn't know what a drunken wasp might do, especially if stepped on with a bare foot. But like some humans, once the power of the juice passed through them, they crawled off in humiliation and heavily flew themselves away.

In 2005 I learned the black grapes were ripe by hearing, at about three in a mid-August morning, unknown sounds just outside our bedroom window. I went out to the deck off our bedroom and switched on the lights. That, together with a flashlight, highlighted a handsome racoon sitting on the rafters, eating grapes, one at a time. He stared at me and continued eating, happily. I found the long extender pole we use for window cleaning and poked at him with it. He finally ran away along the roofline. I went to bed, was nearly asleep when I heard him again. I poked him again; he lost his balance and crashed to the deck. This time he didn't come back. The next day Kit and I brought out the ladders and snipped away most of the bunches of grapes. We did leave the raccoon a couple of scraggly bunches, which he returned for a couple of nights later. We heard and ignored him. Or her.

That was the August we were adopted by a ring-necked pheasant. He lived with us inside the fenced-off area in back, munching on grass seeds, staying out, as far as I could tell, of the vegetable garden. I was raking our boules court when I heard a sound in the brush, and there he was, maybe eight feet away, glancing my way occasionally but mainly unperturbed. The first summer of animals unafraid of me.

Also that summer Kit's brother Ed and his wife, Donna, visited us, they of the boating accident, and he and I went out fishing several times. Our last time out I suddenly caught sight of something rising from the water, a black shaft four or five feet high, maybe one hundred and fifty feet behind the boat.

We both stared. The fin quickly connected itself to the black and white body of the biggest killer whale I have ever seen. It swam by us, breaching eleven times, at its closest twenty-five feet away. A huge feller. A transient. These whales are not nice guys; they often destroy immense schools of fish without bothering to eat them; they prefer sea mammals—seals, sea lions. His cousins the resident pod whales are smaller and gentler. This one was impressive. We stared after him in naive admiration. Luckily he ignored us. No reason for staying around, as he'd have scared away any fish. We headed back to the marina to tell the tale.

3.

As in the summer of 1968, when Kit and I too survived our naïveté and lived to tell our tales. I'd finished teaching my first year at UCSD. It was a time when serious amounts of fellowship money were available for academic travel and research; one merely needed to apply. So I received a grant for a research project that would eventually lead to my second academic book, *Theater and Propaganda*. My dissertation would be my first, and it was in part because of a debt I owed regarding the dissertation (though the man I owed it to didn't know me) that I'd applied for the fellowship. The thesis of my dissertation, using the work of Kafka, Samuel Beckett, and Alain Robbe-Grillet, claimed that however strange their texts may appear, they were in the end all realists. I argued, for example, that Kafka in *The Castle* and *The Trial* was not producing some "absurd"—a notion in vogue at the time—narrative, rather he was merely reproducing the bureaucratically ridden Prague he knew, releasing Josef K. into it; such structures came to be known as Kafka-esque. I was worried that this argument would disturb some academics until I found a book, which included black-and-white photographs, called *Kafka and Prague* by Emanuel Frynta. In his work Frynta had taken text from many of Kafka's stories and set it beside and below photos of the Prague that Frynta lived in, relatively unchanged since Kafka's time, highlighting Kafka's talent at describing the actual. I wanted to go to Prague and thank the man who had with one text given my academic future a much more solid foundation.

The grant I'd received was for spending four weeks in August seeing the new theatre bursting out in the major European capitals. We left Elisabeth, then almost five, and David, ten months, with first my parents in Manchester, then Kit's parents in Ottawa. Kit and I would go to Prague, Munich, Paris, and London. But for two weeks prior, we would visit friends, Gretchen and Ivan, who lived in northern Nigeria, sub-Saharan Africa, their town located fifteen miles from the edge of the desert. We'd met them on the boat coming back from our year in Provence for my final semesters of graduate work. They'd been elsewhere in Africa for two years, and in the fall Ivan would be going to Harvard to begin a PHD in linguistics. But a year in Cambridge left them yearning for Africa. So Ivan applied for, and got, a job at a boys' teacher training college in Katsina, a Hausa town of a hundred thousand inhabitants, with a salary two and a half times mine when I started at UCSD, a two-year contract, and he at that point without even an MA. The only problem with the immense income, there was nothing to spend it on. They had written to say that if we could get ourselves to Europe, they'd pay our way to Katsina, our company their treat to themselves. The offer being one we couldn't refuse, we said, "Of course." (They never did pay for our tickets, at least not directly. Instead they sent us a thirty-inch-high antique wood carving from Mali of a pregnant woman sitting on a birthing stool, worth at that time more than the cost of the tickets. We never sold it because we fell in love with it and paid for the trip to Nigeria ourselves.)

We flew to Madrid and quickly on to Kano, a city in northern Nigeria of then more than two million people. Neither Kit nor I had ever heard of the place, part of our Amero- and Eurocentrism that this trip would, we hoped, begin to displace. Ivan and Gretchen met us there and drove us to Katsina, about five hours away through the last green countryside before the desert. Along the way they filled us in on the politics of the school. Run by the US Agency for International Development (USAID), it was, Ivan claimed, a base and cover for CIA work being carried on in central Africa. Only a couple of years earlier, the Hausas had killed or run off all the Yorubas in Katsina; we would see hundreds of one-time Yoruba houses burnt to the ground. Ivan and Gretchen were concerned about their role there, but on the whole they lay low.

So, acting non-politically, Ivan with his immense energy had started a small zoo. When he learned that the boys at the school knew next to nothing about the animals and birds living in their neighbourhood, he sent out word that anyone who brought him an example of the local wildlife would be appropriately rewarded. By the time we arrived they'd been there a full year. The zoo held three dozen species of birds, several hyenas, rabbits, two small wild cats. Its major centre of attraction was the snake pit. More than a dozen pythons lived down in it, and two cobras. Boys from the school, local adults, as well as kids from Katsina and the surrounding countryside, could visit the zoo by paying the admission price, one penny. The money was used to buy some of the meat to feed the animals and birds.

Ivan gathered more meat especially for the snakes by stunning lizards with a slingshot. He'd taught himself to use it first for self-defence—it would have been dangerous for him to carry a pistol—and only secondly as a lizard-stunning machine.

The high point three afternoons a week came when Ivan

climbed down into the pit to feed the snakes their live lizards. The pit was fifteen feet deep, since several of the pythons were twelve feet long and could practically stand on their tails as they slithered up the walls; at first it had been eleven feet deep, and a couple of snakes had escaped. In the pit he would work the snakes, teasing the cobras and wrapping the smaller pythons about his body. He'd been, he told us, scratched by one of the cobras, and had twice needed help in loosening a python from around his torso. We watched the show several times, with no little concern, along with Katsinans, whose eyes bulged from their heads as they watched Ivan's antics. He had become known as the snake man of Katsina; for eighty miles around, when a python slithered into someone's barn or attic and refused to leave, Ivan was called in. He'd brought half a dozen snakes to the pit in this way.

Ivan was a short, wiry man, a Belgian, highly intelligent and equally highly macho—a trait necessary if one would climb into a pit filled with snakes. Katsina was one of seven Hausa emirates. The emir of Katsina owned a stable of polo ponies. Ivan had never played polo. By the time we arrived he'd become the fourth man on the emir's second team, the only white man riding in polo competition in any of the emirates. As such he had access to the horses. He suggested one day that Kit and I and he go riding across the countryside. I'd never been on a horse before, didn't know how to ride. No problem, they'd get me a quiet, tame horse, I'd enjoy it, we'd be out only an hour. So I agreed. I didn't like the English saddle, no pommel for holding on to, but I grinned and bore it. After an hour riding over countryside completely foreign to me—I recognized not a tree or plant—my butt was sore and the insides of my thighs burned. Then Ivan announced we were lost. Despair. We rode another two hours, with me in increasing agony. At last Ivan identified a landmark, and the horses, too, recognized they'd soon be approaching the stable. Their ambling increased to canter, from canter to gallop. Suddenly I heard Ivan behind me urging his horse to pass mine, and my horse instantly took flight. I have no memory how I held on; somehow I did. Only when we reached the stable did I learn that my horse was no polo pony but had been trained as a racehorse. As soon as it heard a horse behind it try to take the lead, it increased its speed. Ivan had known this the whole time. I was furious with him for a couple of days, newly reminded of my anger each time I refreshed the salve on my inner thighs.

One day a young Katsinan boy arrived to tell Ivan a red fox and her kits had been spotted out by the small airport at the edge of town. We headed off in a couple of trucks accompanied by a team of boys from the school armed with shovels, to bring the animals back to the zoo. They spent over an hour first blocking the dozen or more escape holes, then digging down the holes one at a time. They found the female in a burrow and captured her by throwing a tarp over her, scooting the thrashing animal into a cage on the bed of one of the trucks. The two kits that had been with her were easier to handle; they didn't know what to do and were more afraid than angry. We brought them back to the zoo, leaving the mother in a larger cage and bringing the kits into the house. Gretchen made a nest for them in a basket with a blanket at the far end of the living/dining room. The kits played with each other, gently fighting like cats. When the little ones were brought to the mother in her cage she refused to nurse them, so Gretchen fed them from a baby bottle.

A couple of days later someone brought the zoo two baby rabbits. Since these, too, had to be fed from a bottle, Gretchen put them in with the kits. For days the little foxes and the little rabbits played happily together. Kit and I, tending toward pacifism, wondered if by rearing such animals from literally the same bottle they could learn to live in peace. One morning as we sat at breakfast we heard a couple of little clicks from the basket and got up to take a look. Two small pretty foxes, no rabbits. Just a bit of fur on the blanket. So much for rosy dreams.

A few days before we left, Ivan introduced Kit and me to the emir of Katsina. A large man who lived in a palace behind twelve-foot-thick walls, husband to two dozen wives, father of over a hundred children, the emir greeted us warmly. He showed us about his throne room, and was especially proud of a gold medallion given to his father by King George V for that earlier emir's bravery in the First World War.

The next evening Ivan and Gretchen held a party in our honour. First thing in the morning it was my responsibility to choose between three noble goats, one of which would be the centrepiece of our evening's feast. I made my choice, a handsome fellow with a brown forelock. Three men bound the animal's hooves together, a fourth held his head back, and the slaughterer slit his throat. A fifth man with a bucket caught the blood as it gushed from the goat's throbbing artery. The animal died quickly and was taken away. The pit in which it would be roasted had been prepared the night before and glowed with huge coals. The afternoon was given over to bringing in the entertainers for the evening, a dozen exotic dancers, in their other lives ladies from several of Katsina's brothels. The party began as the sun set. The guests, including the emir and the black teachers, arrived at Ivan and Gretchen's compound; none of the white USAID teachers were invited. Cold beer was the drink of choice. The drumming began, then the dancing, teasingly erotic. The boys from the school, also not invited, had climbed trees outside the compound, or clung to the fence around it, eyes bulging, shouting the dancers on. Skirts twirled, glimpses of bare breasts. Beer was consumed. And then we ate: roasted goat meat, delicious, the memory of the dying animal forgotten. With it, hot pepper soup and some mashed root that made a paste, the idea being to dip the mash into the soup with one's fingers and consume them together. Ivan, macho though he was, ate little of the soup. The guests watched me, the white outsider: how would I handle the soup? I've always loved hot peppers, still eat half a dozen jalapeños a week, so I blithely dipped away and swallowed. It was indeed hot, and also very good. I worked up a visible sweat finishing my bowl and was cheered by some of the guests. Which naturally made it clear that I'd better get seconds. Which brought on a louder cheer. I ate this more slowly, and with more mashed root, but finished it. The dancers came back, we drank more beer, the night ended, and we went to bed.

I would have traded the next day for any six hours on the back of my racehorse. I had never known how long the human bowel, upper and lower, was. For thirty hours I felt every inch as it digested hot-pepper-soaked root-mash.

Two days later we flew off from Kano to Munich, from black to white literally and metaphorically. There we saw several plays, including the opening of Maximilian Schell's *Hamlet* in which he shocked the bourgeois Bavarian audience by having retranslated the play—it's usually done in the early nineteenth-century romantic Tieck-Schlegel translation—turning the "To be or not to be" speech from the traditional, accepted as truly Shakespearian "*Sein oder nicht sein*," essentially, To exist or not to exist, to "*Leben oder nicht leben*," To live or not to live. He spoke this not as melancholy self-questioning but as a challenge to all the theatregoers. Boos, raspberries, and loud cheers from the electrified audience. This was 1968.

From Munich to Prague. Prague summer. The Czechs had announced themselves free of Russian domination. The skies above, like everyone's futures, were sunny. We had an address for Emanuel Frynta at the heart of the old Jewish quarter. The first morning, after asking a number of people, we found it. He lived on the fourth floor of an apartment building dating from the last third of the nineteenth century. A dark, heavy stone stairway circled an elevator shaft. The elevator didn't work. We walked up and found his door. I knocked. Someone spoke. I called out, "Herr Frynta?" I heard the door unlock, and it opened. A man in his forties wearing slacks and a sweater stared at us, glanced carefully about the empty hallway, and said to us in German, "Come in." We did. He brought us to a living room, sat us on a couch. "Will you have tea? Coffee?" Tea, we said. He disappeared. Kit and I looked at each other, shrugged, examined the room. The walls were lined with bookcases, the cases crammed full. I wondered if he had a copy of *Kafka and Prague* around. He returned with a teapot, a small mug of milk, and three cups on a tray, and a plate of cookies. He set them on a little table and poured. We thanked him. Then he sat in a chair opposite us. "Now," he said, "what are your names and why are you here?"

So began a conversation that lasted all day, into the night, and we met the next day as well. His wife had arrived. She spoke nothing but Czech, Kit had only her French and English, but the four of us talked, Emanuel and I translating by way of German, about our lives, domestic, intellectual, political. Life was good for him at this moment, Prague summer. I mentioned I had a nagging fear that it might not last, that one day the Russians would come marching in. He doubted it: they couldn't dare, what with the eyes of the world now fixed clearly on Czechoslovakia's new freedom. We said we were seriously worried about Russia; he said the West was always too worried about Russia.

He wanted to know about America. He'd heard that in Harlem in New York rats attack small children in their beds but knew this was a Communist lie. We had to tell him it was true. He defined for us what an intellectual was: a person who earns a thousand less in his country's currency than he needs to live on. He and his wife kept us there for dinner.

The next day Emanuel, Kit, and I spent walking around his neighbourhood. He showed us where Kafka was born, lived, went to school, went to synagogue, worked. He showed us the gargoyles on the castle, terrifying and "absurd" in the novel, here large as life. And he found for us tickets—sold out, impossible to get without reservations months in advance—for the evening to Laterna Magika, the remarkable theatre ensemble that used live performance and film in interaction on the stage. Clearly this was part of what I'd received my research money for. I must have thanked him half a dozen times, one way or another, for having written *Kafka and Prague*. We saw him again the following day, briefly, before we left.

We promised to stay in touch. Over the next weeks Kit and I saw a lot of theatre. We returned to the United States, picked up Elisabeth and David in Ottawa. Elisabeth was delighted to see us. David had completely forgotten us. We were strangers. He had adopted Margaret, Kit's mother, as his own. We were deeply upset; what had we done? But Margaret, ever a wise woman, told Kit that now she had to be sure only she fed David every bite he ate. No one else must give him food, especially not Margaret. David cried to be fed by her, but she turned a deaf ear to his despair. After twenty-four hours Kit and David had rebonded. It took me a little longer because in those days feeding children was women's work. We returned to California, and life went on. The Russians marched into Czechoslovakia, deposed Dubcek, reasserted their dominance. How naive we had all been.

I wrote Emanuel several times but heard nothing in reply. Seven years later when I was teaching at McGill I met a Czech woman and asked her if by chance she knew him. It turned out she did; his life had become a misery, the authorities wouldn't let him do any intellectual work and his writing couldn't be published. I again wrote to him, saying I felt dreadful for him and for his fate, I told him that his work was, and will be, remembered. A couple of years later the Czech woman informed me she'd heard Emanuel had killed himself. He had nothing more to live for.

In one sense, the geographic, I've wandered far from the road across the bog. But in another, all those distant yet distinct places, all those graphic memories, have been stirred up by my bog tending, brought out of the buried murk into the light. These past months, in these past chapters, they've crept out of my memory storehouse, sometimes by association, as often through lateral remembrance paths. They have become, for me, again vibrant, agitated, drawn with a good bit of the colour of the original.

August is approaching its end. A few dragonflies have been flitting over the bog and landing on the dry, warm dirt of the road for most of the month, but over the last couple of days I haven't seen any. It's the best year ever for the fig tree, about thirty plump fellows coming ripe, this year serially. We love to eat figs as their ripeness peaks, simply quartered or wrapped with prosciutto, while we sip glasses of cold Pinot Blanc and stare out across the strait as the sun is setting. In past years they've all ripened within couple of days of each other. It's not easy to wolf down a couple of dozen figs in three days, far more satisfying to spread the pleasure over a couple of weeks and to share figs with friends.

And we have been blessed with our own Himalayan black-berry jungle. We noticed two years ago that on the land next door a few scraggly vines had shot up, likely the offering of defecating birds some years earlier. Last year we could reach a few berries through the fence. This year the brambles have shot through and have sent roots down on this side as well. The branches are laden with large, sweet blackberries, some over an inch long. We've picked several quarts in the past two weeks. The Himalayans are the last of the blackberries. Midsummer brought the black caps, smaller and rarer than those we now have, and late spring we had blackberries on trailing vines, most of which went to birds.

The Himalayans are, technically, an invasive plant. There is some consensus on the island to uproot certain such invaders, but the blackberries are too lush and sweet to take them out. It's mainly tansy ragwort, *Daphne laureola*, and Scotch broom that receive this treatment: expeditions are mounted annually to remove the broom from one of the provincial parks (GaLTT, the Gabriola Land and Trails Trust, has a device that can uproot the broom; one can rent it for forty dollars, though it's free to members—a membership in GaLTT is forty dollars).

Everything has ripened except my tomatoes, which are just beginning to redden; not enough sun. We'll have to remove a few large firs so more light can reach the garden. But that's a project for the fall. For the next few weeks I'll be gathering up seed pods from peas and beans, more seed from the chard and kale, from the arugula, the cilantro, and the red lettuce. Time to plant garlic and rutabagas for next year, and the last of the old lettuce seeds. We'll get one more crop, which, though feeble in comparison to the summer's bounty, will be welcome in November.

The year has come its cycle. It feels right to be mulling on the regenerative force in seeds that will bring fresh produce to the table in next year's round. For a few months the garden won't need heavy-duty tending. The red-winged blackbirds should be back in the bog by January. They'll find our feeders and steal seeds from the finches and sparrows, from the nuthatches and towhees and chickadees. And we'll refill the feeders all winter. The bog water is low, but autumn rain is coming. Soon it'll be up to full height. We'll have to get the bog road raised a couple of inches before then. The bull lilies are rotting down, but they'll be back. The leaves of the maples are sliding from gold to brown; in less than a month they'll have fallen off. But the firs, cedar, and arbutus will stay green all winter.

I'm looking forward to the next cycle, the repetitions, the renewals.

A FULL CIRCLE, OF SORTS

September 1. Had I not noted, a year ago, the return of the dragonflies, I would not now be so moved, so impressed, to see them back again, and in large numbers, just about to the day of their reappearance last year. The bog road is rich with them, the large blues, the stubbier crimsons. They give me pleasure.

I watch as two of the crimson mate in the position known as the wheel, seeing their copulation almost from the start. Moments before, the male would have spotted the object of his desire. Now he twists the tip of his tail under his thorax to reach an abdominal pouch, where his penis is located; his sperm develop in the tail tip, but to mate he has to load up his penis with the semen. Then he flies up after her, behind and over her. His legs grab her body and hold on, the two flying in this kind of tandem. They land here on the bog road, his tail now up and around to her neck, her tail half-circling his abdomen. His tail grasps her fully, his penis intrudes into genitals located at the tip of her abdomen, and he fills her with his seed. I can see the pulsations.

I play voyeur for maybe five minutes, leave before they finish. They could be at it for up to an hour. I have to get to the cottage. When they're done she'll find a small protected place in the bog and deposit her fertilized eggs there. In the spring a new generation around the bog, their home and mine.

ACKNOWLEDGMENTS

Thanks are due to a number of people who have helped me rewrite *Bog Tender*. Several have read all or part of the manuscript and have generously given me their comments—my writer friends Carol Bergman, Susan Crean, Sandy Duncan, Patsy Ludwick, Heather Menzies. Kit has, as always, made many insightful suggestions (hard for her, as she is also a character in this book). Great thanks too to Rhonda Bailey, my highly perceptive editor; this is the sixth book she's worked on with me. And to Ruth Linka, publisher at Brindle & Glass—I go on deeply appreciating the faith she has in my work.

A National Magazine Award recipient and winner of the Hugh MacLennan Prize for fiction, GEORGE SZANTO is the author of several books of essays and half a dozen novels, the most recent being *The Tartarus House on Crab*. A fellow of the Royal Society of Canada, George is co-author of the Islands Investigations International mystery series, which includes *Never Sleep with a Suspect on Gabriola Island*, *Always Kiss the Corpse on Whidbey Island*, and *Never Hug a Mugger on Quadra Island*. Please visit georgeszanto.com.